A Season of Eagles

[handwritten inscription and signature]

"Josie RavenWing is a true poet, Wisewoman and Spiritwalker. In *A Season of Eagles* she weaves a beautiful, lyrical tale about will, power and Spirit, made all the more beautiful because it is true. She dares to share with her readers her personal journey of transformation and by doing so, encourages us all to risk the journey ourselves."

—Beverly Engel
  Author of *Women Circling the Earth*

***

"Josie RavenWing's *A Season of Eagles* is a classic tale of initiation and the shapeshifter's journey into power, wisdom, and compassion, a book that inspires each of us to reach beyond the limits of reality as we in the industrialized cultures have been taught to perceive it."

—John Perkins
  Founder of Dream Change Coalition
  Author of *Shapeshifting, The World Is As You Dream It, Psychonavigation* and *The Stress-Free Habit*

A Season of Eagles

Josie RavenWing

Writer's Showcase presented by *Writer's Digest*
San Jose New York Lincoln Shanghai

A Season of Eagles

Published by Writer's Showcase presented by *Writer's Digest*
an imprint of iUniverse.com, Inc.

For information address:
iUniverse.com, Inc.
620 North 48th Street
Suite 201
Lincoln, NE 68504-3467
www.iuniverse.com

The events of this book are true but most of the names of the characters have been changed to protect their privacy. Except where specified as otherwise, all poems included at the beginning of this book and at the beginning of each chapter have been written by the author.

ISBN: 0-595-09510-0

Printed in the United States of America

This book is dedicated to all those who summon the courage to walk the path of Mystery.

Epigraph

...Pageants of mystery, enraptured we unfold
Dancers spin in ecstasy while new stories are told
Bodies dissolve, and return as webs of light
Radiant by day and luminous by night...

By Josie RavenWing from her music tape *Trail of Power*

Foreword

A Season of Eagles is the story of one woman's triumphant unfolding of her spiritual will. I had the profound satisfaction of witnessing this rebirth and acting as occasional midwife.

Having seen many turn back from the gritty task of finding real power and *will*, I can congratulate Josie with deep appreciation for what she accomplished. She became a woman of power.

Her encounters across the Southwest now fill the pages of her book some years later. She still doesn't fully know some of what she found and encountered during that season, and neither does anyone else. Her life is a flood of mystery, and will not be defined and held prisoner by fragile human thinking. Her world is one of *will*, and is difficult to fathom. The stories in her book may seem a far-fetched fantasy to many. And one edge of Josie's search for spiritual truth began as a dearly held and perhaps far-fetched fantasy. Yet her desires became reality. Her own *will* became her teacher.

Josie already had considerable spiritual power when she passed into this season. What changed was the new way in which she began to use her *will* out in the world. The beings and forces she found there exist for all of us. Any of us have the choice to gather personal power and to face the mysterious unknown. This is man's fate. And woman's.

During her season of eagles, Josie exchanged normal society for a magnetized world of enchanting, beautiful power. I'm glad to see her share her accomplishments in this book that challenges limiting beliefs.

Sean

Acknowledgements

There are many beings and forces that have contributed to this book. Among them, I thank the person known in this book simply as Sean, who has been a teacher for me in many arenas and for his invaluable assistance in the editing of this book. I also thank the Dineh (Navajo) people of Arizona who welcomed me into their homes, their ceremonies, and who adopted me into several of their clans. And finally, I thank the endless power and beauty of Mother Nature and all the creatures and spirits who have taught me that the human world is only a small part of the unfathomable web of life, the great Mystery.

List of Abbreviations

N.A.C.   Native American Church

Introduction

According to human calendars, a season has a beginning and an end, marked by solar equinoxes and solstices. Yet nature, despite its solar exclamation points, is not so neatly delineated. Who hasn't noticed that leaves sometimes begin to turn before the autumn equinox, snows fall before the day of shortest light, or warm winds push through the winter like buds bursting before their time?

So it was with the season of eagles. Most of the events described in this book took place over a decade ago, within a three-month period: a season. Yet elements of the season were gaining momentum from the cumulative energies of my entire past, gathering like a soft breeze that finally, in the season of eagles, became a wild spirit wind into which I launched myself and took flight.

I played a role in stirring up the elements that eventually carried me into a season of mystery and power. So did fate. For years my role had been to seek out and engage in practices that would hone my spirit. I quested for knowledge and awareness of the numinous power I was certain existed inside the delicate envelope of the human skin, in the hidden song of the wind, in the secret light of creation. I had glimpsed that light in a vision at age one and had sought deeper contact with its mystery ever since.

When I was in my late teens, a powerful shamanistic dance master first showed me that people are fluid energy bodies. For eight years under her almost daily tutelage, I became adept at entering enhanced perceptual states. In those states, my awareness expanded to include "seeing" while dancing with eyes closed. I learned to draw power from the Earth's emanations, the sun and fire, to adopt the liquid quality of water into my very bones, and to ride my breath like the wind itself.

Meditation became a second teacher: for my mental and emotional body. Daily meditation soon brought into stark relief the foundation of Western philosophy, "I think, therefore I am," showing me how the surface layers of identity are based on our thoughts and the dictates of our emotions. Calming my emotions and bringing my mind to stillness helped me forge a deeper identity based on a foundation of Spirit: the infinite, silent expansion of the Self into realms beyond thought.

Over the years, I also nurtured my spirit through forms of artistic creativity. I learned that when the human imagination is freed from habit through creativity, it can become a vessel of the infinite Spirit. The act of creation was, for me, both a means to consistently surprise myself and to enter the flow that is continuously generating, sustaining and transforming the universe.

I became more challenged when I went hunting in the current jungle of spiritual teachings and teachers. This expedition lasted many years, up to the period I've introduced in this book. I emerged wiser but not completely thrilled with all of my discoveries. I did find treasures of knowledge, but frequently I was disappointed when many of the teachers I encountered were not what they claimed to be. Somewhat discouraged and disillusioned, I resigned myself to the possibility of going on alone.

Then my life changed suddenly and irrevocably. I entered into an intense and demanding process with a man who goes by many names. In her book *Buffalo Woman Comes Singing*, Brooke Medicine Eagle calls him Dawn Boy, sprinkles the pages with many of his teachings and devotes the twelfth chapter to her experiences with him. In *A Season of Eagles*, he has asked to be known simply as Sean.

Sean had the temperament of an eagle, in that he was more interested in the spiraling heights of spiritual dimensions than in the closer contact of emotional relationships. And like the eagle, he fiercely guarded his independence and need to hunt—to hunt knowledge and power. Often alone, he could seem as aloof as an eagle in his eerie, and his vision was keen and far-sighted. His call to spiritual awareness sometimes seemed harsh, but he had lofty ideals toward which he urged himself and others.

Sean gave me many tools for my own spiritual development, and to this day I am still integrating what I experienced with him. When we began our journey together, I adopted an attitude toward Sean's knowledge and beliefs that was similar to the one I use when visiting a foreign country or culture: enter fully into it, see what I can learn by being a part of it, and do the sorting out later! In some respects he was not an easy person to be with, and in my mind sometimes I call him "Sean the Challenger," but for everything there is a season, and strange bird that he is, he played a key role in my season of eagles.

But there were other characters that emerged on the landscape after our season began. My own spirit stepped forward to play an increasingly active role, as did Nature—or "Mother," as Sean called her—and power itself. I even had several challenging encounters with the famous Carlos Castaneda and other well-known contemporary spiritual figures. And there were many amazing beings hiding in the background, ready to play their parts as I was carried high on the wild spirit winds.

During the season of eagles, I physically left behind all those I'd previously called "friend" by moving suddenly to Arizona, where I spent the majority of my time either alone in the desert or in the intermittent company of Sean.

Whether alone or with Sean, my old modes of relating to myself and to others were slowly—and sometimes painfully—stripped away. A different relationship was simultaneously strengthened: my relation to the unknown, to dreaming, to Spirit. A storm of power swept through my life, and nature played its part with great exuberance. During that season, avalanches of eagles and other omens rained from the heavens, and the winds sometimes roared and stilled with gestures of Sean's hand. Even my own body participated, convulsing with inner earthquakes set off by my spirit's efforts to adjust to massive confrontations with power. Sean and the universe became

my dance partners in an intricate display of immense energy and primal creativity.

In this dance—which stretched across myriad environments and sometimes included other humans in its choreography—the primary theme was
the development of what Sean called the spiritual *will*. This "energy-muscle,"
which is most concentrated in the human belly, is both the means to and
source of as many spiritual experiences as an individual could ever hope for.
As with our physical muscles, staying spiritually toned and functioning at
peak performance requires exercise, stretching and strengthening of *will*.

Most of what Sean shared with me centered around awareness and use of
will. Although he would often use his power to nudge my *will* and give me
access to some experiences I couldn't yet reach alone, both of our goals were
to make increasingly *will*-full efforts of our own. Sean's beliefs reinforced my
own: that we humans don't have to sit around hoping that Spirit may touch
our lives some day. We can be responsible to ourselves and use the many spiritual practices available to strengthen our *will*. And then we can go exercise
it in the world to serve both ourselves and others. My book *The Return of
Spirit: A Woman's Call to Spiritual Action* offers exercises and applications of
will for those interested in putting such information into practice.

Our experiences often follow our beliefs. Sean dared to believe more
steadfastly and with more *will* in the power of Spirit than anyone I'd ever
met, often leaving Western reason in the dust. His unusual experiences
followed the strength of his beliefs and are beyond many people's ability
to fathom. He was well read, had studied world religions and spiritual
paths from East to West. But much of what Sean knew came from his own
direct spiritual interactions with the earth, plants, animals and less tangible forces of the great Mystery. He accompanied me on a similar path of
knowledge, enticing me into a living myth in which the miraculous
occurred and was accepted.

Over time, the myth gained momentum and I circled on its power
through a season of eagles.

One

"Would you like me to change your life?"

The day had begun in such an average way. My morning shower and quiet breakfast offered no clue that the afternoon's events would catapult me into an unparalleled season of transformation.

Late morning, I got a long-distance phone call from my friend Colette. We'd first met at a seminar several years earlier and had hit it off, talked by phone periodically, and had once taken a spiritual journey together to the Olympic rainforest.

"Hey, Josie!" she now exclaimed through the telephone. "I'm headed your way with a friend of mine. I hope you're going to be home in a few hours, 'cause that's when we'll be landing on your doorstep."

"Sure I'll be here. This is great. Your visit gives me just the inspiration I need to straighten up the house, especially since you haven't seen my new place yet."

"Oh, don't worry about that," Colette laughed. "I'm just looking forward to seeing *you*. It's been ages."

"You drive and I'll clean. Just get yourself here in one piece. And by the way, who's the friend you're bringing?"

"Oh, just a guy. You'll meet him soon enough. Bye."

Luckily there was just enough time for a quick cleaning frenzy. By the time I'd finished getting both myself and my home ready for company, my energies were a bit scattered. I estimated I had about half an hour until my guests arrived. A patch of sunlight invited me to the living room floor, and I sprawled on my back in the middle of it to relax and center myself. A soft breeze blew through the open windows, a cool and perfect counterpoint to the steady warmth of the sun on my skin. My body sank dreamily into the carpet, while my awareness began to float in that delicious state between wakefulness and sleep.

While one part of my consciousness was anchored to my body by its attention to the rise and fall of my breath, another part began to drift back in time through the fluid universe of images and memories, carried by the sunlight's mellow warmth…

I was about a year old and was awakened from my afternoon nap by the brush of Spirit. I opened my eyes, grabbed the enamel white rails of my crib and pulled myself to my chubby little feet. The softest, most sublime gold light was pouring into the room, and that light gently permeated my entire being until I was filled with an ecstatic energy. Gazing rapt and wide-eyed into the luminosity, I became intoxicated with something even sweeter than my mother's milk.

I remained within its embrace until the door to my room opened. My father had come in to lift me from my crib, and child that I was, my attention became immediately distracted from the exquisite vision in which I'd been absorbed. And yet, even as the years flew by with an increasing multitude of distractions of all varieties, I never entirely forgot it. The light suffused me with power, bliss, and a drive to seek it out again wherever I could find it from that day forward. The golden energy expanded past the walls of my childhood home to become the path of my future.

That source of light had since given me spiritual songs, dances and ceremonies, even healing power to use with others in the service of Spirit…

…The sound of someone knocking at the door pulled me back through time. Momentarily disoriented—caught between two worlds—my body rose from the floor and tried to regain its land legs.

I wobbled to the door. Colette swept in first, and as she was giving me a hug, her friend slipped quietly by. As Colette drew away, she introduced us.

"Josie, this is Sean. Sean, Josie." Despite the functional introduction, I didn't quite register Sean's name, because his azure eyes caught my attention so completely that Colette's words faded into the background. In a few moments, those eyes went through an impossible number of changes. They actually seemed to be putting on a dance for me, moving in tiny, intricate, subtly shifting patterns, until I was absorbed in their glow, in their gem-like sparkle.

I felt slightly dazed as those eyes finally shifted their gaze away from me. The fact that I couldn't recall Sean's name seemed to set a pattern for the future. Even years later I was to find myself occasionally drawing a blank when I'd think of him, or start calling him by someone else's name.

Shaking off the disorientation, I led my guests into the living room where Colette began to methodically examine every object I had on the walls, tabletops, or windowsills. At the time, I was an avid collector, especially of unusual rocks and minerals. This had been a calling of mine since early childhood when I'd first seen a dull, bumpy brown rock split in half, and had been entranced by the world of crystals within. From that geode on, I was hooked.

The bulk of the other objects were craft pieces from various places in the world where I'd lived or traveled. Weavings, carvings, fetishes, pottery and musical instruments were strewn throughout the house.

I had a few favorites among them. There was a large, circular, almost flat woven Yemenite basket and a Bedouin camel hair throw rug from my travels in the Middle East. Some Argentine bolas and a beautifully carved and colored *Bolivian* gourd spoke of my year of pampas and mountain *altiplanos*. A woven cedar basket with whales and eagles dancing around its curved sides always brought to mind the aging Quillayute woman who made it. I'd met her on the trip to the rainforest with Colette. Other favorite objects were from the Southwest and Mexico, places to which I'd returned on many occasions.

Colette was a rather competitive collector herself and scrutinized, commented on and grilled me about many of my ethnic "treasures." During the process—which ended up going on for a good hour—her friend leafed through some books, put them down fairly quickly, sat quietly in a corner, and at one point drifted out of the house so unobtrusively I wasn't even aware he'd been gone until I saw him return.

I was slightly embarrassed by then, feeling like a barely adequate hostess to this stranger. Years later I became even more embarrassed by his retrospective commentary on my decor. He said it was all like a giant trap for people's attention, and that Colette and I had basically wasted an hour in the trap, time that he felt could have been put to better use.

Shortly after Sean came back into the house, Colette excused herself to go use the bathroom. As soon as she left the room, he came over to where I was sitting on the floor. Without any preamble, he looked me once again in the eyes and said, "Would you like me to change your life? I can do it with a single touch."

I said, "Yes."

I shocked myself. First, I knew nothing about this person beyond his acquaintance with Colette. I hadn't had a chance to ask him about his background or profession, or even to make social chit chat. Second, I did not ask him how my life would be changed, although for some time I'd felt an undefined need for change.

It seemed that my usual patterns had been placed somewhere in temporary storage. Whatever was suspending them also had put me into a state of trusting abandon. I didn't even question whether or not Sean *could* change my life, although I'd had experiences of *darshan* before with East Indian teachers who could transmit life-changing energies with the touch of a hand or feather. I simply said yes.

Sean immediately moved behind me as if there was no time to spare, and pressed lightly on my back. I felt an intense, slightly electric sensation near my left shoulder blade, and then nothing else.

As I sat there, waiting for lightning or drum rolls, all was quiet. Finally my thinking mind emerged from wherever it had been hiding, assessed the situation, and figured it was safe. As far as it could tell, nothing had happened, nothing had changed.

Then Colette came back into the room and marched over to a small clay figurine of a bat goddess.

"What's that? That's a really unusual piece, Josie."

Diverted from contemplating the possible effects of Sean's touch, I replied, "Oh, I got that recently in Mexico, shortly after a rather strange experience."

"Really? What happened?"

"Well, I was in the Yucatan visiting some ruins that were off the beaten tourist path. They were interesting, but one day I finally got bored with the crumbling pyramids and went wandering toward the edges of the jungle. After breaking through some dense growth, I suddenly found myself teetering at the edge of a large *cenote*, at least ten feet across and just as deep! A tall palm tree was growing out of the bottom, and I immediately felt drawn to go down into this hole."

"Oh, no," said Colette, "another Josie escapade. I hope you were careful."

"Moderately," I grinned. "One side of the sunken area was a little bit sloped. I found a fallen tree to use as a ladder for getting back out just in case I needed it, dragged it over to the hole, and lowered one end. Then I grabbed my day pack and made my way down the sloping soil to the bottom. So I was being careful and adventurous both, Colette."

"Mmm. Go on."

"At the bottom of the *cenote*, the air was slightly cooler and had a humid, earthy smell. As I looked around, I saw the side of the hole that had been in the shadows. It was actually an opening into the Earth!

"Fortunately, the flashlight I'd tucked in my day pack was the kind spelunkers wear to leave their hands free, you know the kind I mean? I placed it on my head and looked around for footprints or tracks on the ground. Even though I was in the mood to explore, I wasn't about to enter a jaguar's lair. I was also curious if any humans besides myself had been there in the recent past, but there were no prints of any kind."

Thus encouraged, I'd set out on an adventure.

As I continued telling the story to Sean and Colette, my memories of the experience were vivid. The earth had slanted slightly downward under my feet, and within twenty meters of walking upright through a fairly wide passageway, it opened up into what was to be the first large chamber of the labyrinth. As I turned my head to examine the chamber, my flashlight played along the cave's carved walls and ceiling.

Along one wall was what looked almost like a frozen stream of whitish shapes imbedded in the surface. I walked over and realized it was a long, wide band of fossilized seashells. The area was far inland, and yet a sea-bound river or the ocean itself must have carved out these underground passages. I carefully extracted several shells from their ancient home, wanting a physical reminder to connect me later to this exotic time and place.

The air was a bit closer now, and very still. There is something unique about being in a cave, completely surrounded with the Earth's energy. Some people don't like it—they feel in danger of being crushed.

I not only liked it but felt somewhat protected from the many vibrations, electrical and otherwise, zooming about on the Earth's surface. The hidden quality of this mysterious underworld enticed me. Being there alone enhanced the adventure. I was just nervous enough about the last part to be careful, for no one knew of my whereabouts and I was unwilling to end up a fossilized skeleton myself.

I slowly made my way through ever-narrowing passageways, always memorizing visual cues that would keep me from losing my way on the return journey. Finally it seemed I could go no further. I sat down to rest and then noticed a shadowed opening in one corner. Crawling over on my hands and knees, I peered into a tunnel, no more than two feet in diameter. Mild claustrophobia quarreled briefly with excitement, but the lure of the unknown won out.

Flopping down on my belly, I started pulling myself along snake style, or combat style, as the case may be. I slithered forward in this tiring manner for some time through the narrow tunnel. The air was getting heavier and I was drenched with sweat.

Suddenly, I felt a sound. I didn't really hear it at first, but rather sensed it with my body. Its vibrations built rapidly until they were almost audible. Then I felt the air around me stir slightly, and I froze. Before a thought could register, I was even flatter on the ground with my nose on the earth and my arms over my head and ears. First a few, then dozens, and finally hundreds of bats were flying past in the scant bit of space between my body and the top of the tunnel. I turned off my flashlight, afraid the light might aggravate them further.

Evidently, my movements had made enough noise to disturb the creatures from some nearby abode. Now, in total darkness, horror movie scenarios created images of them getting tangled in my hair, or worse, of me being devoured by vampire bats. My heart drummed against my ribs. Adrenaline rushed through my body, commanding me to choose the primal response of fight or flight. The immense and rapidly mounting pressure of having to deny both impulses and remain motionless was almost unbearable.

This was the tightest spot I'd been in since descending through the birth canal. *What am I doing here in the belly of the Earth?* I moaned silently, acutely aware that I had no chance of human rescue. I was certain the bats were preparing to feast on my flesh. Thousands of tiny, sharp teeth and piercing claws touched my skin's imagination.

The air was whirring from the river of leathery, invisible wings. My hands were clammy. The darkness was total, as was my fear. Just as my inner coward reached the edge of hysteria, a stronger inner voice yelled, "Shut up, you pitiful excuse for a warrior!"

Suddenly it was as if someone had switched the off/on button. The insult served its purpose, and I began to sober up. I slowly regained control of my breathing, grateful for my years of meditation practices. It took a while to subdue the panic attack, but I did become resigned to the fact that getting up and running was not an option. Finally, after what felt like hours, the last bat was gone. I nervously switched my flashlight back on and began slowly, and as quietly as possible, inching forward again. My muscles were loose and shaky, but they worked, and the inner warrior-adventurer was now back in power.

Within a few more meters, I was out of the tunnel and in a giant chamber. The chamber of the bats.

There were several still hanging upside down on the ceiling of the cave. I decided they must be really heavy sleepers but, nevertheless, I moved about as quietly as possible. Not much was different from the first chamber, except for a truly impressive amount of bat guano on the floor. I wandered around silently, rolling my shoulders and discharging the remnants of adrenaline and tension until I reached the back of the chamber. Only a species much smaller than I could have gone any further through the narrow crevices that remained.

So I sat down on a patch of relatively guano-free earth and tried to absorb the uniqueness of this strange dwelling. My trembling muscles had finally relaxed, and I rested peacefully with the sense of wellbeing that comes from surviving a crisis. My limbs began to feel heavy and warm, and as I gazed at the sleeping bats, I was tempted to take a nap myself. *Except for the smell, it's rather pleasant here*, I mused in a drowsy sort of way. *It's quiet, with no traffic noises, no telephones ringing, no bills to pay…It might make a nice little retreat site…*

My eyelids began to droop. I heard one of the bats return to the cave, and the amplified, solitary flapping of its wings triggered a memory from years earlier…

It is the autumn of 1976. Across the Canadian border, the weather is cool, the overcast skies typical of the Pacific Northwest. I am in my van preparing to head toward Seattle after having attended a spirituality symposium in Vancouver, BC, one of the first of its kind. It is night, and a thick fog is descending on the city of Vancouver. As I begin my drive, a feeling comes over me that tonight's drive is to be some kind of test for me—of what nature, I'm not sure. But what should have been a journey of a few hours ends up consuming almost twelve.

The first difficulty is getting out of the city. Because of the increasingly dense fog, I become disoriented in an endless maze of city streets and can find no one to give me directions. After several hours of going in circles, I finally arrive at the freeway entrance and head south, wondering what else the night has in store for me. Whatever it is, I am determined to persevere.

Once on the freeway, the fog worsens—a blinding presence as real as my own hands but impossible to touch. I seem to be drifting through another world, silent and foreboding. My speedometer slowly drops from thirty miles per hour to twenty, to ten, to five. My fatigue increases and my eyes grow so bleary from straining to see the road that I finally leave the freeway and find a small area off the road to park my van. I lock the doors, get in the back and collapse into my cozy flannel-lined sleeping bag. As I begin to drift, images from the weekend float through my head… I see an Indian praying to the Great Spirit for guidance…strange masks of Haida, Kwakiutl, Makah float by my inner eye…the chants of thousands of voices echo in my ears…and I sink deeper toward sleep.

Suddenly, a loud noise from within the van startles me into total wakefulness. I lay frozen, heart pounding, senses on red alert. The noise comes again. It sounds like a huge creature is flapping around the inside of the van. But what could it be, and how could anything that sounds so large have gotten in here? Images of pterodactyls and giant bats dive through my mind, and I begin to sweat in the cold night air. Once again I hear the hair-raising sound, and dive under my sleeping bag, certain that if this is part of my test, I am undoubtedly going to fail, if not die. Then, a long period of silence.

Finally, I get up my nerve, emerge from my cocoon, and gingerly slip out to find the light switch on the ceiling of the van. I see no monsters and—gaining courage—begin to methodically search every nook and cranny of the van's interior. Nothing. Bewildered but hopelessly wide awake, I know there is no way I'll be able to sleep, so I get in the driver's seat and find my way back to the freeway.

I proceed at a snail's pace through the impenetrable night, dazed with exhaustion and disturbed by the mysterious sounds and images that had awakened me.

Finally, the first gray light of dawn appears, and the fog begins to dissipate. Eventually, the sun breaks through and I find myself in a beautiful little valley. I breathe a deep sigh of relief, and think, whatever it was, perhaps I've made it through my long night of testing.

My thoughts, however, are premature, for minutes later I am plunged back into thick mist. Within several moments, I find I have no traction under my wheels. I have hit the driver's nightmare. Black ice. The van begins to hydroplane along the freeway, picking up speed with every passing moment. My mind races frantically, trying to review what I know about driving on ice. Do I brake, turn the wheel—what!? Finally, I am going so fast that I am terrified I'll crash into some other car in the fog, and I cautiously tap the brakes. Immediately, the van begins to careen, and before I know it, I am in a full spinout.

Everything goes into slow motion. As it does, I see a glowing arrow shoot out of my chest and head straight for the heavens, carrying my fervent prayers for help and protection. Instantly I am surrounded by a brilliant spiral of light and am filled with a calm certainty I will survive. The van eventually slows to a stop in the middle of the freeway facing oncoming traffic. Then, I hear a booming Spirit voice from behind me say, "Flash your lights off and on, off and on. It's the only way they'll notice you in the fog." So I do. Who am I to question disembodied voices at this point?

Cars miraculously part like water to either side of me. I'm concerned about how I'll ever get off the freeway in one piece, but the voice does not advise me again. After several minutes of suspense, miraculously a large semi stops and blocks the lane next to me from traffic. I manage to drive to the side of the freeway and park the van. The truck driver comes over to see if I am okay, telling me I've been fortunate. I agree, thank him for his help, and the good Samaritan departs. Then I get the post-crisis shakes, tremble for a bit, and give thanks to unseen forces for the help and the fact that I am still alive.

As I recover, I realize I was premature in letting down my guard and thinking my test was over when I saw the brief break in the fog. For the rest of the journey, I decide I will stay more alert to possible challenges and obstacles to my progress. How can I know what else this test might include before I reach my home?

As another bat fluttered into its niche, I was roused from my reverie, and the memories wafted off into the cave like *copal* smoke. Guessing the afternoon above was growing late, I decided I'd best start my return journey.

I breathed in the acrid air and wondered if any human had ever sat where I was now. Then, placing my hands on the earth to push myself to my feet, I felt something under one palm. My flashlight illuminated a piece of clay pottery sticking out of the earth. Heart thumping, I brushed the dirt away, and dozens of pieces, small and larger, emerged. They were unpainted but were etched with geometric line designs. Thrilled but trying to be respectful, I finally settled on taking only a few pieces with me as additional reminders of my experience. Somehow I felt they were meant for me.

Murmuring a quiet thanks to the cave, to the ancients who'd once sat here with their clay pot, and to the current bat inhabitants, I quietly went to the tunnel and snaked my way back out. No one accompanied me this time.

What had seemed like an endless descent into the Earth somehow shrank on the return trip, and soon enough the dim light of the sun appeared in the distance. Finally I was scrambling up my "ladder" into the golden-green jungle air, safely on Earth's surface once again.

***

By the time I finished telling Sean and Colette my story—which included finding the unusual but personally symbolic bat goddess figurine from a street vendor a few days later—it was twilight and my guests had to be on their way to some evening event. After a good-bye hug, Colette was bounding out the door and down the stairs.

Sean was a little slower to leave, and a sudden impulse made me tell him to wait for a moment. I raced into the other room, and came back

with an object in my hand. I had him hold out one of his palms, and said,
"Here, I brought this back just for you." It was one of the fossil shells from
the bat cave. A gift seemed appropriate to someone who'd just professed
to change my life, and only the gods knew when or if we'd ever meet
again. And I *did* somehow feel I'd brought it back for him.

Sean thanked me courteously, and as he went down the stairs he
turned, smiled, and said *"al dios y el viente!"* ("to the gods and the wind")
and then he was gone.

***

Sean's touch catalyzed a shift of my consciousness in such a subtle manner that I barely noticed it at the time. Though I wasn't to fully realize it
until much later, that day I crossed into a dream, a myth of power, and
Sean was already standing on the other side of the door where the winds
blew wild and free....

Two

...Green the frame, as green as spring can be
Blue its strings tied to infinity
A whirlwind blows through so free and pure
Milky Way its runway bright and clear...

from "Quatro Mas o Menos"

After that day at my home, I didn't see Sean again for months. Not only didn't I see him, but within a few days I basically forgot about him. It seems strange that I could forget someone who'd said he was going to change my life, but over time I noticed Sean's impact created a variety of fluctuations in my consciousness.

A second interaction with him months later was brief and baffling.

I was at a large outdoor gathering, and suddenly there was Sean, appearing out of nowhere. I was momentarily stunned, but I knew Colette was around and thought perhaps he had come with her. We exchanged greetings, but I was harried, having just made a commitment to help with food preparations.

"I'm sorry, Sean, but I really can't stop to chat right now," I said.

"That's okay," he smiled. "I'd just like you to give this to Colette, if you would," and he placed something in my hand.

I looked down, and there was a magnificent, inch-long beetle. It was no longer alive, but its colors were lively enough. Iridescent emerald green, peacock blue, even gold all glistened off its shiny back.

Oddly, I'd recently seen some identical beetles in Mexico at the Lagunilla sorcerers' market. They were scattered amidst an exotic array:

packets of herbs, rattlesnake rattles, feathers, and dried objects I couldn't identify. I spent hours at the market, buying bags of *copal* incense, for which I had a great fondness, and grilling the vendors mercilessly about the unidentified dried objects and their uses. *"Senora, digame por favor, que esta en este paquete? Y para que se usa?"* ("Please tell me ma'am, what is in this packet. And for what purpose is it used?") I pestered on and on until it was a wonder I didn't have a whole market of irate sorcerers driving me off with curses and lightning bolts. However, they patiently tolerated me and even seemed to be intrigued with my audacity and presence among them. For some reason I was drawn to the beetles, so I picked one out and bought it. It was now in my home in a little glass box with some tiny crystals for company.

"Oh," I said, about to tell Sean of the coincidence. "I—" and he immediately cut me off by putting a finger over his lips. Then he smiled as if to ameliorate the brusqueness of the gesture.

I was a bit taken aback but spoke no more on the subject. Then I saw Colette across the crowds, and said, "There she is now. Are you sure you don't you want to give her this gift yourself?"

I assumed that when possible, most people enjoyed giving gifts directly, partly to see the other person's response and to receive the ensuing gratitude. I was to learn Sean was socially unconventional. The kind of interactions he preferred usually involved invisible (to most) exchanges of power and awareness of spiritual *will*.

"No," he said decisively, "I want *you* to give it to her for me. Please, just tell her who it's from, that's all." Then he reached out and touched me briefly on the belly, exhaled forcefully and disappeared back into the crowd.

At his touch, once again I felt the same unusual electric energy I'd felt—and promptly forgotten—when he first touched my back. And once again I briefly acknowledged and then forgot this unusual form of *darshan* or energy transmission, focusing instead on my mental confusion. I didn't understand anything about this situation, not what Sean's goals were, if he had come with Colette, why he stopped me so abruptly from talking about the beetle—none of it. However, I was now stuck with a mission, so I shrugged and hurried off to deliver the gift to Colette.

I was about as brief as I could be, just dropping the beetle into her hand with the message, and then I was off to the food preparations. Years later I remembered the incident and I asked Sean what that had been about.

"It was a sorely needed reminder of Spirit," he said, "at a time in Colette's life when she needed it. She'd become more interested in having an emotional relationship with me than in having one with Spirit. Since she was irritated with me, I felt I could more easily give her a spiritual gift of energy through you than directly myself," Sean finished pensively.

After the day of the beetle, I'd promptly forgotten about him again. I wasn't to see Sean until more than a year had passed.

Between the time of his offer to change my life and the next interaction, my life had indeed been steadily changing. However, the process was subtle at the time, and it unfolded in stages that I never associated with that afternoon in my home, that first touch to my back, until much later. The main thing I was aware of was a growing sense of life's fleeting quality, and a certain urgent pressure to take inventory and figure out what I was doing with mine.

One night, about eighteen months after I first met Sean, this need to take stock had compelled me to burn the midnight oil with pen and journal in hand. I began the process by asking myself what I'd been seeing and doing with my twenty years of adulthood, and what was still missing.

The clearest thread was that my spiritual life was more important to me than anything else. It had been the basis for most of my major decisions, including those about work, lifestyle, choice of friends, and where to live.

During and after my graduate work in psychology in the mid-70s, I'd been involved in the early stages of the now-burgeoning holistic health movement, integrating my expanding studies of dance therapy, psychology, shamanism and other spiritually based healing systems into my own approach as a holistically oriented counselor. I had a healthy respect for both the expertise and limitations of Western physical and psychological medicine, and I was at heart a pragmatist in my field: I used whatever worked best for a client at any point in time.

Meanwhile, I kept seeking means for my own spiritual development. I could see that two kinds of experiences, each beginning in my early twenties, had affected my journey's goals. One was reading the growing number of books by yogis, shamans and other authors who described vivid and unusual spiritual experiences. Like many others, I was affected by the writings of Carlos Castaneda, self-reported student of the nagual sorcerer don Juan Matus of Sonora. Whether true, as he asserts, or fictional, as some suspect, the spiritual adventures he wrote of described a world and quality of teacher that I longed for in my own life and inspired me to begin to strengthen my spiritual muscle—*will*—as best I could without don Juan's help. Over the years I'd practiced various disciplines and gradually became aware of a certain amount of power centered in my belly where, according to don Juan, *will* was located. This reassured me I was on the right track. Occasionally I even could sense the power flowing out of me, primarily when I was focusing my *will*'s energy into healing actions such as giving polarity therapy treatments. Apparently strength of *will* was the key to diverse realms of spiritual experiences, so I was motivated!

The second early element that set my sights high was an extended training with my shamanistic dance teacher. She is a rare jewel of a woman who teaches her students to enter states that expand their awareness of the energetic movements of the inner and outer cosmos and how to dance with them. Having been exposed to her and to the inspiring spiritual books in my younger days, I was launched on the active spiritual quest.

As my journey continued, I found a fairly high level of spiritual quality in the holistic health field and enjoyed expanding my knowledge of nutrition, herbs, and body/energy therapies. I also pursued a keen interest in shamanism and the power of ceremony, read any anthropological and biographical material I could find on the subjects, and attended what related events I could.

What I learned motivated me to practice years of meditations, vision quests, occasional fasting, and a variety of personal ceremonies. Some people I met took similar advantage of the exposure to shamanic "technology." Others fell into the trap of going to numerous gatherings for the weekend "high" without incorporating any of the multiple tools and teachings they learned into consistent spiritual practice.

As I met various shamans, indigenous healers and medicine men (rarely women) who were teaching the primarily Anglo public, my interest focused increasingly on three areas: their personal power, impeccability, and the results of cross-cultural interfaces.

A growing number of Anglo Westerners were being exposed to spiritual traditions of other cultures, and I saw how the glamour of the exotic was sometimes blinding. The situation was a challenge. It took hard work to separate out those teachers with real knowledge and personal power from the charlatans, and to be on guard for those using their position to seduce women or intimidate Anglo "pilgrims" with their role of authority. As in any situation, our personal naivete or insecurities can cause us to give our power away or misuse the power we wield, and I found that the spiritual teacher/student arena was no exception.

Although I gained knowledge and valuable insights into many areas of spirituality over the years, including shamanic ceremonialism, I also experienced disappointments and began to wonder if I'd created impossible expectations. Was I fated never to find the level of teachers and teachings I'd been so determined to find twenty years earlier? In this growing spiritual crisis, even my friends were beginning to wear on me inexplicably. I also realized I'd been slowly losing inspiration in my professional life. The entire situation was unnerving.

By this point of my prolonged taking-stock process, it was three in the morning, and I'd decided what I really needed was to go on a solitary spiritual retreat. Soon! I'd gone into retreat enough times in the past to know from experience that usually I emerged with increased clarity and spiritual renewal. I was obviously in need of both. I immediately began planning to head for the mountains the following weekend, and went to bed in a better frame of mind having made this decision.

***

My retreat started out as I'd imagined, and was blessed with perfect Indian summer weather. For forty-eight hours I did very little but soak up the sun, drift in and out of dreaming, and try to figure out what I really wanted to be doing with my life.

I'd been to this mountain retreat site in the past to vision quest and enjoy its rugged, natural beauty. Cottonwood and evergreens displayed their greenery against the slopes by day, and by night deer, coyotes and the occasional mountain lion wandered the open spaces still available to them. A few Indians occasionally used the place for their own vision quests, sweat lodges and other ceremonies, but much of the time it was uninhabited by humans.

I'd had several unusual experiences on my vision quests. During one quest, in the middle of the night while I sat praying, I suddenly heard what sounded like heavy human footsteps just up the mountain. I was instantly unnerved, for there had been no slow approach of these sounds from the distance to where they now were—quite close! It was as if they came out of nowhere. And it was virtually impossible for anyone to have gotten through the security fences surrounding the site.

As I sat trying to calm myself and figure out what was going on, a second pair of heavy steps rang out on the rough, gravelly hillside perhaps thirty feet from the first pair. At that point I threw out an energetic shield of protection and prayed out loud for insight as to the meaning of these events. Although the footsteps were now silent, I peered into the night in the direction from which the sounds had first come. Suddenly I saw two tall, glowing forms, each hovering in the approximate location of the original noises. They shimmered in the night for several moments and then disappeared. There were no more footsteps after that, and I became convinced I'd been visited by two spirit allies of some sort who had come to test my power and courage. I felt that if I'd given in to my fear they would have overwhelmed me. But because I kept my intention clear—that I was there to learn but that I would not be threatened by them—they allowed me to witness their presence and thus expanded my awareness of the mysterious universe in which I lived.

The second unusual experience happened during a seven-day vision quest at the retreat site. Once again I was alone on the land. On the fourth night of fasting, I was suddenly moved to pick up my drum and begin singing a powerful Lakota vision quest song I'd learned from a medicine man. My voice rang out in the crisp air, bouncing off the mountainsides and soaring toward the star-filled sky. I sang the song four times through, turning and facing each cardinal direction one by one, and I became filled with a fierce, ecstatic power. As the last drum beat faded into silence, suddenly I heard a loud, deep male voice booming out a "ho!"—a common Native American expression of appreciation or agreement—coming from just outside my circle. Again, I was startled, heard no rustling or footsteps marking human movement toward or away from me after this solitary exclamation, and had to conclude once more that I'd received a spirit visitation. It was to the site of these mysteries that I'd now returned for retreat and renewal.

Oddly, just before leaving for the mountains, Sean phoned me. He was going to be passing through town and wondered if I'd like to meet with him.

In all honesty, the first thought that went through my mind was that I simply didn't have the energy to deal with him, no matter how fascinating he might be. I told Sean I was going to the mountains, and perhaps he'd like to wait until another time.

"Well, you could give me the directions and we could leave it up to fate," he said quietly. "I probably won't make it. But it may be quite a long time before I'm in the area again, so on the remote possibility it works out, why not tell me how to find you?"

I deliberated. I found myself in conflict, and I wasn't sure why. I knew I needed this retreat, and yet there was something ineffable stirring in my spirit, prompting me to pay more attention to Sean and the unusual energy he carried. Still in conflict and guessing he'd never find me, I ended up giving Sean vague directions and the combination for the security gate, then promptly forgot about him. A few days later I was enjoying my mountain retreat, sunbathing and staring at the shadows on the nearby pond. Suddenly I caught movement out of the corner of my eye, and I saw someone walking up the path in my direction. At first I didn't even recognize the man. Until he got closer and started talking, I was momentarily alarmed that some stranger had found his way through the security gate and up into this private sanctuary. Then, as I scrambled for more clothing, I was relieved to realize who it was.

By the time Sean drew near, I was feigning nonchalance. He strode over and without a word, immediately touched my belly at the navel area. This is a fairly unconventional greeting in any circumstance. For a brief moment I wondered if this was some strange sexual advance and was trying to figure out how to respond, although there had been nothing sexual in any of our previous interactions. Then the spiritual aftermath of Sean's touch took hold and elicited some eerie equivalent to hours of meditation. My mind became utterly silent and I entered a state of heightened awareness.

When he'd touched my belly, I now realized he'd sent a strand of his spiritual *will* to connect with mine. (I later learned that Sean regarded the belly as the area of the body where the *will*, our primary spiritual "muscle," is most strongly concentrated). The area around my navel felt alive and filled with a calm power. Immediately after his touch as my mind stilled, a brief and sudden wind roared through the trees, first off to one side of us, and then another from behind me. In a third direction a raven gave a quick burst of calls. Sean followed each event with his blazing eyes, forcefully drawing my attention to them.

The next several hours in his company had the quality of a dream. Once I realized his touch was no sexual advance but rather a greeting to my own *will*, I became quite relaxed. Not only did I relax, but Sean's presence and my own spirit cooperated in such a way that I entered a state of abandon similar to my response eighteen months earlier when he first asked if I wanted him to change my life.

Shortly after his unusual greeting, I put on my tennis shoes and we went walking around the area. Whenever a butterfly or lizard would cross our path, Sean would pause. In a lighthearted mood, we would pay the utmost attention to the creature's movements and what direction it was travelling, as if this mattered deeply. Sean's attitude toward the ravens, however, was distinctly different. Several large ravens were quite vocal much of the time, and Sean made intense gestures with his hands and *will* that seemed to first pull the ravens out of the trees to circle around us and then to turn them away until they would go into hiding once again. Watching his mood change with the ravens and seeing and hearing the ravens' quite bizarre calls and behaviors alerted me that an unusual interaction of power was occurring between all of them. I was the witness.

I followed Sean through a dense area of wild sage, finally crawling on hands and knees until we found a small opening not quite big enough for both of us to sit. Sean began to break and bend some of the branches to enlarge the space and give us more room, and I joined him. We pulled and wove the slender stalks until we'd created a spacious nest. Then we sat back to back, surrounded by the pungent fragrance of the sage and the steady drone of honeybees.

As the bees satiated themselves, I became intoxicated sitting in the silver-green nest. Bolts of energy surged through me, concentrated most intensely in the area of my back which Sean had pressed on at my house. I felt both electrified and dreamy. After a while we stood up—a minor challenge for me due to my altered state. I was wobbly as a young bird about to take first flight.

The moment we emerged from our nest, Sean moved behind me and, with his left hand, lifted my left arm straight out to my side so it was extended parallel to the ground. With his right hand he reached around my other side and covered my navel area: the *will*'s center. His breath was a mild wind against the back of my neck.

Then we began slowly turning in a circle. We stopped at each cardinal point with our left arms extended in its direction. The first time we pointed north, some intense raven calls erupted from that direction. They were hiding perhaps a few hundred feet away, but were even more powerful than earlier. As we turned to the east, the same thing happened. The west and south seemed eerily silent in contrast, but months later Sean told me his spirit allies, the winds, had been there in one of the directions. Unlike my noisy encounters with spirits in those same mountains in the past, the winds were silent. I didn't recognize Sean's allies at the time, but the power coming from the ravens was more than enough for me to deal with.

We continued in our slow revolutions a number of times. Every time we'd point east and north, the raven sounds would explode, getting increasingly intense until shudders of energy were going up my spine and I became slightly cross-eyed. Apparently my circuits went on overload, for I have no memory of how we extricated ourselves from the sage jungle and made it to a circular clearing. What I do remember next is that I, with great abandon, was performing some kind of cat-like dance around Sean, crouching, springing, batting at invisible things in the air. He stared at me, eyes glowing like blue flames. Finally, he pressed firmly on the top of my head, murmured something inaudible, and then was gone as suddenly as he'd arrived hours earlier.

After he left, the entire afternoon quickly became a surreal memory. Weeks later Sean reminded me of the sequence of events that day in the mountains, and gave his view on some of what had taken place.

"One of the things I was doing, Josie, was trying to help you face the power of the four winds and bond your *will* to them. Women can develop deep spiritual relationships to the different winds. As one of your ongoing practices of awareness, you might want to begin paying attention to the wind, especially when it is blowing consistently from one direction for several days. Then notice what effect the west wind—for example—has on your mood, your physical energy, mental state, and even your dreaming and *will*."

"What's so significant about the wind coming from one direction for a few days?" I asked curiously.

"Sometimes," Sean replied, "power occurs in four-day patterns, including changes of the wind, and will build over those four days to an energetic climax. Once you start paying attention to a wind in its four-day cycle, you have to follow all the way through or the wind, especially the west wind, might get pissed off at you." He didn't mention at the time what would happen if it did, but implied I'd rather not find out!

We went on to discuss various bits of information we each had on the subject. Sean said every wind has its own unique impact, particularly on women, although men can also be effected by them. I told him that in the Middle East, the effect of the wind on the human temperament has been well known for at least a thousand years. There are even legal exemptions for behaviors during one particular kind of wind. Occasionally, a *chamsin*, a hot dry wind similar to California's Santa Anas, will come out of the Middle Eastern deserts and wail ceaselessly, sometimes for days. Not only does sand and grit get in everything, but people's moods are strongly effected. Some experience only a general irritability that ends when the wind changes. For others, their normal control can slip over the edge into acts of violence. Over centuries, the *chamsin's* influence became so apparent that allowances for it were made in the judicial system. Crimes of passion, ordinarily severely punished, often went completely unpunished if they took place during the *chamsin*. Sean added that the northern Chinook and the Nigerian Harmattan winds are also known for their powerful disruptive effects on the human psyche.

Other kinds of winds can be calming. Because of a mysterious connection between the wind and the womb, Sean said it was advantageous for women to note the effects of the four directional winds. Eventually, most women would find that one of the four is "her" wind or direction.

"If a woman can gather enough personal power over time," Sean told me once, "with effort and discipline, eventually she will be able to coax some of that wind into her womb. After that, she will have a solid spiritual connection with it."

I felt the truth of much of what he'd been saying from my own experiences. The wind sometimes had profound effects on my moods, which ranged from restlessness or apathy to creativity and exhilaration. And I looked forward to forming a more intimate and active relationship to the winds, to testing what Sean had said and finding out for myself if it was possible.

"Over the years I've seen that most women have an affinity with one directional wind," he continued. "But with spiritual training, some can balance themselves with all four and come into an alignment with near-infinite power. That day in the mountains I supported your *will* in making a 'contract' with all four winds, even though you might have had no conscious awareness that that's what was going on.

"And maybe some day you'll be strong and balanced enough to take on a whirlwind. Whirlwinds have a unique spiritual power because they hold a moving and equal balance of all four directions. People call some of them dust devils or *diablandos*. They are definitely a spiritual force to be reckoned with, so get ready, Josie. There just might be a *diablando* waiting to test your power somewhere down the road."

Three

--- --- --- --- --- --- --- --- --- --- --- --- --- --- --- --- --- ---

Prowling dreaming's edge
Jaguar will fans out the silver net,
Green its eyes on night's vague promise
Spirit need the force that drives…

from "Hungry Spirit Hunting"

New and haunting rhythms of the unknown were pulsing through my life. The staid interludes of the known and familiar were becoming shorter and shorter. Sean's presence was ushering in a unique quality of experience that defied thinking analysis, and only weeks after our mountain encounter, I found myself once again entranced, sitting across the table from him in a Mexican restaurant. He'd already informed me we only had a few hours, so we were in concentrated time.

Just before going into the restaurant, while we were still in the parking lot, a large, pale moth flew over our heads. Sean moved behind me, covered my *will* center with one hand and extended my right arm with his straight toward the moth. I could feel his whole body become tight and hard as a stretched drum skin pulsing with power. The moth suddenly dipped and weaved from the energy contact as if it had become drunk. Then it recovered and disappeared into the night. Sean shifted to my side, glanced at me briefly with eyes glowing like sapphires, and then we turned and entered the restaurant.

After a light meal of soup and tortillas, Sean began to tell me a story relating to why we'd come to this particular restaurant. As I settled into the padded red vinyl of our booth, my gaze wandered around the large but

simple room, lingering here and there on the walls where voluptuous fla-
menco gypsies danced on black velvet canvases, then taking in giant som-
breros, potted cacti and rainbow-hued Mexican blankets. The scent of
chili, cilantro and corn filled the air.

"Some years ago, I believe in the late sixties," he said, laughing to himself
and shaking his head, "Angelina, a Mexican sorceress I knew of, came here
and put on one of the most amazing performances I've ever seen. She came
in disguise as a sick and decrepit old street lady. I was here for dinner, and the
restaurant was full. Angelina shuffled in, dressed mostly in black, with tangled greasy hair and gross dirty bandages wrapped around one forearm and
both legs. She leaned on a cane that wobbled convincingly under her weight.

"This horrendous apparition immediately headed for one of the booths
where a family was sitting. Standing at the end of their table, she began to
complain to them about her health. Wouldn't they let her sit with them,
she queried, looking as pitiful as she could while gesturing that all the
tables and booths were full.

"The family immediately capitulated, and soon regretted it. Angelina
loudly carried on for some time about being alone and old and sick, with
no one to care for her. The doctors she'd seen were all incompetents, she
attested, just trying to take advantage of a poor old woman. She described
her symptoms to her captive audience, including details of oozing sores on
her arms and legs that wouldn't heal, and even offered to unwrap the
hideous gauze so they could see for themselves that she wasn't exaggerating!

"By that point, the parents of this family had gone from trying to be
polite, to being silently irritated, to finally turning shades of pale green
and on the verge of losing their tortillas. They tremulously declined her
offer, although their children's eyes widened in hopeful anticipation. She
had already started to unwrap one arm slightly, and glared at them as if
she couldn't believe they could turn down such a marvelous opportunity.

"Finally she shrugged, looked around the dining room, got up and
headed for her next victim. The routine was repeated, at a slightly louder

volume and with more drama, for the benefit of a well-dressed business-man, who was doing his best to hide from her behind a newspaper.

"After she had him squirming, she continued on to another table of two young women. Soon Angelina had corralled the attention of the entire room with her energy alone. When she wasn't seated at a table, she had a different means of holding everyone's attention in a fierce grip.

"She would stand with one hand on the table itself, immediately claim-ing the territory. Then she'd go through a serious of riveting non-verbal contortions. Sometimes she would clutch at her throat or chest, adding agonized moans to the gestures. The most unnerving thing to me was what she did with her face. She somehow had mastered furrowing her forehead so that the wrinkles converged from all directions into the center, where the Hindus place the third eye. This created an indentation that would get deeper and deeper, turning into a dramatically shadowed dark hole.

"Once she achieved this phenomenon, as her demeanor of torment reached a crescendo, Angelina would invariably glance in my direction. I tell you, it was a struggle not to get sucked into that black hole, which I was sure would be the end of me or worse!

"I had to keep steeling my emotions against the drama of her pain, ordering myself not to get drawn in. This became especially difficult when it looked like she was working herself up to some epileptic type fit. Just as her body started jerking, she regained control, hobbled over to my table, and tried to bully her way into sitting across from me. I told her a flat 'no way.' Nothing was going to convince me to sit with that black hole in her forehead across the table from me!

"After a brief staring match, she finally moved on, and had covered almost two thirds of the restaurant patrons before she shuffled her way back through the room, mumbling to herself, and left. The whole room breathed a collective sigh of relief, as if a threatening storm had finally passed and they knew they were safe.

"I was probably the only one who was a little disappointed," said Sean, his eyes dancing with delight. "For me, it was true love mixed with true terror. That woman was a consummate actress. No one would have guessed that under her scruffy outfit was a powerful sorceress, and yet Angelina had the attention of all the patrons wrapped up tight. Oddly enough, the restaurant personnel themselves didn't act at all concerned. None of them asked her to leave or objected to her behavior in any way."

"Maybe they knew what she was and were afraid to," I guessed out loud.

"No, it was her conscious use of power that soothed them and kept them unruffled."

Sean then continued his story. "Just as we'd all settled down and were back to eating and enjoying their meals, in walked Angelina again! There was an instant hush in the room, and you could almost feel the customers wanting to slide under the tables and disappear. She took up where she'd left off making the rounds until she interacted with every table she'd missed earlier. Not one person told her to leave them alone. They all seemed to feel obligated to listen to her tale of woe, her complaints and minute details of failing health. She really was like some grotesque mirror of how a good many people carry on conversations. Most people just love an audience for their complaints. I think this is part of why they were so trapped in her presence.

"By then, a few tables had emptied, and she went to sit alone at one of them. Once again, everyone thought they were off the hook, but Angelina wasn't quite finished with us!

"A waitress did go up to her then and politely asked for her order. The old woman complained loudly that she was much too sick to consider eating, and glared at the waitress as if to dare a contradiction. The waitress met the challenge admirably, and quietly suggested that she might like to order something to drink.

"Evidently Angelina agreed, because the waitress left and soon returned with some water and a cup of coffee. Needless to say, all the customers surreptitiously followed the transaction. I was the only one truly enjoying Angelina's performance, paying serious attention to every nuance and action.

"She rearranged the water and coffee slightly after the waitress left, stared at them for a while, then moved them a bit more. Then she lifted the coffee cup almost to her lips before setting it back down in the saucer. Angelina captured our attention in this manner for another fifteen minutes or so. Sometimes she'd hold the cup close to her lips for longer, or vary the time she'd take to shakily raise or lower it. When at last she fumbled in her ragged old purse for a few coins for the coffee, everyone was thoroughly exhausted from the suspense. And she never did drink one single sip.

"As she made her grand exit, she gave a final pitiful glance around the room as if to say, 'see, I told you I was too sick even to eat *or* drink.' And then she was gone."

We sat in silence for a while, as I digested this story along with my dinner. I felt vaguely disturbed. The story had me wondering what I would have done if I had been there for Angelina's performance. I did some mental squirming, remembering times when I'd demanded an audience for a litany of complaints myself. Often it was in the show-and-tell context in which one person would start on the things wrong in his or her life, and then I, along with others, chimed in with our grievances, not to be outdone. Perhaps this was the human tendency the sorceress was trying to reflect—the aspect of ego that doesn't care how it gets attention as long as it gets it—and the reason Sean related the story.

Partly to divert him from any possible mind reading, I excused myself and went to the restroom. After I returned, Sean and I sat a while longer at the restaurant even though we'd long since finished our meal. For him it was a place where sorcery still shimmered from the walls themselves, and he'd returned to it time after time over the years.

After the Mexican dinner, Sean filled the remainder of the night with tales and teachings of power until, as dawn's first light touched the sky, he headed east. Once again I had no idea when I'd see him again. But somehow I was certain I would.

***

As fate would have it, not long after that evening I first met Carlos Castaneda.

I knew over the years there had been some controversy about the authenticity of his books. From my own readings, I'd noticed that some details were either contradictory within the context of his own books, or with information from outside sources.

Whether or not his stories were fiction, Carlos detailed a map of the human spirit and the effects of social pressures on it in a way that felt deep and made a great deal of sense to me. In addition, I'd found some of the practices he described were spiritually effective. Although Carlos has had a minimal personal interface with the general spiritually interested public, his writings alone inspired many people toward spiritual activities and explorations of other realities.

Sean happened to phone me a few days before I met Castaneda, and we discussed the potentials of the event at length. One of the things I appreciated most was what Sean suggested about acting *will*fully when I met Carlos.

"You have a fantastic opportunity to act with power toward Carlos rather than simply being a passive spectator. Probably most everyone else will just be gawking, so if he's what he claims to be, he'll notice the uniqueness of your spiritual attitude."

So often when we get a chance to be around "celebrities," even spiritual celebrities, we tend to fall into the passive mode Sean had described. I was enthused about taking an active spiritual role in my upcoming encounter. However, the evening I was to meet Castaneda, I also felt a flurry of excitement at finally being face-to-face with this legendary figure whose books had sparked so many dreams and experiences over the years. I dressed in my fanciest Oaxacan *huipil* to honor the man who had written at such length about his experiences with Mexican sorcerers.

Carlos in person was both dynamic and articulate. The other people who had been invited to meet him seemed as excited about the situation as I, although Sean may have been accurate about the ratio of gawking to spiritual attention. Nonetheless, we all sat in silent fascination as Carlos began to speak of some of the events in his books.

I kept trying to focus my *will* and power to remain concentrated. However, after listening to him talk for a while, I lost track of what he was saying and found my head had slowly tilted to the left so I was looking at him sideways. Not only that, but I realized I'd been experiencing myself as floating horizontal to the ground for some time before I was aware of the new position of my head! I was in a very strange state. My intense determination to be *will*ful had evidently inspired my *double*—my astral body—to set up maneuvers of its own. It took me a while before I could readjust my head to its normal upright position, as if some dreamy lassitude had overtaken my muscles.

As my mind shifted back to more normal awareness, I gathered Carlos was now talking about "la Gorda," a female character in his books who had been Carlos's partner in the *art of dreaming*. As they dreamed together, they'd retrieved many forgotten memories of events that had taken place in altered states of awareness in their individual and shared past.

Carlos spoke about what had happened to la Gorda since the last mention of her in his books. Evidently, over time she had become increasingly greedy for power in an unbalanced way. "La Gorda" means the fat one, which she had been when don Juan found her. Although she overcame her greed for food and became lean, her ego's need for power took its place in an equally obsessive manner. Carlos said she was like a wolf in her hunger. This lust consumed her, and translating into a physical form, finally manifested in a blood clot that exploded in her brain and killed her. Whether true or allegory, the story packed a punch!

The author-storyteller launched into a series of other anecdotal tales of power and of his own earlier search for knowledge. What stood out the most, however, was what he had to say of the nature of social aggregates. I listened with great interest.

Carlos described a few kinds of these groups, such as co-workers, families, groups who party together and fellow students. He said that in almost every kind of aggregate, over time there is a tendency for individuals to trade in the mysterious unfolding of their own spirit for extended membership in the group. This seems to be an inherent pressure of the social aggregate, and it takes hard work to overcome the quicksand of social pressure.

Nevertheless, he asserted it was possible to do so, primarily through perfecting the *"art of stalking"* and utilizing it as a barrier against the pressure.

Spiritual stalking is a means of ameliorating the effect of the continuous onslaught of social attention, with freedom as its goal. One can interact with and *stalk* oneself, and in fact, this is really the core of *stalking*. It entails controlling the quality of attention we place on ourselves: primarily how we think about ourselves, and the emotions we aim at ourselves. *Stalking* also involves gathering power through reviewing our past social interactions and taking back the energy we have invested in others. Practicing the *art of stalking* in interpersonal exchanges can involve extravagant disguises and behaviors to keep other people from putting the practitioner into limiting boxes. This art can also be more subtle and involve being more intentional about what we share of ourselves with others.

If we are engaged in *stalking*, the pieces of information we *choose* to hand out would be consciously selected for the purpose at hand. We must ask ourselves what impression we want to create and with what goal in mind. Do we want to lull others with predictability, keep them guessing with unpredictability, or some of each?

Someone might say this is manipulative and devious. In a sense, that is true. However, people are *always* manipulating their environment, and are frequently devious. We separated ourselves from our primate ancestors long ago when we began to manipulate the raw materials of the earth and create tools.

The differences with *stalking* are the goals. Some people manipulate for material wealth, some for a job, some for a mate, most for social acceptance. *Stalkers* do it to keep their connection to their own mysterious spirit and its freedom. And they do it with honesty, in that they are quite aware of the purpose of their behavior. Most people will rarely admit to the extent of their manipulations, since the majority of us regularly lie to ourselves!

One of the main principles of the *art of stalking* involves the disruption of habitual patterns. When we disrupt a pattern, no matter how great or small, we immediately make space in our awareness for the "left-side"—in Castaneda's terminology—or spiritual unknown. As we break more and more habits, the more of the unknown we can touch and the freer we become.

Carlos also mentioned a second alternative to social pressure.

"Sometimes one simply has to leave the social aggregate or aggregates one is in. This becomes necessary when the aggregate is so confining that without enough strength of *stalking* one cannot find freedom within it."

His statement was an omen for me. As I'd begun to realize before my mountain retreat, I'd been feeling weirdly hemmed in by the groups around me—professional, social, even the larger community of the city residents. I needed a major change in my life. I wasn't sure quite how and when it would happen, but it was looming. Carlos helped me immensely to identify some of the dynamics and begin to muster some momentum.

At the end of the evening, I gave him a ride to his next destination. As I was driving, at one point he patted the exact place on my back that Sean had pressed with his promise to change my life, an area Sean called the "dreaming point." Soon after that evening, Carlos began appearing more frequently in my dreams. I believe his contact with my back forged an energetic link between us that made this possible. I also believe it reconnected him, through me, to Sean, who he'd met briefly about seventeen years earlier.

I returned the favor just before we parted, by making the spiritual gesture Sean had suggested in advance. It was a subtle motion of my left hand, but apparently power was moving through me and it caused Carlos's body to noticeably jolt. I masked my surprise at this result, waved good-bye and drove off thinking about the years I'd spent reading his books and the reality of having finally met him. I wondered what Carlos had made of my gesture, and if he'd keep the dinner "date" he'd promised me earlier in the evening.

He failed to keep our date because, as his secretary told me when she called, he had to suddenly leave for Mexico. Although I was somewhat disappointed, I decided to go to the restaurant where we'd discussed meeting to see if he might show up anyway. As I arrived, I kept telling myself this was irrational behavior on my part, but despite my mind's commentary on my actions, something was driving me to pursue the original plan.

I waited for some time in the lobby, having checked to see that Castaneda wasn't already seated at a table. After half an hour had passed, I resigned myself to a no-show and went out to the parking lot. I felt strange, uneasy, as if there was something I was missing in this situation. I lingered at the door of my car, looking around the lot for a clue to my disquiet. Then I glanced up at the night sky and froze with disbelief.

Floating in the darkness was a massive, glowing outline of an abstract, geometric form. It easily covered a third of the sky and hovered almost over me at some distance. I blinked rapidly to make sure I wasn't having some kind of eye problems, but the form remained constant. Shivering slightly, I wondered if I was seeing my first UFO, although the shape didn't really look like a craft of any kind.

Feeling a bit intimidated by the spectacle, I searched the parking lot to see if there were any other humans nearby. A man stood about thirty feet away, facing away from me in the direction of the glowing apparition. My first thought was that perhaps Carlos had made it after all, but as I approached him, it was obvious this man was taller and was a complete stranger. Nonetheless I stopped at his side and could see that he was definitely looking up at the sky.

"You see it too, don't you?" I said with no preamble.

The young, dark-haired man turned and smiled at me for a moment before returning his gaze to the heavens. "Yeah, it's really there, whatever it is."

We stood side by side in silence for a while, riveted by the mysterious form above. After a good ten minutes had passed, we wandered to one side of the parking lot and sat on the ground to continue watching. Not a single car came or went during that time. The young man began telling me he'd frequently seen strange lights bobbing through the skies on his numerous backpacking trips into the mountains and guessed the universe was big enough for plenty of weirdness. He seemed bemused and not at all intimidated either by his earlier experiences or by the current glowing presence above us. I too had seen many inexplicable things in my life, but never anything quite like this.

As we sat and watched over the course of an hour, the form began to slowly shift until it resembled something identifiable: the outline of a giant, luminous eagle. I stared in amazement, certain this mysterious omen would reveal its meaning to me some time in the future. The eagle remained in place a long while before finally disappearing into the cobalt skies. Without speaking again, the young man and I looked into the infinite spaces of one another's eyes, nodded at what we'd shared, and then turned and walked away, never to see each other again.

Carlos had failed to show up, but power had kept its appointment with me nonetheless. And the season of eagles had launched into full force, with its teachings of freedom in the face of social pressures and patterns.

By the time I did see Carlos again, my social aggregate was gone and my whole life had changed.

Four

"Fate is the shepherd of power."

Sean

Spirit power came knocking at my door once again, and as it was no stranger to me, I answered the summons. I responded by travelling to Arizona, a few weeks after the Mexican dinner, to a ceremony a Native American acquaintance had invited me to attend. Ironically, the acquaintance never showed up. I wouldn't have gone if I'd known that in advance, since I knew no one else who was attending and would be far from home. However, I don't regret the turn of fate that led me there.

As it happened, at the last moment Sean decided to join me. And the season of eagles continued to surprise me with its mercurial shifts and changes.

When Sean met up with me in Arizona, once again I didn't recognize him at first. I walked right by him, and later when he greeted me I feigned nonchalance, like I'd known all along it was him and was just being mysterious myself.

He didn't speak for the first hour or so, but simply drove the car directly to a secluded, snow-covered forest just outside Flagstaff where we sat in silence. Although I was enjoying the natural beauty and freshness after the hours of recycled airplane air, I was somewhat unnerved at first. Here I was far from home with a near stranger in a strange land, and this silent treatment didn't resemble anything close to a normal social encounter. Not that any of our past interactions had either! Finally, in a series of spiritual gestures that were now familiar to me, Sean touched my belly and the dreaming point on my back like a doctor taking a pulse. I knew he was "reading" my *will* and I wondered what he was learning.

Then, before we went back into the nearby town to rest up for the ceremony, he broke the silence and told me something startling about his trip
to Arizona.

"I picked up a hitchhiker a day's drive from here," he said in a subdued
voice. "I was going to pass him by and then something made me stop.

"Charlie's fairly young, maybe seventeen or so, and seems to be in the
process of leaving home for good. He's half Apache, and you might find
his unusual spirit intriguing. Charlie wants to come to the ceremony with
us, so you'll have plenty of time to be around him."

I found myself both curious and slightly annoyed at the change of
venue. I was still suffering under the delusion that *I* was in control of this
journey rather than Spirit! Later I regretted not having taken even more
advantage of the situation, for, as it turned out, we were to have only the
briefest time to enjoy Charlie.

Looking back at some of my impressions, Charlie had many energetic
similarities to Sean. He could be charming, thirsty to learn and experience, intense, open to Spirit, and sometimes immensely aggravating in his
confidence that crossed over into arrogance.

One of the most extraordinary experiences took place the first evening
the three of us spent together. After our time in the forest, Sean drove me
to a cafe in Flagstaff where Charlie was waiting for us. Dinner was spent
in relative silence, so I figured Sean had probably already suggested to
Charlie that he not chatter unnecessarily. Every once in a while Charlie
and I would catch the other in brief, speculative looks. I wondered what
Sean had told Charlie about me.

When we returned to the motel room Sean had reserved for the three
of us, he asked Charlie and me if we'd sit on one side of the room while
he sat on the other, facing us. Charlie folded all six feet plus of his brown,
lanky form into some pretzel-like contortion in which he seemed quite
comfortable, in true adolescent fashion. I leaned against the wall with my
arms wrapped around my knees. I was a little fatigued from the day's travels and was still trying to adjust to the fact of Charlie's presence and to

being with Sean again. Nevertheless, I gathered myself to pay attention to whatever Sean was up to next.

As I stared at him, suddenly he began to unfold his *will* through his eyes. The phrase "dancing with his eyes" is perhaps more descriptive. They shimmered and darted like silver-blue fish flashing in the sun. Such was the power of his efforts—combined with the collective spirit of the moment—so that in seconds all of us were in heightened awareness. Charlie and I were riveted in our attention, and I could hear both of us breathing deep.

As Sean's *will* unfolded into the room, it seemed to be carrying much more than just his own energies. Charlie and I each experienced this quite differently.

Charlie, as he later reported, saw everything in the room dissolve into light until he couldn't see Sean's human features any more. In that light, he then saw a variety of colored balls bouncing around.

Simultaneously, I was feeling an intense pressure building in the room, and hearing invisible energies begin to pop and crackle through the walls and into the space. First Sean, and then the entire room started to glow. Suddenly I felt another distinct presence joining us. As I looked around, trying to locate the source, my heart was racing. I glanced back to Sean for a clue, and found myself witnessing a subtle but extraordinary change in his face, until it was transformed into someone who resembled him, was slightly older, but was definitely *not* some future glimpse of Sean...

I gaped. Charlie, the way Sean described him later, entered into a soothed, non-thinking, inebriated state. Right before returning to more normal awareness, he too got a glimpse of someone else looking out of Sean's face.

Finally Sean closed his eyes, and we were all released from the intense grip of the experience. After a few moments of stunned silence, Charlie and I simultaneously began babbling about our experiences, like two puppies trying to enthusiastically extricate themselves from a tangled blanket. We finally got ourselves slightly sorted out and Charlie spoke first. Then

I described the other face I saw superimposed on Sean. The latter was at first surprised, and then delighted.

"I'm going to say something from my own perspective about what just took place," he said, sitting up straight and taking a few deep belly breaths. "The eyes have a peculiar power, and can be used for other purposes than perceiving the world.

"Ordinary people with flirting and mating on their minds often use their eyes to signal and pull another person's energies toward sex." Out of the corner of my eye, I saw Charlie sit up straighter, suddenly hanging on every word, and I laughed inside over his obvious interest in this aspect of the discussion. "They don't have to have any spiritual training or be a sorcerer to signal sex or seduction to one another," continued Sean. "Sexual energy has such an innately strong connection to *will*, and *will* expresses itself so directly through the eyes, that it's a natural talent for most people, and linked to the survival of the species.

"Most people rarely use their eyes in a powerful way for anything besides sending sexual messages or expressions of deep anger. I'm a little different. I've been trained to use my eyes to shift other people through various states of awareness that have nothing to do with sex. This is partly because of my ability to summon *intent* with my eyes."

"How do *you* define *intent*?" I asked, having always had difficulty grasping the descriptions of this term in Castaneda's books.

"*Intent* dwells at the source of power, and the direction power takes is part of the shape of *intent*," he continued. "Another part of its shape is created by the human *will* and the *will* of all other life forms. Therefore, when I cajole *intent* through my eyes, and someone else is following my eyes with theirs and thus with their *will*, I am able to help them align with *intent*. Then, together we all face the power flowing toward us. Where that will carry us at any given moment is unknown, both to myself and the others. Does that make it all clear to you, Josie?" he teased, seeing my eyes glazing slightly.

"Well…Give me a few years and I'm sure it'll all come together for me."

Sean grinned, nodded and went on. "In my youth, I once met a sorcerer down in Mexico, in the Oaxaca city *zocolo*. He approached me immediately upon first laying his eyes on me, and suggested I come to his place in nearby Mitla. I was shocked at his appearance. He looked like a slightly older version of what could have been my twin brother.

"I accompanied him to his one-room, ascetic home. There, on a small shelf, sat a photograph of what turned out to be a Sufi master. My 'twin' gestured that I should sit down and make myself comfortable. Then, silently and with no later explanations, he took some fabric out of a dresser drawer and slowly, almost ritualistically, wrapped it around his head till it formed a turban. This transformation from Mexican cowboy to Sufi master was eerily calm and sedate.

"In fact, the overall effect he had on me was deeply soothing. Despite the unusual ritual and circumstances, I felt sublimely comfortable, as if looking through a mirror at myself. I trusted him implicitly, and he seemed to know me and why I was there in Oaxaca. This became more apparent as I looked about the interior of his home. There, on a counter against one wall, sat a large transparent bag filled with *ololiuhqui* seeds, the very thing I'd been searching for in the Oaxaca market. They seemed to be glowing like a beacon in the night, and I knew I'd leave with some of those seeds.

"Various spiritual transactions took place during the relatively brief time I spent with him, and out of those I nicknamed him the Great White Shark nagual. This white-skinned twin of mine had spiritual connections to Sufi and Mexican traditions alike. He was deeply involved with Miztec, Mazatec and Zapotec Indians in the Oaxaca region, and had married an Indian woman and become a father to their several mixed-blood children. Since that time together many years ago, we've had a mysterious access to each other through our link to *intent*.

"I don't know all of what he was doing or why his power came through me so clearly tonight. It was some kind of gesture especially toward you, Josie, but beyond that I cannot say. Some day perhaps you will 'see' its meaning."

I was fascinated with Sean's story, although still mystified as to how the Great White Shark nagual had managed to appear through Sean's face the way he did. I'd seen channelers before, most of whom I'd thought questionable, and the majority went through a ritualized rigmarole to get ready for the "entities." To my relief, none of this had taken place with Sean, no strange voice passed his lips. In fact, he was as surprised as the rest of us. He'd simply made room for *intent*, flexed his *will*, and bingo!

Over the next five or six days, the three of us were around each other almost constantly. I'm not sure any of us ever completely reverted to normal awareness during that period. Every time I look back at that week, it has the quality of an incandescent bubble of time suspended dreamlike from any kind of normal continuum. Much of the time I think we were all as content as we could ever hope to be.

Sean played his part in weaving our energies back and forth through each other, out to the "left," and back again with all the flair, thoroughness, and visionary accuracy of an immensely skilled and experienced weaver. Color by color, warp and woof, the tapestry came to have a life of its own. I was the grounding force, anchoring at least a corner of the tapestry to the Earth, and Charlie was the young hunter, intent on making the absolute most of his new world.

We ended up attending two ceremonies together rather than the one originally planned. The Dineh (Navajo) seemed to enjoy us as much as we enjoyed them and had invited us back. Between the first and second ceremony we traveled around a bit. I wanted to go shopping in Gallup, so one morning we drove east past the Painted Desert and miles of vivid red rock cliffs. We crossed the New Mexico border and arrived in Gallup in the early afternoon. While I went around to the various shops, delighting in the array of turquoise and silver jewelry, hand-carved fetishes, beaded earrings and packets of medicinal and other herbs, Sean and

Charlie went off on a walk, having no interest in shopping and eager to stretch after the drive.

We met up several hours later, me happy with my purchases and Sean and Charlie glowing from the brisk winter air and some mysterious male spiritual bonding. After a good night's rest, the next day we did some hiking in the desert so we wouldn't be restless at the evening's ceremony.

The day after that second ceremony, as the three of us headed east through Albuquerque in high spirits, a police officer pulled us off the road for no reason. We were not speeding or disobeying any other law. After an hour of questions and intimidation tactics that both angered and unnerved me, the officer told us he was going to have to hold Charlie as a possible runaway. Try as we might, there was nothing we could do. We had to leave him there.

I felt terrible about the whole situation, but Sean seemed to have some kind of calm faith. "If it's within *intent*," he told me, "we'll see him again some day and I'll continue supporting his spiritual development. And if not, we'll wish him well on his path. Guard your emotions and don't lapse into melancholy, Josie. Keep a fierce grip on the power and mysterious beauty of everything we shared. You don't want to lose that as well, do you?"

"No, but it's really a struggle not to hate that cop right now," I muttered. Charlie's presence on this journey had taught me a great deal, and my initial mild resentment of including him had been transformed into appreciation. I'd learned once again the lesson of abundance: that there is always enough to go around, whether it be love, spiritual energy or teachings. And Charlie's boundless enthusiasm for life and Spirit were infectious. It delighted me to see him and Sean interacting as spiritual comrades.

As I reflected and tried to send Charlie blessings to see him through his current difficulties, Sean and I continued driving east. We had been invited to a third ceremony in about a week, and decided to use the time in between to do some travelling. Spirit power joined us for the journey.

Shortly after leaving Charlie, Sean pointed up to the sky ahead of us. We were about halfway between the Arizona desert and the Louisiana bayous. In defiance of our loss of Charlie, it was a bright, glorious day in the Texas Panhandle and I had to squint for a minute to see what Sean was pointing at. Finally I saw a large bird high in the sky, flying swiftly in our direction. Sean stopped the car, and we both jumped out to get a better look. He began to breathe deep, yoga-style, and I followed his example while keeping my eyes on the sky. My belly began to grow taut and my *will* unfolded and reached out toward the bird. My attention sharpened. A large golden eagle was heading our way!

I'd never seen one before in the wild, and was enthralled with its majestic flight. If that wasn't enough, however, off to our left we saw another large bird heading on a crash course with the first.

They didn't collide. They did cross paths suspensefully close to each other. The second bird was a *bald* eagle. I was astounded. After crossing, each bird then changed directions a quarter turn and continued on its separate way. Sean commented later that the interaction was a four-direction omen, and that we should remember which way each bird came from and which way it turned. He said we might need to refer to the information later as the meaning of the omen unfolded. Sean was surprised to find a bald eagle as far south as Texas, and even more surprised it turned and headed even further south toward Mexico.

The odds against seeing eagles are somewhat high but not unheard of. The odds against seeing a bald and a golden in such proximity are off the graph. This had been a true "big Texas event" of epic proportions! And Sean assured me, with a broad wink, that if I just paid enough attention, I'd see more eagles on this trip. I was to learn from experience and from Sean's stories of his past, that eagles were often around him, dropping out of the sky in regular omonic showers. But this event had its own unique properties, even in Sean's experience. He felt that it was a massive intersection of power. I felt like I was the recipient of a mysterious gift whose meaning I didn't quite get yet.

As we continued our journey across the U.S., the big plains stretched ahead of us like a western movie. I'd never traveled across the south and was enjoying the vast, enticing panorama of new scenery. Sean seemed to have a near endless stamina as a driver so we covered hundreds of miles each day.

His promise was realized as we saw half a dozen other live eagles before the Texas plains dissolved into the greenery of Dixie and the swamps sent out their humid greetings. In fact, by the time we saw the last few we were getting giddy and bursting into uncontrolled laughter from the over-whelming numbers and power. We also saw some unusual road kills: birds, armadillos and other creatures I'd never seen before. Sean took an entire dead marsh hawk and feathers from other birds we found to give to the Dineh at the ceremony when we returned to Arizona.

Once we stopped by the road to look at some very unusual bird we'd just passed, thinking it might be yet another kind of raptor we'd never seen. We jumped out of the car and raced back down the road to the strange lump we'd just passed. To our dismay and then uproarious delight, it turned out to be a life-size, realistically painted rubber mallard!

As we passed through Arkansas, I experienced several tense hours when the interior of the car began mysteriously filling with smoke. We kept stopping and looking under the hood, but it was not coming from there, nor from any other source we could locate.

I became convinced the car was going to blow up at any moment and suddenly wished I was home. I was going to be stranded in the middle of nowhere with this person who I'd been enjoying immensely, but who was now acting weird. He staunchly refused to stop at a gas station and have an expert look at the car, insisting we'd figure it out. Was this a male thing, or what? He didn't seem to share my growing concern about the car and our own welfare, and the whole situation was getting on my nerves. As I rapidly approached the point of screaming with frustration and anxiety, Sean suddenly told me he'd finally figured out what the source of the problem was.

"What is it then?" I snapped, my tension spraying the words out like little bullets.

"Well," he said very seriously, "I think its from some kind of strange, fiery power emanating from your womb. In fact, I'm quite certain that's what's causing all the smoke in here."

"What!" I yelled indignantly and with some embarrassment. "That's ridiculous. I've never heard anything so absurd." Nonetheless, I surreptitiously glanced down just in case, but saw no smoke rising from between my legs.

Sean burst into laughter.

"Oh, I'm quite certain about it," he maintained. "It's probably one of those female tricks to keep me intimidated and in your control."

At that, I did my best to give him a blank and unrevealing stare. My mind was racing to figure out if believing his claim, or at least acting as if I did, was a useful tactic or if it would get me in water deeper than my ability to navigate. Apparently Sean mistranslated my inner turmoil, because after glancing at me he exclaimed gleefully, "I knew it! You're just trying to hide your power from me, so you can catch me unawares. What a formidable warrior you're becoming!"

I was stymied. I'd never had anyone ascribe so much potential power to me, even in probable jest. Feeling slightly anxious about impending engine explosions, and both flattered and dubious that the source of the smoke could be my female power, I valiantly tried to maintain an air of silent and mysterious inscrutability.

Finally we stopped the car one more time to look for the car's physical correlate to my alleged fiery power. We tried the one place we hadn't looked before by lifting up the back seat.

Somewhere in his past travels, Sean had evidently picked up and later lost a small hitchhiker. A mouse had found a temporary home under the seat, built a nest, and then disembarked further down the road. It was this nest of various bits of paper, hair from the stuffing of the car seat, and other unidentifiable miscellany that was now visibly smoking.

At that moment I realized I'd been sitting in back resting right over the nest shortly before the smoke started filling the car. I sneaked a quick look at Sean out of the corner of my eye as I remembered this alarming evidence. He was standing with his arms crossed, and on his face a small grin was slowly spreading.

No more was said on the subject.

***

A few days later at the most eastern point in our journey, another event illustrated both Sean's sometimes bizarre sense of humor, his audacity, and his level of self-assurance in unusual circumstances.

New Orleans had always seemed an exotic flower growing in U.S. soil. It was one of the few cities of this country that I'd always wanted to visit, especially in my youth after hearing about Mardi Gras. We arrived there in the evening, hungry and road-weary, and headed straight for the nearest restaurant. We ended up at a fast-food place in a somewhat rundown section of town. As we finished our meal, an elderly black gentleman approached us, carrying a well-worn Bible. "May I join you folks for a few minutes?" he asked, and Sean made a gesture of welcome toward the seat next to him.

Sean was generally respectful of anyone's religious/spiritual beliefs, and apparently enjoyed a good dialogue on their various strengths and weaknesses. During our long drive, I'd been impressed to discover him quite knowledgeable of all the worlds' major religions as well as many smaller ones old and new. He'd read extensively and attended various church services and other kinds of ceremonies. This evening, he mostly listened for a while. When the older man had spoken his piece, he asked where we came from and why we were in New Orleans.

"Oh, we're from out west," Sean said vaguely. "We came here to see the sights, maybe hear some good music. But you want to know why I'm really here?"

"Why's that, young man?"

"Well," he leaned over confidentially, "I'm here to teach the black folks how to dance."

Once again I began to wish I was anywhere else but there, preferably as far away as possible from this obvious lunatic. *Here*, I thought, *is reckless-ness and conceit unparalleled in my prior life experience.*

Of course, I hadn't seen him dance yet either.

Our after-dinner guest seemed duly impressed and amazed.

"Say what?!" he responded.

"I think you heard me, brother," grinned Sean, with a quick wink in my direction.

"Thas' really the case, man," he said, "you're here to teach us black folk how to dance?"

"That's absolutely right."

Dead silence. Then deeper silence. Then a period of obviously pro-found inner contemplation. Followed by a slow and elegant pulling of his Bible from the table top in front of him to his chest.

And finally came "Whoo-ey" and a shake of his head from side to side. This word and motion were repeated quietly three more times, with downcast eyes. I was riveted by the drama of the moment, and by the deep terror that at any second he might announce the news to all his black brothers and sisters at the restaurant.

"And feel free to tell all your friends," said Sean, twinkling his eyes at me.

You fool, I thought. *You're going to get us killed.*

As if to confirm my fears, the man stood up abruptly and looked around the restaurant. I trembled.

Then he looked down at Sean, and they locked eyes. *High noon*, I thought.

As I watched breathlessly, I saw a slight twitch at the corner of the older man's mouth. There, I saw it again at the other corner. Slowly, to my great shock, it turned into a big, brilliant grin, which was soon accompanied by a low chuckle.

"No jive?" he asked once more.

"No jive," Sean drawled in his best Texanese.

The chuckle turned into a somewhat louder laugh, and the laugh steadily developed into a booming belly laugh.

"Thas' the best news ah heard in a long spell," he gasped, palm out. He and Sean gave each other some skin with ritualistic grace, both laughing uproariously now, and then the older man began to wander his way through the restaurant. One hand was clutching his Bible to his chest, the other was clutching his belly as he laughed and hooted his way out onto the street.

As he passed the window we were sitting by, he yelled "And ah *will* tell *all* mah friends!" And then he trailed off into the night, his laughter and further "whoo-ey"s bouncing off the buildings of the near-deserted street.

I sat there in shock, and for lack of anything better to do I glared at Sean.

"You shouldn't have worried," he said, his eyes sparkling like a Mexican hat dance. "I never travel to New Orleans without my mojo. Besides," and he paused a moment for effect, "when I was just thirteen I started the first rock-and-roll all-male voodoo dance troupe at my school. And you haven't seen me dance yet," he grinned.

A few hours later, I had that memorable honor.

We asked the locals where the best dance place with the biggest dance floor was. When we walked in, every face there was at least several shades of skin tone darker than ours, from cafe au lait to shiny blue-black.

I'd extracted a promise from Sean on the way there that he wouldn't make a public announcement of his mission when we arrived. Nonetheless, I was a bit tense, being one of the only two apparent honkies there, though after a bit of sun I'm often darker than cafe au lait myself. This was winter.

However, no one blocked our entrance or hassled us in any manner. As we made our way through the crowd toward the dance floor, I felt at least as nervous as the many times I'd waited backstage for the curtain to go up.

Throughout my teens and twenties I'd been a choreographer and performing dancer on numerous occasions. I'd also danced for a few years
with a Zimbabwean dance troupe, and had learned some pretty wild
moves that I'd integrated into my already eclectic social dance style. So I
hoped I wouldn't disgrace myself in New Orleans. Sean was an unknown
and wild card.

The floor was crowded, the air hazy from smoke and humidity, the
music was hot and swinging low, comin' for to carry me home. By the
time I was dancing I no longer cared where I was. Energy was pulsing out
the soles of my feet and spreading onto the dance floor. My blood heated
up. My long hair curled and crackled in the electric field around me. *Let's
get down!* was my last coherent thought.

I glanced at Sean, and then looked twice and thrice. Wearing his old
Texas toad boots, his Armageddon boots, as he called them, he was a sight
for sore eyes. Mexico meets the Congo via Dallas comes close to describing his dance style.

Sweat began flying like drops of mercury from Sean's skin as he shim-
mied and shook, boogalooed and Texas stomped, leaped, twirled and slid
across the floor. Then he moved in and got belly-to-belly, *will*-to-*will* with
me, and gripped my back on the dreaming point. I gasped as our joint
energies slammed into each other and fused. Then we started sending
them swirling around the dance floor. Our *wills* wrapped and wove their
way like a serpent through the crowd, touching everyone's spirit as theirs
touched ours, urging them and ourselves on and on, until it seemed the
place would explode.

Finally and mercifully, the music began to cool down, and as it did, we
slipped off the dance floor and rode the ebbing wave of energy out into
the street and mild southern night air. Soft strains of jazz and blues echoed
from several places in the nearby French quarter.

I never did see any of New Orleans in much detail beyond the fast
food place and the dance hall. After a few hours of deep sleep in a

dingy, dilapidated motel room I didn't *want* to see in great detail, we were on our way back to Arizona.

We'd driven over two thousand miles round trip for a few hours of dancing in New Orleans.

I felt it was worth it.

Five

...Women of daybreak and women of night
Women of darkness and women of light
I reach out to you with my spirit and song
Will our dance be short now or will it be long?

    I gaze in the pool and I see what I see
    Images of you and some images of me
    Shadows of clouds passing, mirrors of delight
    Winds rippling changes, reflections so bright.

History 'twines 'round our feet like a snake
What parts will we leave and what parts will we take?
O mystery swirls round the questions I ask
Far into the future my line has been cast...

                        from "Pool of Reflections"

Dallas shimmered on the night horizon, a flashy Texas jewel of dazzling neon, tinted glass and big ambitions competing with the star-studded skies above. It was a welcome sight after a long day of driving.

We'd taken Interstate 10 out of New Orleans, streaking by Baton Rouge, Lafayette, Lake Charles and across the Texas border through Beaumont. At Houston Sean headed north on I 45. As soon as I realized we would be going through Dallas, I had a sudden idea of where we might spend the night.

"Pull off the freeway and stop at that gas station," I said. I want to make a phone call. There's a woman I know in Dallas who might enjoy a visit."

"Really?" asked Sean with curiosity, doing as I asked. "Who is she?"

"Her name is Rose, and she's come to several seminars I've given here over the years. I think I've become sort of a role model for her," I laughed a bit self-consciously.

"What do you mean?"

"Well, Rose has been a spiritual seeker for a long time, but most of her teachers have been men. I think meeting me and seeing me teach began to give her more confidence in herself and in the possibility that women could be at least as powerful as men. Rose was abused by some of her male relatives when she was growing up, and the spiritual circles she's been involved with here have been pretty male-dominated, so she's had a rough time believing in herself and other women.

"I guess I've helped her, especially since her separation from her husband Robert. I've offered her comfort and helped her see some of the competition and male-female games that go on in her spirituality group. I had to deal with it myself when I taught in Dallas. There are all these power plays that go on constantly, with everyone jockeying for their place in the pecking order, and some of the guys weren't accustomed to seeing a woman in a spiritual teaching role. So I got to open their minds a little," I grinned.

"Anyway, at this point, Rose and I bounce back and forth between a student-teacher role and more of a friendship. She's a character, this Texas Rose, and you might enjoy meeting one another."

A few minutes later, following profuse gasps of surprise and delight coming from Rose through the telephone lines and a very brief conversation, I was writing down directions to her apartment on the outskirts of Dallas.

When we arrived several hours later, Rose flung open the door and embraced me with "Hey, y'all, this is great, come on in, what are you doing here, who is this guy?" in a non-stop Texas welcome.

I made introductions and Rose then proceeded to give us the grand tour of her home. We trailed after her slender form from room to room as she rattled out a non-stop commentary on the decor and furnishings. Finally we returned to the living room, where I sank into the sofa and watched Rose pour our tea with her hospitable southern grace.

Sean broke the brief silence with a question. "So what's with the clocks?" he said with a grin. I turned to him in puzzlement, wondering what he was talking about. "You've got seven clocks in this house and not one of them has any hands. Are we out of time or what?"

"I hope not," Rose laughed. "You just got here. But I don't quite know how to answer your question, Sean. You're going to think I'm a nut case. Now Josie, here, she already knows I'm kind of off the wall so it won't bother her any, but you've just met me and should have at least a few hours to think I'm a normal human being."

"Don't worry, Rose," I interrupted. "I don't think there's much you could say that would greatly shock this guy. C'mon, give. What's this all about?"

Rose looked at Sean dubiously, as if trying to judge what she really could say. Then she took a deep breath and plunged into her story.

"Well, to tell you the truth, you two are the first people I've seen in about a week. Frankly, Josie, I've been getting real burnt out on all the little intrigues and power plays of the 'enlightened' group of people I've been hanging out with. I mean, for a bunch of folks who are supposedly more interested in their spiritual path than anything else, things get pretty funky.

"So I just decided I was tired of all the gossip hot-lines, the late-night calls from the newcomers to the group who want to tell me their life stories, the guys who want my help for their 'sexual healing', the mountains of crap, in other words." She closed her chocolate-brown eyes and shook her head wearily.

"I just felt like I was losing myself in all these people, and decided to shut my doors, turn on my answering machine and go into retreat. It's really a miracle I answered your call, Josie. I don't know what made me do it."

I smiled, not sure myself but trusting in the motions of Spirit. "Maybe we'll all find out before we leave," I said. "So how has your week of solitude been?"

"Well, it's been great but weird. I've been doing a lot of journal-writing, trying to figure out some bizarre dreams I've had over the last year and generally get back in touch with myself. And one day it came to me that I should just take all the hands off my clocks. I don't know where that came from, but I've been in this kind of timeless space ever since, getting up in the middle of the night and writing, sleeping at odd hours, just letting things flow. I feel like I'm going through some kind of heavy snake power transformation. You know, shedding layers of old stuff or something?" She glanced at Sean with slight embarrassment, as if waiting for some judgment or derision.

Instead, he nodded and closed his eyes for a few minutes. Rose looked at me for advice, but I just shrugged and we sat in silence. When Sean opened his eyes again, he said, "Your dreams this past year have been a reflection of your struggle for personal power, and they're lined up at the edge of your spirit."

Rose's eyes widened. "I don't understand what you just said but I know exactly what you mean!"

Sean burst into uproarious laughter and I grinned at the two of them. It was a great delight to watch Sean interacting with one of my friends, especially such a freewheeling spirit as Rose. Then Sean asked her a question about her dreams. This led to a several-hour discussion, during which Sean pointed Rose toward deeper and deeper levels of the mystery of her own dreams and spirit while simultaneously helping her make more sense of both. I finally began to fade, worn out by the days of driving and the lateness of the hour.

"Oh, Josie, I'm so sorry," Rose said, suddenly seeing my fatigue. "You must both be exhausted, and here I am keeping you up until all hours. Let's call it a night, okay, y'all? And Sean, thank you. This has been really profound. Do you think you guys can stay for a while tomorrow? I'm just so glad you came and I'd like to at least spend the morning with you before you fly off to wherever."

With promises of more time in her timeless home the next day, we all drifted off to our respective beds for the night.

The next morning, Sean said, "Guess what, Rose? Josie went to see the famous Carlos Castaneda recently. And between you and me, I think Josie's own power surprised her."

Rose got all excited and immediately demanded to hear all about the evening, so I filled her in on what seemed relevant at the moment. What Carlos had to say about the pressures of social aggregates seemed particularly germane to her present struggles, and she nodded vigorously as I described it.

Sean took up the ball at this point, and made some comments of his own as we sat around the kitchen table. "People have a strong drive for social security, and our sense of security often stems from having our world be as predictable as possible. We feel more comfortable if we can just get to know others well enough to predict as many of their future actions and responses as possible. And the more comfortable we get, the more we seek out the intimate details of each other's lives. We do our utmost to try to eliminate the unknown!

"Finally, we breathe a sigh of relief when we feel we have everyone flattened out. We *know* these people, and they know us. All mystery has been vanquished; we are safe at last. And our friends are those people we've been the most successful with in this process. Isn't that part of what's been happening with you and your circle of friends? Is there room for mystery between any of you at this point?"

I'd already heard some variations of this theme. Sean felt a grasp of the issue was critical to personal freedom and spiritual awareness. Over time, I began to understand why. Most of us completely accept our social conditioning, and as long as we do we are unable to see the traps and limitations it creates for our spirits.

Rose mulled over the information, and slowly nodded in response to Sean's question. "I'm not sure there is much room for mystery, and think I see what you're saying about social conditioning, but where's the beginning and end of that kind of thing? Isn't it pretty ingrained in us humans?"

"It's a deep pattern, for sure," he replied, "but that doesn't mean it's unbreakable. I'm sure you're aware the whole social cycle begins with the primordial nucleus of our parents, to whom we're deeply bonded. Adults are fairly fixed and rigid in their personalities, thinking, and behavior. Children, on the other hand, are extremely open energetically. So that child is like malleable gold on which the parents stamp a signature of all their attitudes.

"If we want to please our parents and insure their affections and protection in this big world, then our range of behaviors is fairly limited by the standards our parents are comfortable with, through temperament and their own conditioning."

"Isn't that the truth," Rose laughed. "I always knew some of those rules were more for my folks mental health than mine! I was always trying to sneak around those damn rules."

Sean grinned. "Yeah, I was a little that way myself. A lot of kids try to find more freedom through 'covert operations'. They try out various actions alone—or sometimes with siblings and friends—that they hide from their parents. This can be exhilarating in the moment. But often the price later is a sense of guilt. We're often uneasy when we upset the balance of power, even when it's a positive move.

"And yet, we increasingly need that sense of autonomy and freedom, and one way we get it is through hiding some of our actions from our parents. We learn to put on certain emotional masks to reassure them all is well, or we lie."

"In adolescence," Sean said with a note of admiration in his voice, "there is one last major bid for freedom as we begin to be less dependent on our parents for survival. Parents wring their hands when their children grow into this stage of teenage rebellion. We test the limits, break the rules, we're chastised, and we test the limits again. Then, almost exhausted by our daring and defiance, we collapse into the embrace of the larger aggregate and become fixtures in our own right. We are now adults. The malleable gold, first stamped by our parents, is set to cool in the cultural mold into which it has inexorably been cast."

Here he paused for a few minutes while Rose and I mulled over what he'd said. The last part seemed to be true for most people, but, as I gazed out the kitchen window at a bird soaring in the distance, I decided the information really didn't apply to me. After all, *I* was different. I was more independent, more free-thinking, more adventurous, more…

"Remember the decision you made to completely acquiesce to your parents' plans for you at age nineteen, Josie? And again at age twenty?" said Sean with an uncompromising stare, bluntly cutting through the wonderful illusions I'd just been entertaining. It was like a psychic punch to the guts, and I flushed and broke into a sweat as I recalled exactly what he was talking about. Rose gave me an anxious look and asked what Sean was meant.

"I guess I've been caught with my metaphorical pants down," I admitted, "just when I was thinking some of that stuff didn't apply to me. I'll tell you what Sean was referring to. At nineteen, I was living in the Middle East when the possibility of war suddenly became imminent. I'd developed friends and an attachment to the land, and decided to stay if war broke out. I was doing volunteer hospital work at the time, and I guess I envisioned myself as a potential heroine. I was young, passionate, idealistic, and was being swept up in the pre-war fever and fervor.

"When my parents found out I meant to stay, they were horrified and pulled every trick in the book to try to dissuade me. Finally they both convinced me my father was on the verge of a heart attack due to his anxiety about me. If he died, my mother told me ominously, it would be my fault.

"I felt cornered and furious with them for their manipulations, and then again with myself for giving in to them. I left the country before war began, returning home to the world my parents believed was safe. After having been the somewhat daring rebel throughout my adolescence, knuckling under from guilt-producing threats did not sit well in my gut. Nonetheless, a year later, I did it again. I was weary from my parents' ongoing pressures against my struggling spirit, and this time bowed to them by marrying a man I only wanted to try living with at the time. It was a mistake, despite having some positive aspects, and the marriage eventually dissolved."

As I sat pensively for a while recalling these events, I realized just what Sean had meant. Not without remorse and regrets, I'd slid into the mold that had always been waiting for me. It was quite deadening until, like the phoenix rising from its ashes, I began to extricate myself through my spiritual pursuits.

"Don't feel bad, Josie," said Rose. "We've all done things that go against the grain to get someone's approval. Anyway, you've come a long way, baby."

"Thanks, Rose," I laughed.

Seeing I'd grappled with my emotions, Sean continued. "Between early childhood and adulthood, there are a few more aggregates that are powerfully formative.

"Besides our family, there is school. Each year we're faced with new authority figures that we must try to please or be willing to face the consequences. Then we have our peer groups who likewise can exert considerable pressure. A little later in life, we're constantly up against an invisible contract defining behaviors for marriage and parenting. We sign without bothering to read the terms and we continue weaving our way deeper and deeper into the social fabric until, for most people, their deeper spiritual identity disappears."

As Sean spoke, I became preoccupied and slightly nervous, as if he were trying to quietly pull some rug out from under my feet.

"Giving in to the control of an aggregate is most of our life," Sean concluded. "To get out of the invisible prison, we must engage in a ferocious struggle. It takes real guts to look at how other people's expectations and judgments have defined and controlled us. The social aggregate is a monster!"

he smiled, crossing his arms and gazing into the air. "The only way out of its clutches is to know and be perceptive of the enemy, to strategize one's actions, and to keep a fierce grip on one's emotions and mind."

Sean leaned back in his chair, seemingly content he'd made his point. Rose appeared lost in thought, while I became increasingly uneasy. Finally I focused in on some of the issues preoccupying me, which had to do with the conflict between social structures and conditioning and the need for freer, more fluid interactions.

"Okay, you guys, I've gotta say something here. People are tribal, right? And a tribe needs a certain amount of knowledge of—and standards for—its members to function well. We're all part of the big human tribe, and then we've got smaller tribes like your group of pals, Rose." She nodded in agreement.

"But," I continued, "most tribes traditionally set aside blocks of time for being *un*known to each other as well, usually through spiritual ceremonies. To facilitate this more mysterious space, sometimes masks and costumes were used, sometimes psychoactive plants, but a time was always created for behaviors that are different than normal social interactions.

"In fact, during such ceremonies people were *encouraged* to put aside their normal identities and to identify with something different than themselves. That might be a force of nature, an animal, or a supernatural being from their mythology. Drumming, chanting and dancing also helped the participants get 'outside' themselves and allow each person's spirit to spread its wings. I think we need these opportunities to counterbalance being too known to ourselves and to each other.

"But look at contemporary white Western society. As an extended tribe, our culture rarely takes advantage of powerful ceremonies. We've rejected the unknown! I think societies have a need for both: structures that bring stability and the known, and structures where we can be unpredictable, unknown and deeply spiritual."

"That's true," interjected Sean. "I think the reason you're having so much trouble with your little tribe, Rose, is because more energy is used in fostering ego than in supporting the unknown.

"Hmm," said Rose. "I hear what you guys are saying and I think I agree, but can we get down to some nuts and bolts here? I mean, is there a practical way I can take what you're saying about social conditioning and mystery and use it in my day-to-day life? I don't want to keep getting so drained that I have to lock myself in my house for weeks at a time so I can be mysterious and unknown, y'know what I mean?"

"One thing that would help would be for you to exert more control over yourself in your interactions with other people," Sean replied, "and figure out who in your circle drains you and who energizes you. Another would be to gather more power and learn to hold it better, instead of leaking it out all over the place. Nobody owns you, Rose, and they don't own your attention, either, unless you give it to them. You don't have to be part of that gossip hotline you were complaining about. Try keeping more of the details of your thoughts and activities to yourself, for starters. And when people start bending your ear about others, either tell them you're not interested or find ways to change the subject.

"If people want to tell you their life stories and you don't want to listen, you can deflect them by telling them they'll become more spiritually powerful by doing something creative with their need to express themselves, like writing a poem, painting a picture or doing a personal ceremony. Even though it's too bad you were driven to lock yourself into the house from social stress, look how powerful it's been for you to write, dream, meditate and do your own rituals this week. You can make space every day for some of those activities, and if you're doing that for yourself, your suggestions for others to do likewise will carry more weight."

"Yes! Yes! That's good," said Rose enthusiastically. "People don't own me, they don't own my energy, my attention, my time; gather more power, Rose" she muttered, looking around for paper and pen. "I've got to tack this on my bulletin board so I don't forget."

I looked fondly at my Texan buddy while Sean shook his head in bemusement.

While Rose wrote notes to herself, Sean and I finished packing and took our bags to the car. Sean gestured for me to go back indoors without him, and then bent and began rummaging about in the car.

I found Rose tacking up her last note and slipped behind her to gave her a hug. "It's sure been good to see you, Rose. Thanks for putting us up on such short notice."

"Oh, please," she said. "It's been a hoot for me, just what I needed. By the way, Josie, where did you find this guy? I've been dyin' to ask you, but we haven't had one moment alone. He's really unusual, wouldn't you say?"

"I'd say so," I laughed, uncertain what else to tell her. I didn't really feel like going into much detail at the moment, and fortunately Sean returned just then and I simply whispered in her ear, "I think Spirit sent him." Then we turned toward Sean, and Rose's jaw dropped.

Sean was holding the marsh hawk we'd found in Louisiana. He stared at Rose, his blue eyes flashing with intensity, and then began to do a dance with the brightly striped bird, spinning his body and power around the house like a dervish. As Sean raised and lowered it by the wings, it appeared as if he was bringing life and power back into the hawk. Rose stood there agape, completely mesmerized by this strange apparition diving and prancing about her living room, beads of sweat flying off him like tiny diamonds in the wind.

Then Sean swooped the bird toward the top of Rose's head, and one of the pure white down feathers separated and floated slowly to the floor at Rose's feet. Sean bowed, and in the same motion reached his hand out, plucked the treasure off the floor, and presented it to Rose.

"This is obviously for you," he said, his dance completed. "Keep it and use it to remind yourself of everything you experienced from the minute we first crossed your doorstep. And please don't talk to anyone about my dance or show off this bit of feather down to your friends. They won't be able to relate to the power of it, and it will cause you problems to discuss it with them, believe me. In fact, it would be best if you kept the whole visit to yourself for a while until you've integrated it and made it your own. Not talking about a powerful event for some time gives the power a gestation period in which it can grow and deepen. Later, you can better choose if, why, and when you're going to discuss any of it. Remember, nobody owns you and you have the right to remain silent."

"Right, right," exclaimed Rose, jotting yet another note to herself. "I have the right to remain silent! That's great, y'all! Thanks. Thanks so much."

Then, in a flurry of promises to stay in touch, we said our good-byes and Sean and I headed down the road.

As we drove north out of Dallas, the sky rapidly turned steely-gray and ominous. Within a half hour we were in the middle of a sleet and ice storm which slowed our pace to a crawl and made the freeway dangerously slick.

"This storm is an omen about Rose," Sean said abruptly as I clung to the dashboard with sweaty palms. Memories of my black ice spinout long ago kept rushing by my inner vision and I was unable to relax.

"What do you mean?" I asked, not taking my eyes off the darkening road ahead.

"Like this storm, her life and the way she deals with power are going to become slippery issues for both her and us," he predicted, "and at some point both are going to temporarily slow the two of us down the way the storm is doing to us now."

"How do you know that, Sean? What is it that makes you certain this storm has anything to do with Rose?" I was genuinely curious, since Sean often spoke of omens and their significance.

He pointed to his belly and said, "*Will.* That's one way I know. Second, look at the timing. The weather was clear until after my dance with the hawk feathers and my caution to Rose to hold the power to herself. Then clouds suddenly rushed in and now we have this storm. And finally, I know because of the way in which power prompted me to do that dance in the first place. That hawk's power wasn't for her. As you know, it's for a Dineh man in Arizona who really needs it and will know what to do with it. And yet power gave Rose a chance and a test when it prompted me to dance, and it left her a small physical reminder—that bit of down.

"The whole time I was dancing, Spirit power filled me with a sense of caprice, as if it knew Rose was probably going to blow it but was kind enough to give her a chance anyway. You wait and see, Josie. Power is going to push on her weaknesses and expose them, despite her promises and good intentions. Her tendency to run her mouth is going to create a big mess, and we're going to get to deal with some of it."

"Oh, great," I moaned, although I know we often learn from our "mistakes." "I hope you're wrong, but if you're not, isn't there some way to avoid this?"

"No. The only thing we can do is to prepare so we're not taken entirely by surprise and to look at it as an opportunity to strengthen ourselves. This ice storm is challenging, but it won't last forever, and neither will the aftermath of Rose's 'failure'.

"Just remember, spiritual power isn't chosen by everyone. Like the wind, it may blow by many people's lives, and those who have made a space for power may end up with some, but that's not the end of the ride. Then they need to learn how to manage it properly. This ceremony we're headed for just might teach us a thing or two about managing power."

As we drove through the dangerous center of the storm, I wondered just what it was I would learn.

Six

...At my heels dust devils race
Toward a point in inner space
Who will win is yet unclear
But coming very near.

Heaven knows and holds its truth
While living flows like aging wine
Into a bowl held by the young
And beggars all in a line, in a line....

from "Find Them"

The late afternoon sun touched the red rock cliffs that rolled on and on like a backdrop of crimson velvet, and the molten tones with their purple shadows accentuated the intense turquoise of the sky. But the warm tones of this tableau were deceptive, as the actual temperature was near freezing. A few sheep grazed on tiny tufts of dry winter grass, and the typical tipi-style of wood stacking sprouted near every hogan we passed. The Southwest air was perfumed with the soothing, redolent scent of burning juniper, and the ice storm and its intimations of danger were an almost-forgotten dream from another land.

We were about twenty miles from where the third ceremony was to take place, driving down a back highway that was virtually empty except for an occasional pick-up truck driven by Dineh. Suddenly Sean pulled off the pavement and stopped the car. As two ravens flew silently by in front of us, he pointed up in the air.

"I drove down this road fifteen years ago and saw the same thing!" he exclaimed.

There in the sky, etched with delicate, lacy clouds, was a large and amazing design, a giant fingerprint, spiraling into itself.

"And I was just thinking about a quote that was printed next to a similar design that I'd seen hanging on a wall in your house."

Looking at the sky, I knew exactly which one he meant. A Dineh elder had spoken the words long ago:

"...It is the wind that comes out of our mouths now that gives us life. When this ceases to blow we die. In the skin at the tips of our fingers we see the trail of the wind. It shows where the wind blew when our ancestors were created..."

This delicate tracing hanging in the air before us was compelling. As we gazed at it, in one moment it went from filling the sky to suddenly being quite far away and much smaller, but still intact. Not a breeze was stirring, and what took place was inexplicable. Sean grabbed my belly and dreaming point, and abruptly shook them. I gasped from the effect on my body and *will*. There was a pulling tension between my mid-section and the area of my back around the dreaming point, which was suddenly itching and burning.

As I was trying to sort out these demanding and varied experiences, I perceived yet another apparition in the sky. The sun was somewhat low, closing in on the horizon. On either side of it, equidistant and out a ways, were two smaller glowing orbs of light. They were almost white and had a luminous, pearlescent quality, and a slight hint of all the colors of the rainbow seemed to overlay and extend outside them like a faint halo.

I'd never seen anything like it before.

"Three is one," Sean murmured. A few days later he would explain what he meant, but now he was silent again.

We stood there entranced until the two orbs and the spiral slowly faded away. I suddenly realized I was freezing. After several minutes in the car with the heat turned up full blast, my teeth finally stopped shattering and I was able to speak.

"What were those balls of light?" I asked.

"They're called sun dogs, or sun bows," replied Sean. "They're an omen of some powerful motion of Spirit taking place or about to take place."

I was beginning to get the sense that in Sean's world, there was an ongoing dynamic but silent (to most ears) communication between various forces and his *will*. I had no chance to be dubious about this, as manifestations were a daily deluge. Their omonic quality had begun to rearrange my idea of the kind of universe I inhabited and cause me to pay a great deal more attention to Nature as a source of spiritual meaning and communication.

We Westerners usually aren't attuned to omens. Occasionally we'll note, after the fact, that one event seemed to be a heraldic prelude to one that followed. But people who have lived with a more physically and spiritually intimate relationship to Nature generally seem more attuned with the omonic quality of some natural phenomenon.

Sean started driving down the road again, and I wondered briefly what powerful motion of Spirit might be waiting ahead.

Following the directions we'd been given at the last ceremony, we pulled off the pavement onto a dirt road that meandered like a dusty river into the distance. A few miles and many bumps later, we arrived at a small cluster of hogans, trailers and sheds. A number of pick-ups were already parked there, so we knew we'd arrived at the right place. The vast and magnificent sunset drama of the Southwest cast the desert as a fiery giant surrounding the tiny human dwellings.

We followed Dineh social custom and sat in the car for a few minutes before getting out and going to the door of the largest house. I guessed that this ritualized pause was developed to give the inhabitants time to prepare for guests, should someone arrive unexpectedly.

As the door was opened to welcome us in, the now familiar fragrance of mutton stew and fresh fry bread rushed to meet us. My mouth instantly started watering—I'd come to delight in the local fare. "Ya' at' eh," we were greeted by the middle-aged couple whose home this was, and we greeted them in return. "Ya' at' eh."

Sean and I were immediately invited to sit at the small table and eat. I smiled my thanks, handed our hosts some bags of food we'd brought to contribute to the following day's morning meal, and we sat down. As we ate, scooping and soaking up some of the delicious stew with our fry bread, I occasionally glanced around at the Dineh who were here for the ceremony.

Many of them were elderly, and still dressed in a fairly traditional way, wearing their long hair pulled back in a cloth or yarn-wrapped bun. Their faces were etched with the markings of long years in the relentless desert, and their dark eyes glittered like molten obsidian pools in the firelight.

The women had their gorgeous silver and turquoise jewelry draped in necklaces, wrapped around their wrists in large bracelets, as well as in delicate rings and magnificent hair adornments. The men wore silver and turquoise on rings, watchbands, and belts. Their shirts and jeans were western, and most wore boots. The women were dressed in velvet blouses and almost ankle-length skirts that were full and often tiered in layers. For the winter weather, these were augmented by several underskirts for warmth, as well as by thick leggings. Many of the women wore leather loafers, but a few had on more traditional footgear, which was my favorite article of their apparel.

What at first looked like a type of thick boot was actually several pieces. On the feet were soft, bleached leather moccasins. Then, wrapped around each calf and all the way down to meet the moccasins was a large square of the same color leather. These pieces were held in place by long leather strings crisscrossed around the calves. Finally, underneath the wrapping was some kind of thick cloth padding. This padding gave the women's leggings a bulky look similar to knee-high "moon boots" that somehow ended up looking graceful.

The next younger generation of women and their children were dressed in non-traditional clothing except for some turquoise or a shawl here and there. The younger men dressed like their elders, but mostly minus the long hair in buns. I've always loved cultural variety for its many expressions of art, language and spirituality, and I was now immersed in the particular blend of the Southwest. These Dineh existed in an constant juxtaposition of old and new, as teenagers with boom boxes and Nikes meandered amidst moccasins and traditional ceremonial objects set out in readiness for the night.

After dinner, I warmed myself by the fire of the upright wood-burning stove with my Dineh companions. Sean was off to one side of the room talking to an older man about the origins of some of the chants that would be sung in the ceremony. After I helped the clean-up crew in the kitchen, I was content to sit quietly and listen to the tonal cadences of the Dineh language. The community hummed with shared conviviality. Some of the older ones were napping as they sat on the sofa or lay on the floor, conserving energy before the demands of staying awake all night.

One of these older women who apparently was sleeping reminded me of a delicate bird, her slender bones curled up within her voluminous skirt and fringed shawl. I'd noticed her frequently glancing my way earlier in the evening, looking with her one good eye. This both unnerved and intrigued me. I wondered if she was simply curious about me or if something else was going on, but I too was drawn to stare at her occasionally.

I turned back toward the fire, not wanting to seem too bold or rude. Knowing the ceremony would be starting soon, I tried to prepare myself further by reviewing some things Sean had told me earlier. This was to be a traditional peyote ceremony, and peyote, like all power plants, was a force to be treated with respect.

The first time I'd heard anyone talk seriously about peyote's spiritual value was in the mid-seventies. I was in the middle of writing a thesis on shamanism and psychotherapy, and a friend informed me about a month-long seminar on shamanism taking place in the Big Sur area of California at Esalen Institute. Everything I needed in order to be able to attend fell swiftly in place and I arrived at the magnificent coastal retreat full of excitement and curiosity. Such luminaries as Joseph Campbell, Rupert

Sheldrake, Terence McKenna, Joan Halifax and Michael Harner were among those there to share information and experience. The tangy ocean air and pounding of the Pacific's rolling waves were the ever-present backdrop to four weeks of intensive learning.

Among all these famous names was a man who was little known at the time but who later became an icon for many Anglos interested in indigenous shamanism: a Mexican Huichol Indian farmer and ceremonial leader named don Jose Matsua. Frail in appearance, this quixotic figure—rumored to be in his nineties—perched among us in his exotic, embroidered plumage of traditional Huichol clothing. This was Matsua's first time in the United States, but he adapted to the foreignness of his environment with remarkable aplomb.

Over the course of several weeks Matsua taught us shamanistic healing techniques, told the ancient stories of his people, and eventually led us through an all-night ceremony based on the peyote Deer Dance of his people. In preparation for the ceremony, he spoke of peyote with great affection as one of Creator's spiritual gifts to his people, along with maize and deer meat. Matsua also taught us several Huichol peyote chants, for his primary ceremonial role was that of a singer. The songs had a unique spiritual power that made me wonder about this being, peyote, who had inspired such beautiful and deeply moving music. The peyote chants and Deer Dance ceremony were the most profound aspect of my entire month, and awakened an interest in learning about peyote from direct experience.

In the decade that followed, I pursued my interest in shamanism as well as my love of spiritually inspired indigenous music. I learned a smattering of words from several shamanistic cultures and dozens of powerful Native American chants of many tribes, including peyote songs. I began to feel a connection to peyote, and sometimes when I'd go into the wilderness for days of solitary retreat or vision quests, I'd ask peyote to send me a new song. His spirit was most accommodating, and these new songs strengthened my bond to him. This bond, more than ten years after the Huichol Deer Dance ceremony, was about to be further deepened: not in Mexican

Huichol country, but in a Native American Church peyote ceremony in
the middle of Dinetah—Navajo Land…

***

Heading back west from New Orleans, Sean had brought up the issue
of "power plants" as this third ceremony loomed on the horizon.

"Human beings and power plants, like peyote and 'magic' mushrooms,
can enrich one another's experience and awareness. The power plants are
here on earth partly for themselves and partly for humans. Most animals
don't normally eat power plants, but power plants send out some kind of
energy that has always pulled the human *will* to interact with them. On
their own, these plants are, in a sense, incomplete, and mixing with our
wills completes them. And they undoubtedly feel that without some relationship to them, *our* experience is incomplete."

"You're right," I said as a representative of modern civilization. "These
are definitely foreign concepts for most, and I don't think you're going to
find too many botanists to back you up, either!"

However, energy fields weren't a new concept for me. I'd sometimes
seen them, and frequently felt them. I'd also sensed means for interspecies
communication existed. But I'd always relegated plants and animals to
being passive recipients of *our* attentions, having grown up with the
anthropocentric viewpoint typical to Western culture.

Sean laughed at my comment and continued. "As you know, every
human being has an individual spirit and *will*. The human race as a whole
also has an overall spirit or *will*.

"This is true for other species as well. When people come in contact with
a bear spirit 'totem,' for example, they've touched the spiritual template of
the entire bear population, not just the spirit of an isolated bear. When you
eat some peyote buttons and experience a connection with peyote, it's with
the peyote spirit, not with several little individual peyote spirits.

"I'll tell you something else that hardly anyone else on the planet knows," Sean added, his cobalt eyes glowing with wonder.

"Please do," I said, bracing myself for whatever strange knowledge was headed my way.

"Power plants have an unusual kind of memory," he said slowly, glancing at me out of the corner of his eye as he drove down the highway. "Although individual plants grow and die, the species do not experience death. The mind and spirit of peyote remembers everything that any individual peyote button ever experienced in its lifetime.

Sean paused for a moment to let this sink in. "This memory," he then continued, "includes each interaction peyote has ever had with human beings, especially with those who have eaten him. The same is true for every other kind of power plant, from tobacco to *pajaritos* (a Mexican "magic" mushroom), African *ebogame* to *ayahuasca*. As long as there is still one living member of their species on the planet, the plants don't relate to death and they have total collective recall."

"What you're saying sure makes me want to be on my best behavior with peyote," I said, only half-jokingly. "It's a little daunting to consider that whatever takes place is going to go down in peyote's official book of records."

"Why do you think I'm telling you all this!" Sean laughed. Then he shifted to a slightly different direction. "When we invite a power plant into our body, we become occupied territory. We become occupied by another sentient being. Can you think of any other experience that resembles this situation at all?"

"How about pregnancy?" I said, voicing the first thing that came to mind. "You're right!" Sean exclaimed. "When a woman is pregnant, there are changes in her chemistry, her internal awareness, and her perceptions of the outside world. Many women also have a sense that some psychic communication exists between them and the fetus. Once the baby is born, the communication continues to grow, even though its body is now outside the mother's body.

"When power plants are inside us, they also change our chemistry and our perceptions of ourselves, the world and them, via a direct spirit-to-spirit umbilical cord, or *will*. Even after no physical trace of the plants remains in our bodies, we can maintain an ongoing communication with one another. What's very different from pregnancy and mother/child bonds is the fact that humans and power plants are not of the same sentient specie. Therefore, our interactions need to be approached with the same sense of exploration as if we were going to meet a Martian."

I gazed out the window, watching the last hues of a silver-blue twilight fade swiftly into more somber tones of slate, dark purple, and indigo. I could feel my life changing at an ever-accelerating pace the past month, ever since that day I spent in the mountains with Sean. Already, the person I called "me" was less recognizable. Shifts of identity, perspective and knowledge were tumbling with increasing frequency from the combination of Sean's presence in my life, from the recent increase in my own spirit's activities and from the actions of the greater Spirit. Now I was about to add little green Martians into the cauldron! Was I really ready? My stomach churned nervously, gurgling in harmony with my mental and emotional turmoil.

"If you'd like, I'll share a few things that might help you take more advantage of the encounter with peyote, to strengthen and develop your own *will*," said Sean, as if he could feel my mounting anxieties.

As soon as he said these words, I began to calm down again, as if someone had flipped a switch. They refocused me on the core of my spiritual path, which was the development of my *will*. Once I remembered my goals, my life's purpose, I became centered and confident. I had a direction. I nodded for him to continue.

"When you take some part of a power plant into your body, whether through inhaling, drinking or eating it, its spirit mixes with your *will*. Then you *both* are really inside each other. This can be rather overwhelming, especially in the initial stages, until you each make various *will*ful adjustments to the other.

"To make this a smoother process, I suggest that you introduce your *will* and the plant to each other *before* you ingest it. One of the simplest and most direct ways to accomplish this is to put some of the plant directly on your navel area for a while, intentionally unfolding some of your *will's* energy into it. This is a polite way of introducing yourself!" he chuckled.

"Then you need to talk to the plant, preferably out loud, and tell it what your goals are for taking it into your body. This may sound like a strange idea at first. But really, you already know that energies flow in a more unified, less chaotic manner if they have a directional goal."

I thought about this, and the image came of a river flowing in a well-defined riverbed as contrasted to a flood going every which-way. In the past, I'd noticed that I generally had stronger and more focused energy if I had a plan or goal I was aiming my energies toward, even if it was far in the future. "Yes, I know what you mean."

"Well, both you and the plant are going to feel more comfortable venturing into unknown terrain with each other if you have some defined goals. If you don't, then the plant's power is going to move through you and will push against all your weakest points, just like a dammed-up body of water will keep pushing against any weak place in the dam. If you want a greatly magnified experience of your weaknesses, then don't set any goals!"

I shuddered, thinking such an experience might be informative, but I didn't really relish the idea. "No thanks!" I hastily declined.

Sean nodded. "I don't blame you," he joked, "knowing how many weaknesses *you* have."

"Ha-ha. I really appreciate your confidence in me."

With an impish grin he continued. "Each power plant has its own characteristic way of greeting your *will*. Peyote is one of the blunter ones in that respect. His energy will make itself felt directly in your navel area and stomach. If you don't have a prior contract set up with peyote, and don't immediately start utilizing the energy for some part of your agenda, you may get nauseous, and possibly even vomit. If you do get queasy, you'll know peyote is demanding that you pay attention and be more intentional with his energy."

"How do I know what kinds of goals to set with peyote?" I asked. "I'm not sure I know what kinds of goals would be appropriate, or even what kind of help I could realistically expect from peyote."

"All power plants have one thing in common," said Sean, "which is to help loosen your fixation of attention from normal awareness and reattach it to the left-side: to *will* and to the unknown. Then you identify more with being *will* than with being your usual thinking/emotional self. Here. While we're talking, try putting this over your navel."

I looked down at the object Sean was placing firmly into my hand. It was brown, rough-textured, and had little tufts of white hairs on the top of its round and wrinkled surface. It was a dried peyote "button." After examining it thoroughly and smelling its earthy fragrance, I tucked it under my blue jeans, where it rested nicely in my navel. I had a new belly button!

"Being with peyote is somewhat like dreaming, in its more left-sided fluid qualities of *will*. When we dream, most people aren't aware they're doing so. Most people who deal with power plants also drift like those in a dream, and rarely come to clear, *will*ful awareness. I challenge you to make *will*ful awareness your main goal, Josie, and apply your power and intentionality toward succeeding."

As the night sky darkened rapidly and the first few brilliant stars appeared, I tried to assimilate what Sean had said. He seemed to have some relatively unique perspectives on a variety of subjects, including the human spirit. What he was saying about peyote, dreaming and awareness was very exciting, and I felt myself warming even more to this upcoming challenge.

Suddenly I became aware that my belly was slowly heating up where the peyote button was nestled. Streams of hot energy were flowing from my navel down to my womb area and back up, causing some noticeable mild cramping sensations. The feelings weren't unpleasant, exactly, but they definitely were getting my attention. I finally decided to tell Sean what I was experiencing, since the sensations were intensifying rather than diminishing.

"That's good," he said, nodding his head in agreement with himself. "It sounds to me like peyote and your *will* are already making a contract. Perhaps the nature of the connection with your womb will become more obvious during the ceremony."

After a few more minutes he added, "Don't worry too much about an additional agenda for the ceremony. You still have time to come up with more ideas, and you'll need to keep adding goals throughout the night anyway. Every time more peyote is passed around for us to eat, more power will be released inside us, which will require new agendas to focus the motion of power."

"But Sean, I *am* a little worried about having enough goals to keep me occupied. During the ceremony, I'm going to have a good twelve hours to fill, and I sure don't want to spend the night puking or contemplating my weaknesses because I didn't get my goals organized ahead of time. Give me a few minutes to jot down the ideas you've already suggested, and let me think of at least a few more!" I dug a bit frantically around my handbag till I found a pen and piece of paper, and immediately started making notes to myself. I suddenly could relate to Rose and her note-taking at the end of our visit.

Sean shook his head at my obvious nervousness, but I didn't care. If at all possible, I wasn't going to go unprepared to meet this alien being, peyote.

When my furious scribbling had subsided, Sean suggested one more area of focus to my agenda. "Be observant of who's there and what they do with peyote's power. I've been to a number of these ceremonies in the past. People tend to take varying degrees of advantage of peyote. Some may resist peyote's power, and some may drift aimlessly with it. And some may have a very powerful and dynamic connection to peyote, so you might want to keep your *will* on the alert for them..."

***

As the heat from the stove warmed me, I realized in my drowsy state that I'd been hearing the muffled, modulating rhythms of some kind of drum coming from outside the house. I found out soon enough that it was the ceremonial water drum being tuned in the nearby hogan. This signaled that the beginning of the peyote ceremony was at hand, so people started to drift out of the house toward the hogan.

I felt an immediate stab of nervousness, and went racing to the bathroom one last time before joining the others. Then I stumbled through the dark across the rough ground until I reached the hogan, which was squatting in the night like a giant mushroom. As I opened the door, the dazzling brightness of the fire welcomed me, and I looked about for Sean. He was across the room staring intently at the fire, and had prepared a space for me by his side with some cushions and blankets. I walked around to join him, smiling at the people I passed as they murmured greetings in Dineh.

Everyone was seated on the dirt floor along the walls of the octagonal structure. The fire had already been lit in the center of the hogan, so despite the cold night, indoors it was once again quite warm. The burning wood was arranged in a V pointed away from the east-facing door toward the place of the "roadman" or ceremonial leader. Only the end of the logs burned, occasionally dripping coals from their tips to create a glowing orange mound on the reddish earth.

Between the coals and the roadman was a simple earthen altar. It was shaped into a large crescent moon that extended its arms to embrace the flickering fire. Sean told me that throughout the evening, the firetender would periodically spread the coals out until finally they'd form an entire half-moon shape with striations extending through it in a sunburst pattern. By morning, the shape would almost completely fill the space outlined by the moon altar.

While we waited for the last few people to arrive, Sean whispered one more piece of advice into my ear. "During your time with peyote, try to be careful about closing your eyes. Peyote can carry you toward dream-like states even with your eyes open. If you close them, this tendency increases

and you might enter a kind of groggy, aimless condition. This benefits neither you nor peyote, so if you do choose to close your eyes, be aware of
the risks, and have a clear reason for doing so. The worst time to close
your eyes is if you get tired during the night. That's the time to do the
opposite of your inclination. You need to get up on your knees and sit
straighter, willing yourself through your attentive posture back into wakefulness and awareness. You'll see how effective this can be." I listened
closely, and nodded I'd understood.

Once all twenty-five or so of us were seated, the roadman, wrapped in
a special red and navy blanket traditional to his role, introduced himself
and his assistants. He placed a small woven cloth on the ground directly
in front of him, and laid a rattle, staff, and eagle fan upon it after carefully
blessing each object with cedar incense and sage. He also blessed a small
object and placed it on the top and center of the moon altar, directly in
front of him. This was the special "chief" peyote button. Next the head
drummer similarly blessed his water drum and "beater," as well as several
containers of peyote and peyote tea.

The roadman then passed tobacco and dried squares of corn husks around
the circle. We each rolled our own cigarette, placing the tobacco in the corn
husk, and then licked the edge once it was rolled to help keep it glued. These
cigarettes were used for initial prayers and as a unifying force. Only four puffs
were required to pray and make a spiritual bond with tobacco, and inhaling
was not necessary. The tip of a cottonwood "lighter" stick was always kept
glowing hot at the edge of the fire for the specific purpose of being used to
light prayer smokes throughout the night.

The opening prayers were primarily for the benefit of the sponsor who
had asked for this ceremony to help out a sick relative, but we could also pray
for ourselves. The firekeeper brought the cottonwood "lighter" around to
each of us in turn, and everyone puffed on their cigarettes to keep them lit
until he'd gone completely around the circle. Then the roadman began praying out loud, which meant it was okay for everyone else to begin doing likewise. I pulled on my fat cigarette, sending clouds of smoke swirling around

me. The tobacco had been mixed with ground "bird's eye" (a seed resembling fennel) and a special smoking sage, rendering the taste and smoke quite sweet and aromatic. Since we could pray for ourselves as well as for the sponsor at this time, I did both, asking Creator to help me learn as much as I could this night about my *will*, peyote, the power of this kind of ceremony, and about some of the other specifics on my agenda. I ended by declaring myself willing to try to serve others during the night if I saw a way to do so. I found this ritual very calming, and was finally able to relax a little more. Once our prayers were done, the remains of the cigarettes were collected and placed at the tips of the crescent altar.

Next, a bundle of pungent local desert sage was passed around for everyone to use to purify ourselves, touching it especially to the top of the head, the shoulders and down to the hands, and then down the front of the body. Some individuals paused during this pattern to spend time working on areas in need of extra attention. When it was my turn, I used it determinedly, particularly on my belly, to make sure my *will* was in the best shape it could be for the unknown. Then, like the others, I inhaled the fragrance of the sage deeply, pressing the bundle against my nose and lips before passing it to the next person.

Now the peyote was coming around in a bowl followed by a bottle of brown liquid. My stomach contracted again and I closed my eyes for a moment to try to calm myself. Was it nervousness, my *will's* recognition of peyote, or some of both? The sensation intensified as peyote got closer to me. I saw it was being offered in two forms, dried and in tea. I watched as the others downed the powder and saw an occasional slight grimace as they did so.

Finally the bowl of pulverized peyote buttons was in front of me, and I poured some of the dry, yellowish powder into my hand as I'd seen others do. I held it over my belly for a few minutes and talked silently to peyote as Sean had advised, saying what I wanted to do with its energy, and asking it to spread as rapidly as possible throughout my entire body so I wouldn't get nauseated. Then I put it in my mouth.

I was more than grateful by the time the tea arrived. Having a mouth-ful of the grittiest and most bitter tasting powder I'd ever ingested set my taste buds jangling and my mouth watering. It took considerable effort not to gag. The warm peyote tea was a much- needed chaser, and I used it industriously to rout out the pockets of grit tenaciously clinging to my teeth, tongue and palate. The tea was also strong tasting, but a bit milder than the powder.

Once it was all safely swallowed and on its way toward my stomach, I glanced over to see how Sean was managing. He smiled at me and smacked his lips, as if to communicate how sweet and tasty peyote was. It must be an acquired taste, I thought to myself, hoping I'd acquire it before the next batch came around. Sometimes peyote was called "medicine," and at this point I thought it a bitter medicine indeed. However, the term actually referred to its properties of healing body, mind, spirit and heart. Those who used it regularly expected cures and miracles as a matter of course, and stories abounded of both.

The singing began as soon as the peyote had started its way around the circle. The beautifully beaded staff, sage bundle, and beaded gourd rattle were passed, held tightly together, followed closely by the water drum. The drum was a cast iron kettle partly filled with water. Over its top was stretched a piece of tanned elk hide, fastened and intricately laced onto the kettle with some thin rope. A slender lathed and carved wooden stick was the beater, and I learned later that sometimes these sticks were made of finely polished ebony. By periodically sloshing the water to wet the hide, and then pressing against the hide with his thumb, a skilled drummer could produce a soul-stirring variety of resonant, liquid tones.

The person holding the staff and rattle could choose to "lead sing" four songs, or simply pass the instruments along to the next person. The songs were of a specific genre called, not surprisingly, peyote songs. Each song had been inspired by peyote at some time, and each was now part of a shared, ever-growing body of music for the ceremonies. Since I'd already learned several dozen peyote songs, tonight I would be able to hold up my end of the singing.

As it turned out, I was the only woman out of the roughly one quarter female population that night to "lead" the group with four songs when the staff was passed, although the other women weren't shy to chime in once someone else began a song.

As I was the *bilagaana*—the stranger among them—my singing came as a great surprise to all but Sean, who'd encouraged me in this endeavor. Despite my initial nervousness about forgetting a song midstream or making some other mistake, it was a great thrill to sing with the drummer backing me up on the water drum. Each time someone took up the rattle to sing his or her four songs, that person had the attention and focus of the entire group, especially of the main drummer who would come around the circle to kneel by whomever was going to lead the next set of songs.

When it was my turn, I, like the other singers, began by shaking and swirling the rattle as I searched for the beat of the first song. The typical peyote rattle is made of a gourd mounted on a beaded stick and is filled with tiny pebbles often gathered from an anthill. At the top of the stick, a tuft of horsehair waved back and forth as I shook it. The fine braided strands of soft, bleached-white deerhide attached to the base of the stick bounced and twirled.

As I rattled, the drummer likewise began "tuning" the drum, finding the most resonant part of the hide but waiting for me to establish a rhythm. Once I'd done so he synchronized with me, following my beat intently, and off we raced into the heart of the music! Usually I would sing alone for a bit until the other participants recognized the song, and then they would add their voices and occasional harmonies. The experience was deep and joyous for me, and later in the night became the emotional climax of the entire ceremony. Each time the drum came around, I became more confident and at home with my ten minutes or so of singing my heart out, and increasingly looked forward to the next opportunity. Although I didn't speak the Dineh language and many of the older Dineh present spoke little English, as a singer I could openly communicate to them my heart's appreciation and my spirit's delight for being welcomed at this sacred moon altar.

As the night progressed, I was grateful for every suggestion Sean had given me in advance, especially for the fact that I could address peyote and expect a response. I have a somewhat sensitive stomach, and about an hour after eating the first round of peyote, sure enough I began to feel queasy. I immediately talked to peyote and begged him to redistribute his energies quickly, as I most definitely did not want to spend the night puking. Somehow an image came to me that I should breathe slowly into my belly and direct peyote's energy down to my womb, so I concentrated and was able to feel the threat of nausea drain out of my stomach, and an energy started to fill my womb. Then, as if I'd been pregnant and was now to give birth, I sent peyote from my womb, not *out* of my body, but equally throughout all my cells, so he would be everywhere in me.

This worked beautifully, and I began to feel a pulse of energy humming through my entire being. I looked at the fire, and the fire was pulsing at the same rhythm, and then I heard the drum, and it was also perfectly synchronized. It finally seemed as if peyote was holding everything and everyone present in a tight embrace.

Then I remembered to try to feel my *will* unfolding into the fire, whose colors had intensified, displaying deeper, more vibrant shades of orange, blue, purple and sometimes an eerie pink. Before the ceremony, Sean had told me, "Don't forget you're going to be with a group of people, and peyote will be in and around each one of us. He will not only deal with each individual in different ways, but he'll simultaneously relate to the group as a total.

"You'll probably notice that throughout the night, sometimes peyote will help you feel a deep and mysterious connection of wholeness with the group. You may feel very empathetic and engaged with everyone there at various times as peyote weaves through all our *wills* toward heightened awareness. And you may also feel alternately quite alone with yourself and peyote, so be ready for the possibilities of both.

"Since the fire is everyone's main visual focus, peyote will often display himself there. He enjoys being center stage sometimes, just like people do. And since the fire will be peyote's central headquarters *outside* our bodies, you can use it for yet another purpose. Periodically during the night, try to unfold your *will* out of your body and into the fire, feeling the changing quality of sensations as you proceed. You can ask peyote in advance to help you with this goal. One of peyote's fortes is enhancing awareness of energy flows. And if you're trying to unfold your *will* toward peyote in the fire, he'll probably be particularly helpful."

"Now that possibility really excites me, Sean," I'd said enthusiastically. For years I had been strengthening and refining my awareness of energy moving through the human body. Although my shamanistic dance master had started me on this endeavor, I'd explored it further through studies of Chi Kung and martial arts, energy-based healing practices and meditation. Direct experience of my own or others' energies was always a magical doorway that beckoned my spirit toward ever-expanding dimensions.

I decided to explore one of these realms: the fire's energy. As soon as I tried to feel my *will* unfolding toward the fire, I had the sensation of a liquidy serpent-like uncoiling of power flowing out of my navel. As it reached the flames, the fire suddenly popped loudly and threw a shower of sparks into the air.

My *will* immediately began trembling with excitement, causing the rest of my body to shake as well. It wasn't an unpleasant sensation. In fact, at first it was rather intriguing and invigorating, but as it continued, I noticed many of the other people were becoming somewhat agitated. Nonetheless, I felt quite at home in the dancing fire, and delighted that my efforts were meeting with such success.

But suddenly, my experience was interrupted by a pressure on my back. Sean was pushing on my dreaming point while whispering rapidly in my

ear. At first I couldn't understand him. It seemed like he was speaking a
foreign language, and I knew it wasn't Navajo.

I looked at him and said "What?!" and as he repeated himself I felt a
giggle rising up at the seeming gobbledygook coming out of his mouth.
As the giggle threatened to explode out of me, Sean fixed me with a stern
gaze and repeated slowly and clearly, "Get a hold of your power and
ground it. You're about to shake everyone in the hogan too far out of their
bodies with your energy, and most of them can't handle it."

I finally understood him and immediately knew what he meant,
sobered myself, and was able to get my energetically excited *will* back in
and grounded. Sean's pressure on my back helped, and finally my belly
and the rest of my body stopped shuddering and I became calm and more
contained. It seemed like the entire circle of other participants breathed a
sigh of relief.

Then I noticed the older Dineh woman with the one good eye, who
was across the hogan from me. She occasionally glanced at Sean and me
from behind a beautiful fan of anahinga tail feathers. Periodically, she'd do
something no one else in the hogan was doing. From her seated position,
she would bend forward from the hip joints until her whole torso and
head were parallel to the ground but not quite touching it, with the crown
of her head aimed toward the fire. Incredibly, she would stay that way for
lengthy periods before sitting back up. As I watched, she glanced my way
and then bent over again into this amazing position.

While I gazed, fascinated, Sean nudged me with his elbow and asked
me in a whisper, "Well, is she dark or light?"

His question thoroughly shook me up, and my mind and heart began
racing. The issue had never even occurred to me that there might be any
dark sorcerers or witches here. This was a church! The woman looked so
sweet and frail, how could it be possible? And yet, why else would he
bring it up? I began to wonder if I was in danger, and a shiver went
through my body.

Under the stress of the moment, I felt my "peyotied" *will* immediately and fiercely fan out around me to create a protective shielding, pushing outward against any possible intruding energies. *How dare anyone try to mess with me on my night with peyote*, I thought indignantly, glaring in her direction.

I maintained my defensive posture for some time, trying to ascertain what kind of threat this woman might pose to me. Despite all my efforts, however, I couldn't seem to tune in to anything. I began to get depressed, worrying that my future chances of spiritual survival were probably minimal if I couldn't even perceive the emanations from a dark sorceress right in the room with me. As I sank deeper into this pit of self-recriminations, Sean nudged me again.

"Well?" he whispered.

"Well what?!" I snapped, having forgotten there was even a question.

"Well, is she dark or is she light?" he repeated, with wide-eyed candor.

"Oh," I gulped, embarrassed and partly confused because of my assumptions. "Um, once you asked, I'd assumed she was dark, but I can't really feel anything negative coming from her," I confessed.

He evidently read my turmoil correctly, for he turned to me again and said kindly, "She's a saint. Not only is she a saint, but peyote absolutely adores her."

Seven

...A moth flies through, she flutters in the breeze,
Soft air currents cushion her with ease,
The universe, it dances with her flight,
She trembles where there is no day of night...

from "Quatro Mas o Menos"

The fire blazed suddenly brighter, and the singing and drumming picked up in intensity and volume in the aftershock of Sean's words. I glanced briefly at the older woman, but the fan she held hid her face in flickering shadows. I returned my gaze to the fire, feeling waves of heat and energy pulsing out and against my forehead, chest and belly. I felt a bit disoriented, and the fire was my anchor.

Then Sean nudged me and I saw the peyote had come around the circle a second time and was sitting in front of me. Like the "chief" button that was initially placed in the center of the crescent altar, the powdered peyote now also appeared to be glowing silvery green. All of my perceptions were becoming keener, every sense heightened to the spiritual essence of everything around me.

As I gathered some spit in my mouth in preparation, I remembered I was about to take in power, not just physical powder. I silently begged peyote to be gentle on my stomach, and gathered myself for this next cycle. A brief surge of trembling washed through me as I faced the unknown again, wondering just how much my sense of reality was going to be altered before the ceremony ended.

As before, it was a challenge to chew and swallow the dried peyote. This time, after spooning some into my hand and passing the bowl along, I waited until the tea was almost to me before putting the powder in my mouth. I quickly used the liquid to help wash down the powder, which worked better, although this time the medicine tasted even stronger. Peyote was a unique and demanding experience to my tongue and spirit both.

After I'd finished, shuddering slightly as I swallowed, Sean began to whisper to me again, taking up where he'd left off.

"Here's something you could add to your agenda for this round with peyote," he said. "The next time our friend bends over to do her fire yoga bit, ask peyote to help you extend your *will* out your dreaming point, where I'll be touching you, and to send it across the fire till it makes contact with her. Then close your eyes and pay the utmost attention to what unfolds. Do you want to try this?"

I nodded, continuing to readjust to the reality that this woman was actually *not* an evil sorceress. Instead of protecting myself from her, I now was about to connect myself to her energetically. Briefly, I wondered to myself why on earth Sean had put me through this whole rigmarole about her in the first place if he'd known she was okay all along. I would definitely demand an answer some time later.

Meanwhile, another phase of the ceremony was beginning. This was the prelude to "midnight water." The roadman took up a new prayer cigarette and smoked it as he prayed loudly over the background of singing and drumming. Sean and I knelt on our knees like the others, spines straight, and added our prayers for the sponsor. Power came rushing through the hogan like a sudden storm, and I glanced briefly at Sean, who was still praying with eyes closed, his face as beatific and serene as an angel in earthly transit. My heart warmed at this new and softer aspect of my travelling companion.

The roadman went outside holding a slender, almost waxy looking eagle-bone whistle, and prayed and blew the whistle at each of the cardinal directions around the hogan. Even through the hogan walls and the ever more enthusiastic singing, the sound of the whistle pierced through the night. Delicate lightning bolts shot through the top of my head and down my spine, and my mind suddenly became sharp and clear.

By this time, many of the Dineh had their ceremonial fans in hand. A symphony of colors and patterns burst around the room as the firelight danced on blue and red macaw feathers, on the many designs of striped and spotted hawk tail feathers, water bird tails, and the occasional prized eagle fan. Some participants moved their fans to the rhythm of the drum and rattle, others held them quietly in front of them, shielding their faces from the heat of the fire. I was entranced with the sheer physical beauty of my simple surroundings, and felt a wave of affection for—and con-nectedness with—these people with whom I was sharing this amazing night. It seemed like we'd become one giant, plumed creature, our songs taking flight toward the infinite heavens.

With a rush of wind that cooled our fire-warmed faces, the door opened and the roadman re-entered the hogan, carrying a silver bucket decorated with a turquoise waterbird, peyote's symbol. In it was midnight water. The bucket was eventually placed in front of the fire keeper, and as he prayed over it with a fresh cornhusk cigarette, the singing surged anew and peyote lifted us up on a green wave of power.

As the wave receded, we entered into a more quiet and sober period. Once again the roadman verbally reviewed the purpose of the ceremony. As the water was passed around for drinking, it both quenched my thirst and re-grounded my awareness of my physical body. I felt the first part of the ceremony had been an "adjustment period" in which humans and pey-ote had mixed and were getting acquainted or renewing ties. We'd arrived together at a new plateau, and many potentials still hovered between now and the impending dawn. Even though there was a brief round of singing part way through, this mid-point quiet space extended over several hours to the "main smoke," when the sponsor and friends spoke and prayed for a good hour.

During that period, when most of the participants' eyes were closed, Sean began to "dance" with peyote. Unobserved by anyone except myself and peyote's elderly "girlfriend" across the fire, Sean was enjoying his connection to peyote. I saw him grab several extended fingers of his right hand with his left, aim them toward the fire and suddenly a loud popping noise came out of his fingers. Immediately some of the burning cottonwood branches bounced and dropped, sending the fire keeper rushing over to rearrange them once again. When the wood was neatly ordered, Sean began to dance anew.

This time he put one hand over his belly and extended the other toward the fire, moving his fingers rapidly in some kind of sign language apparently known only to him and peyote. There suddenly appeared a bright green flame, which remained for at least several minutes. While it hovered in the midst of the fire, something on the ground near Sean's feet caught my eye. It was a silvery, almost transparent-looking insect, about half an inch long and vaguely cricket-shaped. It waved its antennae at me. Once it captured my attention, the creature scurried closer to the fire. Before getting *too* close, it turned left and began to travel toward the nearest tip of the crescent altar.

When it arrived, it climbed uphill to the top of the altar, found the slight indentation of a line that had been ritually inscribed earlier, and followed it all the way around to the other tip. The little pilgrim managed to skitter around the peyote "chief" button at the center.

The line, which is indented all across the center of the top of the altar, was made with a stick before the ceremony began. This simple, literally down-to-earth gesture carries deep meaning for the ceremony. The line is called the road of life, and is sometimes marked with red ochre to signify the lifeblood. Placing the peyote chief button in the center of this line opens the ceremony and signifies peyote is on the road of life with us. The prayer cigarette butts are placed at each tip, signifying the prayers and mystery of the human spirit from birth to death, at the beginning and end of the road of life.

The bug finished tracing the line, descended from the altar, and continued around the fire until it had made a complete circle. It was now in front of me once again. Then it bowed, turned around, and headed straight into the coals where it disappeared. I gasped at this amazing demonstration of purposeful determination on the path of life and in the choice of death, death by fire.

Before any sentimental emotion could set in, Sean gestured again toward the fire, and up out of the coals rose a miniature *diablando* carrying a swirl of white ash into the air. A second, and then a third one rose up, and they chased each other around the fire a few times before vanishing back into the coals. As this entrancing display ended, the green flame dissolved back into blues and oranges, and I realized I'd once again witnessed Sean unfolding his *will*, this time with peyote meeting him halfway as a dance partner. I was delighted at their obvious bond and looked forward to further strengthening my own link with peyote over the next hours.

The main smoke was done, and the peyote was passed around the circle a third time. I took some deep breaths, trying to gather myself so I could decide where to direct this new wave of green power. I was becoming more confident about being able to continue adjusting to it, but now was definitely not the time to slack off and abandon awareness. Just then, I saw the older woman bend over. I glanced at Sean. He nodded and placed his hand on my back. I closed my eyes, focused on my dreaming point, asked peyote for help, and began to try to direct my *will* out my back and toward the woman.

I felt an intense pressure in my head, and then my ears popped, leaving the after-effect of a high-pitched ringing sound. As it faded, everything became completely silent and pitch black. I seemed to be suspended in some kind of transitional void, floating without direction or sense of time. I mused how pleasant it was just to drift. Despite my earlier intentions, slowly I became more and more relaxed, and even a bit drowsy. I could just take a little nap, and…

Suddenly I felt some kind of tug on my awareness and realized I was doing exactly what Sean had specifically warned me *not* to do if I closed my eyes. With more resolve, I told peyote I didn't want to drift and to please help me with my goal.

The blackness began to take on a bit of definition. It was still dark, but the darkness now appeared to have curved walls and ceiling. I realized I was in some kind of tunnel.

"Where am I?" inquired the voice of my mind.

"Keep going a little further," said a different voice, which I knew now to be peyote. "You're travelling through my vagina."

"Your vagina! I thought you were a he!"

"I'm quite adaptable," rumbled peyote's voice, "and right now I'm showing you some of my female side. Hurry up now, you need to get to my womb cave for a rendezvous."

I propelled my disembodied awareness forward. The "tunnel" walls began to have a greenish luminosity, and I could see slight crevices and ribbing until finally the passageway opened up into more of a cave-like space. The same subtle glow shined from its rounded walls.

As I entered peyote's womb cave, I could see two shapes hanging from the ceiling, moving slightly as if in an invisible breeze. At first, all I could tell about them was that they had wings. I wondered if once again I was going to have a bat encounter. Then my vision cleared a bit more, and I could see that one figure was a moth, the other a butterfly. The moth was of delicate grays, silver and mauve, while the butterfly was orange and black.

As I got closer, the moth began to communicate with me telepathically.

I knew immediately that the moth was the form the older Dineh woman had adopted for the occasion. Once that was clear, she said, "That butterfly is an associate of mine. She's a Mexican woman named Constanza, and I'm Emily. My purpose is to acquaint you with different facets of the *art of dreaming*, starting now."

"I thought the *art of dreaming* was something one did while asleep," I blurted after greeting them both.

The moth Emily said, "That is only one of several styles. Another is to dream awake, with or without power plants, and that is my forte, so that is what I'll teach you. I am a weaver. In normal awareness I weave wool into rugs in the tradition of the Dineh. In dreaming I weave strands of awareness.

"Forty years ago peyote first showed me the luminous fibers that connect everything in the universe. When I dream, I will myself into contact with the fiber of whatever or whoever I choose. Then, like a spider, I simply follow the fiber to the being it's attached to. That's how Sean and peyote helped your *will* to find me in dreaming, though you couldn't quite see the process. In time, with enough practice, you'll be able to do this as well as I can."

Emily's moth form slowly unfolded its wings, and closed them again. This languid movement repeated itself numerous times, and I began to feel slightly mesmerized, and then increasingly groggy. Just before I slipped into complete unconsciousness, I again heard Sean's admonition to pay close attention to everything. Whether he was somehow reminding me or my own memory was doing so, I jolted back to awareness. Maintaining awareness was proving harder than I'd anticipated.

The moth was still moving her wings, and now began to turn in a slow circle. During this stately dance, I began to see a slender glowing thread extending from her midsection. With each unfolding of wings, the thread got brighter until I could clearly see its entire length. The other end of the thread was connected to me.

"The more we dream together," said Emily's voice, "the stronger and thicker this thread will become, until finding me will be as easy as picking up the phone. Until you become a little more adept, however, having Sean's hand on one of your dreaming points may help focus your *will* in my direction when you wish contact."

"*One* of my dreaming points?" I asked. "I thought there *was* only one, the one on my back."

"No," she laughed, and the sound was like a cascade of white shell wind chimes echoing in a desert canyon. "I'm afraid we're more complex and mysterious than that. But ask Sean about the others," she said. "He'll describe them for you. He loves making long-winded descriptions of the abstract and indescribable, doesn't he, Constanza?" and the two of them burst into another soft avalanche of laughter. Behind it I heard peyote's distant rumble of accompaniment.

"But now," Emily's voice finally continued, "now is a time for acting. Would you like to go flying with us?"

I reflected briefly on the many flying dreams I'd had over the years, and felt a thrill of anticipatory suspense. My flying dreams were some of my most cherished experiences.

The first time I recalled ever dreaming of flying was both humorous and frustrating. I was about seven or eight years old.

In the dream I was just outside the bedroom where my physical body was sleeping, and I was standing at the top of a flight of stairs. I was wearing a favorite pair of blue jeans and a T-shirt. As I stood there, a voice was telling me how I could begin to learn to fly. It told me to grab my blue jeans at the right knee, and pull it up in the air. I did so and was left standing on my left foot, with my right leg poised in the air. Then the voice told me to grab the other knee and lift it up too. As I complied, I found myself sitting in the air. Next I was told to tuck my knees further in to my belly, and then to extend them straight out behind me.

I was floating horizontal, belly down. I then began to tilt slightly, aiming toward the bottom of the stairs, and floated down easily, eventually ending up taking a slow motion flying tour of my childhood house. It felt completely real.

So much so that when I awoke the next morning, I was certain I'd be able to repeat the experience. With great enthusiasm, I tugged on my same favorite pair of jeans and went racing to the head of the stairs. I lifted my right leg effortlessly by the knee, just as I'd done in the dream. I was halfway there! Then I pulled on my left knee. And alas, it was there that the resemblance to my wonderful dream ended. Try as I might, I could not get the second leg off the ground. Finally, after many such attempts and near broken-hearted with disappointment, I gave up.

Fortunately in dreaming I had much greater success, and over the years, went from that primitive first effort to choreographing aerial dreaming dances and teaching other people in my dreams to fly. There was always a very visceral sensation in my midsection, as if I was literally *will*ing myself into the air.

"Yes!" I said to Emily and Constanza's offer.

"Come get between us then," said Emily. "We'll have to give you a flying form too so we look like we all belong together." As I found myself between them, I looked down, and I too had a moth's body, more vibrantly colored than Emily's but similar in markings.

"We are going to go south into Mexico, where we will introduce you to some of the rest of our spiritual family," said Emily. Constanza was evidently going to be the silent partner in this first venture. Except for laughing, she was quiet the whole time. "They've been anxious to meet you. You must stay right with us now. You don't want to end up lost in space, do you?" and she and Constanza burst into another round of celestial laughter as we began floating through the tunnel and out into the night sky. I had a brief glimpse of the hogan far below, with little fire sparks spiraling up from the chimney, and then we were far away.

Flanked on both sides by my winged escorts, we flew across the desert, and farther over jagged mountain ranges, occasionally spotting the nightlights of cities below. Finally we began to descend. As we approached the earth, I saw a small cluster of luminous elongated spheres arranged in a circle. As we descended slowly into the center of the circle, the glowing shapes appeared much larger. Then the glows began to fade and human forms took their place. As I looked around at the faces, I felt a jolt of familiarity.

***

My continuity of experience was dislodged, and I was suddenly aware of the water drum resonating in my head and someone squeezing and rubbing the back of my neck and base of my skull. I jumped, disoriented and slightly queasy. The area around my navel was contracted; in fact, my whole belly felt like I'd just done a hundred sit-ups.

"Take some slow, deep breaths down into your belly," a voice which I finally recognized as Sean's whispered steadily in my ear.

I nodded slightly, wished I hadn't as a wave of vertigo immediately followed, and began to inhale as slowly and deeply as I could.

"And open your eyes and focus on the fire," he added.

I was momentarily blinded by the brightness. Then my eyes adjusted, and I glanced across at Emily's place. She was just beginning to rise from her unusual dreaming position. As she sat up, she pressed the top of her head rather firmly with her hand for a few seconds. She then glanced briefly at me as if to suggest I do likewise. I did, and immediately felt grounded back in my physical body again. In combination with the slow breathing, I soon felt my stomach muscles relax and the nausea departed.

As I sighed with relief, Sean whispered to me once again, suggesting that I take some time at this point to do a review of what I'd experienced so far.

"Pause periodically throughout the rest of the ceremony," he murmured, "and create sober islands of awareness. Take the time to remember what you've experienced with peyote since the last 'island'. This will force your *will* to tighten up and enable you to remember more of the ceremony in the following days. Otherwise your experiences might disappear into a vague blur. The exercise will also improve your future awareness and memory of nighttime dreaming.

"Each time you sit on your 'island', you can reassess your agenda and see if you want to add any new goals. This kind of intentional shifting back and forth between different kinds of awareness while 'on' peyote is going to strengthen your *will*, make you more fluid, and give you spiritual balance."

Easier said than done on peyote. I began to see how this exercise could be quite strengthening to the *will*. On peyote, just as in dreams, the mind does not operate in its usual patterns, and capturing the elusive quality of memory was a challenge.

One of the first things I began to inventory was my body awareness. Peyote made my kinesthetic awareness more keen than usual, but he was also very demanding. If I became lazy or passive with my awareness, he would usually grab my attention through intense sensations in my belly. This kind of biofeedback was sometimes unpleasant but always effective, and forced me to get control of my awareness again. Then peyote would become most responsive. If I consciously worked to deepen my breathing, the result of physical wellbeing would soon follow. If I directed peyote's energy down to my womb, that's where the energy would go.

Slight shifts in my posture immediately translated into shifts of awareness. When I slumped from lack of focus, my awareness would get increasingly sloppy and I'd feel groggy within seconds. If I straightened my spine, peyote and my mixed energy would rush up it, filling me with a buoyant and very focused enthusiasm.

Peyote heightened my awareness of the effect of the other holy plants used in the ceremony as well. Breathing in the sage each time it was passed around with the staff brought renewed clarity to my mind and a sense of purity to my body. The burning cedar incense calmed my emotions and opened my cells to embrace every molecule of its fragrance. I'd breathe deeper and feel a sense of physical relief. The tobacco had a cooling, sobering effect on my mind, and made room for more awareness of peyote's energy and effect on my body.

I also noticed that each time I ate more peyote, I'd go through several distinct phases. In the first phase my muscles and joints would start feeling looser, and I'd feel peyote's first knock on the door of my *will*. Then those sensations would fade and I'd feel more 'normal' for a while. Next, grogginess would threaten, and if I didn't become active and *will*ful with peyote immediately, queasiness would soon follow.

When I successfully got through that phase, I'd get a burst of energy and become much more alert. I could see how in times past, some Apache runners had gotten good mileage out of their use of peyote for all-night sprints. This burst of energy was not at all like that associated with caffeine or other stimulants. It was an overall sense of concentrated vitality with no nervous edge, and was the direct experience of peyote adding his life force and power to mine.

This extra energy carried the price of a demand to be used. Though I felt twice my usual energy, I also was living each moment with twice my normal intensity. I occasionally looked at my wristwatch, and was usually surprised that what felt like hours was often only twenty or thirty minutes. It was as if time was slowing down in order to make room for the surplus of energy streaming through my *will*.

It was intriguing to unfold my *will* toward Sean. After being with him almost constantly for a grand total of about two weeks, I realized how accustomed to keying off of his various body-centered signals I'd become. These included a compelling use of his eyes, various gestures toward his own body, strange hand/finger signs, and several kinds of touch to my back, belly and sometimes top of my head. All of these signs and gestures alerted me to spiritual experiences that were unfolding, including the movement of our *wills*.

In the peyote ceremony I could see Sean touching others with his *will*. And I too began to more actively participate in this manner. For example, we'd both focus on the individual, and his or her singing would become more powerful. At other times, if some healing or special prayers were taking place, we added our *wills* in support, and more power would arrive in response. This learning situation deepened my appreciation of how connected we all are, and that our focused intentions truly make a difference.

I also tried out Sean's "island" exercise and found my memory in a slippery state. With considerable effort, I was able to recall most of my experiences from the beginning of the peyote ceremony to the dreaming experience of flying to Mexico with Emily and Constanza. I remembered the luminous forms beginning to look like people, and then, nothing. I was certain there had been more, including how I'd gotten back to the hogan. Yet, no matter how hard I pulled, no more fruit could I pluck from this branch of memories.

In my fervor for success in this project, I began to go overboard, searching again and again for the thread that would pull the memory back, but it stubbornly retained its elusive status. *This is* my *memory*, I thought possessively. *Where could it be hiding*?!

Just then I felt something brush the side of my face. I turned, but all I saw was Sean fumbling with something in his cupped hand. I looked over, and he had some little pieces of cedar needles that he was playing with and crumbling. I turned back to the fire. I'd been momentarily distracted from my efforts, but I gritted my teeth and plunged back into the hunt for my lost memory.

Again I felt something brush, or maybe hit the side of my face. Were there some kind of flying bugs in here or what? I certainly hadn't noticed any before. If there were, I couldn't see them. Once more I turned toward the fire, and immediately I felt the same sensation. This time I explored the side of my face with my hand, to see if I could find any bumps indicating insect bites. I did feel a bump on my cheek, only it moved as I rubbed it.

Ech-h-h. Had I squashed a bug on my face? I peeled it off and looked at my fingers, hoping I wouldn't find anything too gross. As I peered at it through peyote's slightly diffusing effect on my vision, I tried to make out what it was. It was green, flat but nubby looking, and slightly damp, evidently from its recent squashing. It looked vaguely familiar, but I couldn't quite identify what kind of bug it could be.

Something hit my face again. This time, when I looked to the side, I saw Sean make a slight chewing motion, turn toward me and blow something out of his mouth at me, right into my face.

Shocked, I looked quickly around the hogan to see if anyone had noticed. However, someone was making a rather lengthy speech, and most of the participants had their eyes closed, either in deep concentration or deep sleep. It was close to three in the morning and no one was watching us.

I began to work up an edge of indignation. No one had *ever* spit at me, and secondly, this was a ceremony, and where was Sean's respect? Then he did it again, eyes sparkling, and I finally realized what the little green thing on my face had been. Sean was spraying me with cedar.

Earlier in the ceremony, the roadman had talked about the role of cedar, which was periodically tossed onto the hot coals so everyone could use the smoke for purifying and balancing their energy. It looked like I was getting my own special little blessing ceremony, and actually, just in the nick of time. I could have gotten trapped until dawn in a fruitless rabbit hunt for that one elusive memory. And at the other ceremony we'd attended, I'd watched a Dineh woman go around the room and spit yellow corn pollen in all directions as a blessing, so what Sean was doing was not really disrespectful of Dineh ways, and was in keeping with many other shamanic traditions. It was simply unexpected in the moment.

Finally I got myself regrouped, and enjoyed the rest of the night immensely. More peyote came around, the music kept improving and I had some enlightening visions. The last time I ate it, the peyote had even begun to taste sweet.

The staff and drum came around a total of four times that night, as did the peyote, and each time that it was my turn to lead, singing was an eerier, more deeply spiritual and impassioned experience. By the last round, for me the drum beat and peyote had merged into a horse. I was the rider as we galloped exuberantly toward the center of creation.

Before the closing water ceremony, the fire keeper swept clean the area around the altar, arranged the coals into their final sunburst form, and respectfully placed the prayer cigarette stubs into the coals. The hogan took on a fresh and orderly appearance. The fire was then built up and everything glowed with light.

After all was in readiness, the roadman's wife, wrapped in a beautiful fringed shawl, brought water in at dawn—the second and last water blessing we were to have—and thanked everyone in turn for being there. When she got to Sean and myself in her speech, she shifted from Navajo to English for our benefit. Each person was the recipient of some specific acknowledgment of his or her contribution to the ceremony. We all drank the water the roadman's wife had blessed with cedar, and then three bowls of traditional morning ceremonial food were passed around: blue corn meal mush, finely chopped meat, and fruit. At first I couldn't relate to the idea of eating, but once I tried, I found each small mouthful reminded my body that it enjoyed this experience of food! Soon I was longing for seconds, wishing I hadn't been quite so tentative when the bowls were at my feet. I was suddenly ravenous! After everyone had their share, we were all encouraged to go outside and greet the new day.

The air was crisp and golden, and there was a light cover of fresh snow on the ground. I stretched, breathing deeply of the invigorating brisk air, my body grateful to be upright and moving after almost ten hours of sitting. Sean came up beside me and motioned to the side with his head. I looked and saw Emily bending over, scooping up snow into her hands and burying her face in it.

I tried it myself, a bit gingerly, but found it both a refreshing face wash and energizer.

The next few hours were very communal but non-ceremonial. The women served coffee along with various breads and rolls. Later, there was a large meal. I helped the women with preparations and serving. Sean kept company with the men, who were taking care of those really important things such as smoking, telling stories and staring at the fire. Gender division of roles on the "rez" evidently wasn't too different than mainstream Anglo society.

As we worked together, some of the women asked me what tribe I was from. My singing the peyote songs had caused them to assume I had some Indian blood. I tried to describe my somewhat mixed heritage, but finally, in the face of language problems and increasing bafflement, I simplified the matter and said I was of the Mongol tribe. Since the most ancient Dineh origins are thought to be in or near Mongolia, perhaps we were distantly related.

I was still very "green," Sean's way of referring to being full of the green peyote, and periodically went outside for a few minutes to enjoy the morning, the meadowlarks and ravens, the wide open desert spaces. I had not only survived my encounter with peyote but felt like I'd made a friend. Just before dawn peyote had assured me that in the future we could use our bond for further communication, even if I never ate him again. Since I had no desire to become dependent on ingesting power plants for my spiritual development, this was comforting.

Peyote was a little like Sean, with a personality that could be blunt and uncompromising as well as humorous and sometimes sensitive. And both could be a little scary in their unusual manifestations of power. I'd learned some things about both of them, myself, and the strengths of this ceremony. I felt rich and satisfied to be alive in such a wondrous universe.

***

Later in the day Sean and I drove several hours to a small town, where we checked into a motel. I fell quickly into a deep and dreamless sleep.

The next day I felt quite alert. Peyote didn't give me any kind of hangover. *Au contraire,* I felt filled with energy and creative ideas about all manner of things. I wrote a poem early on, and felt ready to tackle some burning questions by late morning.

Sean apparently required less sleep and had been out in the desert for hours before I even woke up. So I figured by noon it was fair for me to begin to pester him.

We ate brunch in a local Dineh cafe, scooping up the remains of our chili with fry bread, to which I was becoming happily addicted. As we sat in the warm aftermath of our meal, I told Sean I had some questions from the ceremony.

"First, I'd like to know why you put me through all that is-she-dark-or-light drama, if you knew all along the woman was pure as driven snow? I mean, I really went through a lot of anxiety and turmoil for nothing. Was that really necessary?" I finished, finding myself suddenly quite irritated.

"Yes, it most certainly was," he replied calmly.

"Oh, and why was that?" I said acerbically. "Was it to satisfy your bizarre sense of humor, watching me get all worked up about the situation?"

Sean leaned back in his chair and stared at me in silence for a while. Finally he sighed and said, "Do you really want an answer, or are you just looking for a chance to exercise your emotions? If it's the latter, at least be clear that you're the one choosing to give them some exercise."

If we hadn't been in a public place, I'm not sure how well I would have controlled myself. As it was, I clenched my jaws until my teeth ached. It seemed like my emotions went through more extremes around this person than anyone I'd ever met. Half the time I was around him I felt I had the equanimity of a saint—nothing could faze me—and the other half I was an emotional yo-yo.

I finally took some deep breaths, and began to search for my wandering priorities. After a little looking around, the one that stood out the most that I really wanted the answer to my original question.

"Okay," I said, and exhaled rather forcefully. "Why *did* you raise the issue of dark and light?"

"Because," Sean said, sitting up and then leaning toward me with eyes radiating intensity, "you were in danger."

I gulped, immediately forgiving him for all the nasty things I'd been thinking about him. Then I stopped. "Wait a minute. I thought you finally told me she was a saint. What kind of game are you running here?"

Sean shook his head, as if to disperse a swarm of irritating mosquitoes, and then he repeated, "You *were* in danger, but not from the old woman. You were mostly in danger from yourself."

Before my emotions could hop onto a new bandwagon, he explained himself. "You were starting to become dependent on me, Josie. Because of my particular spiritual training, sometimes my energy *can* protect people from various disruptive and even dark forces, especially when I'm physically nearby. People can sense that at some level and then tend to lean on me too much for their own good."

Sean felt this was not healthy, and stated that he was dedicated to furthering people's spiritual strength, independence and quest for freedom.

"Each person who wants to use and develop *will* absolutely has to begin the task of becoming discerning about energy. And that's part of why I raised the issue. You were in danger of complacency. Your attitude stemmed from an unconscious assumption that you didn't need to check out the spiritual climate yourself. You'd been lulled into a sense of safety and protection, and I was doing you the favor of jarring you awake."

"I get it," I said, raising one hand in a peace sign. I valued my independence, and was quite willing to learn how to take better care of myself. My *will* had certainly rushed to shield me when I became worried that Emily might be an evil witch, and had demonstrated a form of spiritual self-defense.

I knew the probability of ever encountering dark sorcery was a concept that would not occur to most Westerners. The idea of sorcery, dark or light, has generally been brushed aside from "modern" thought, relegated to the realms of "primitive" and superstitious peoples who don't have the advantages of scientific methodology and rational thinking.

However, Sean's perspective was that many levels of sorcery existed in the "modern" world.

"The most pervasive form of *dark* sorcery in Western society," he said, "is what you would call thought projection. Almost everyone practices it. If we dislike someone and don't deal with our own emotions, on an energetic level we can negatively effect the objects of our hostilities every time we think about them. Each time we wish them ill, we are practicing a crude level of dark sorcery.

"Parents are sometimes guilty of affecting their children in a similar manner," Sean continued. "If a child senses one or both parents dislikes or resents them, he or she will have trouble thriving even if no hand is ever laid in anger on that child. Such children will tend to be more sickly, have more emotional problems, and may even become suicides when they're older. Some may tough it out, becoming hardened survivors, but often in the process their protective shells will develop to a point where they can never have any kind of intimate relationship, and thus they suffer emotional isolation. In either case, the 'sorcery' was effective."

I thought about how, as adults, we're occasionally aware of thought projections aimed our way. A black person who walks into a white redneck bar will undoubtedly *feel* the energetic response to his or her presence. So might a woman trying to get a job at some previously all-male place of employment. And, on a more positive side, a popular entertainer can feel the "good vibes" coming from a crowd of aficionados.

"None of this is foreign to us," said Sean. "On the other hand, none of these negative forms of sorcery are identified as such by their practitioners.

"In present day Western society, there are very few spiritually *trained* practitioners of sorcery. Nonetheless, they do exist, both light and dark and shades of gray, and playing ostrich does not make them disappear. The major differences between the two extremes of practitioners are their goals, not their level of power. With enough discipline, either side can attain considerable personal power."

He told me the main goal for dark sorcerers everywhere is control over others for purposes of personal gain—material, emotional and spiritual—often to the extent of making their "victims" virtual slaves. "Light" sorcerers, on the other hand, pursue freedom for themselves and try to foster it in others. Toward these quite opposite ends, some of the technologies may be quite similar and others vastly different.

"My main concern," he stated, "in challenging your perceptions during the peyote ceremony was to engage your *will* in a struggle to discern energies *while on a power plant*. Depending on the plant, most people are more sensitive to energies when mixing with a power plant. However, the bigger issue and challenge is to be able to soberly evaluate *what* one is feeling and *where* it is coming from. On power plants, humans are more experiential and less analytical. For most Westerners, this is a welcome change from their usual rational mode. The novelty can draw them into levels of non-discerning passivity and intoxication. In that state, even though the power plant itself is partly responsible for their condition, they are in fact abandoning the real potential of mixing with such plants: to arrive at heightened awareness. That awareness is the rest of what I was trying to nudge you toward when I asked you about the old woman's energy."

After understanding his motives, I felt more appreciative. I was also relieved to remember that my *will* and instincts had accurately read Emily's energy, even though for a short time I'd thought my perceptions were failing me.

"Are you satisfied on that subject now?" asked Sean.

"Yes, thank you, I believe I am. Now, did you know, and if so, *how* did you know that Emily, as she called herself, was a dreamer and could help teach me about the *art of dreaming*?"

"I can't really tell you much more than that I had certainty. I could feel it with my *will*," he said. "The fingerprint omen in the sky first keyed me in, since it occurred both fifteen years ago and before the ceremony, right above the area where Emily lives. Once the peyote ceremony was under way and she began her fire yoga routine, Emily clued me in herself by the way she related to the top of her head. Peyote later told me about her dreaming abilities."

"Oh, oh!" I exclaimed, getting excited. "That reminds me, I was supposed to ask you about that. I'd almost forgotten something Emily said."

"What was that?" he said, downing half a cup of freshly poured, steaming hot coffee. I winced. Over our time together, I'd begun to wonder if Sean had an iron-coated mouth or very developed heat resistant powers. He could drink liquids so hot that they scorched my hands through Styrofoam cups.

"You always refer to that place on my back as the dreaming point. But Emily said that there were *several* dreaming points. She told me I had to ask you about them, and that you were very good at talking on and on about things that defied definition."

At this pointed synopsis, Sean burst into uproarious and highly appreciative laughter. I had to wait several minutes before the last waves subsided. I didn't mind. I vastly enjoyed seeing someone take such delight in laughing at himself. It certainly was a rarity.

"She is right in pointing out the ineffable nature of this topic," he finally said. "And now that you've both put me on the spot, I find I have nothing to say on the subject."

"Now you're teasing me," I said, my curiosity growing by the moment. "Won't you at least try?"

Instead, Sean suggested we first leave the cafe. We paid our bill and stepped out into the crisp, sunny afternoon air.

After driving a while, we passed Bitahochee, and a bit further down the highway parked on the side of the road and began walking out through the desert scrub, past occasional juniper trees. We eventually hiked up a large hill where we could gaze out in all directions, and sat down to rest.

The snow had mostly melted in this area except for a few patches glittering in the sun. The earth was therefore quite damp and appeared even redder than usual. A good deal of it seemed to have accumulated on the bottom of our shoes. I found a sturdy twig and began to scrape it off my soles while Sean launched into a brief but fascinating discussion in response to my earlier question.

"There are *two* dreaming points on the back, the one I touch frequently, and one just on the opposite side of the spine. The other points I believe Emily was referring to are related, but I wouldn't say it was quite proper to call them dreaming points."

"The two points on the back 'face' the opposite direction as the eyes. Since most people's perceptions of the world are heavily weighted toward the visual, simply shifting the focus to the back and what is unseen by the eyes activates a different aspect of *will*. This is the *dreamer*, which also functions when we sleep with our physical eyes closed to the world. The two points on the back then become like the openings of the *dreamer's* eyes, with the *will* moving and perceiving through them and out into realms of spirit."

There is something about the inherent nature of these two points that is very responsive to the touch of a focused *will* such as Sean's. The response, as I'd already experienced numerous times now, was to shift into heightened awareness and/or dreaming states. As if to provide an opportunity for Sean to demonstrate this once again, two ravens suddenly caught our attention with their calls. They were flying above us, black feathers flashing silver in the sun. Sean stood up and motioned me to do likewise as he moved around behind me.

He put one hand over my navel area, and pressed the left dreaming point of my back with the other. Immediately my belly got hard and my back jerked into an arch as my *will* flung itself out and toward the ravens.

My eyes became slightly unfocused, and I could see a haze of light around both birds. They began to dive at each other and perform an intricate and well-timed dance of aerial maneuvers that was breathtaking and unlike anything I'd ever seen. Finally they flew off. Sean rubbed my dreaming point and pressed my belly for a moment, and then returned to his place. I blinked a few times, pressed the top of my head, found the earth still existed as I remembered it, and sat down.

Sean then went on to describe five other points on the body. He stated that if a person had enough spiritual power and training to be involved with his or her *dreamer* and moved toward awareness of the *double,* then these points were going to be both similar and different.

"Before you go into those five points," I interrupted, "can you define what the relationship is between the *dreamer* and the *double?*"

"I'll say this," responded Sean. "Before the *double* is the *double*, it is first the 'single'.

I blinked, hoping he'd clarify this Zen-like statement.

"The *double*," he continued after a pause, "or energy body, is inside the physical body first, and is a spiritual coherence within us. If a person gathers enough energy and limits his or her energetic indulgences, then over time the *double* will get strong enough to be able to move *outside* the physical body. With enough energy, it can even form a complete and functional replica of the physical body, one that others can touch and perceive: the *double.* Or, it can assume a variety of other forms. The *dreamer*, which you could say is one function of the *double*, is something you can approach conceptually from a more normal worldview. The *double* is like plunging in *over* your head."

My attention was glued to this esoteric explanation. Sean continued, true to Emily's prediction!

"Among all these points, the top or crown of the head is most well known in worldwide spiritual disciplines. It is sometimes associated with dreaming, but I see it as an opening to a variety of spiritual states including psychic and telepathic ones and what's known in some cultures as spirit possession.

"However, just as one needs to guard the top of an infant's head till the bones close together to protect the brain, one also has to shield the spiritual opening there. If novices blast it open without first developing some system of awareness for the process, their consciousness can become diffuse and fuzzy. Their discernment about what forces they're dealing with in that state will diminish. The 'acid generation' and the expression 'far out' are good examples. As people got stoned, they were going as far out as their drug of choice might take them, a state of abandoning awareness in exchange for naive intoxication. People can go so far out that afterwards they don't even remember where they've been, becoming dazed and passive in the process. No awareness, development of *will*, or productive relationships to power plants can come from this approach.

"In the East, students of spiritual knowledge and awareness are cautioned to guard the top of the head, or 'guard the top knot,' until they know what they're doing. That's excellent and practical advice."

I realized that when Emily finished her *dreaming* with me and pressed on the top of her head, she was energetically sealing herself back up. When I copied her actions, I'd immediately felt more grounded and back in my body.

Sean said that the other two sets of two points each are substantially less well known, and he described them only briefly. "Two are on the sides of the neck. Because the neck is the juncture or connection between the head, where thinking takes place, and the rest of the body which is intelligent but *not* thinking, these two points are fundamental in leading our spirit toward the unthinkable. The other two points are located on the sides of the ribs. These points are usually protected by our arms, so to open our *will* out these points entails a specific kind of choice.

"You could say it is from the sides of the ribs that the wings of the *double* unfold their mysterious flight," Sean said, his eyes taking on a soft glow.

He paused for a few minutes, perhaps contemplating the unfathomable nature of the human spirit.

Finally, he again broke the afternoon silence with a few last comments on the subject. He said that utilizing these seven points were ways for the *will* to manifest a variety of relationships to the body itself. Because every person's body is different and has its own distinct history, the way we experience the *will*'s motion through these points may create unique tones of awareness for each individual.

"I just might have a few other things to say about dreaming and *will*," Sean smiled, "but I'll save them for another time. This is pretty rarified stuff to assimilate, and your eyes seem to be glazing over a bit. Shall we walk some more?"

I nodded with some relief, rose to my feet on my nicely cleaned shoes, and got ready to pick up a few new pounds of fresh damp desert soil. Sean, in his typical fast-moving style, was already at the bottom of the hill by the time I had moved from sitting to standing.

Eight

Weave, weaver, weaving,
Spider Woman spins the web,
Dream, dreamer, dreaming,
Casting patterns with her thread...

...Power shimmers from the earth
Pulling on me, pulling on you,
Pregnant Mother giving birth,
Life coming through, life coming through...

from "Canyon Calls"

The phantom touch of lengthening shadows and rapidly plummeting temperatures chased us back to the car. It was a great relief to warm my gloveless hands over the heating vents as our breath became invisible once again. In true desert fashion, there was immense contrast between the noon heat and the now near-sunset chill.

As we drove for a while in silence, I realized that it had been weeks since I'd been on any kind of schedule. I had no idea where I'd be tonight or tomorrow, and it didn't matter very much. I was in a spiritual cocoon that felt like it had been woven in another dimension. Through good fortune I had nothing urgent demanding my return home for a while, and was content to live out one day at a time, although occasionally I experienced a peripheral but stomach-lurching sense of how fast my life was changing moment by moment.

But for now, in the continuing quiet of our drive, my thoughts wandered dreamily. Images from the peyote ceremony and other aspects of this journey flickered through my awareness like Balinese shadow dancers. The presence of the moth woman, Emily, fluttered at the edges, and I recalled her winged dance that had illuminated the bond between us. I wondered when I would see her again, and in what reality.

As I reflected on the peyote ceremony, its uniqueness in the midst of "modern" Western society struck me at a deep level. Here were people trying to respect a power plant as a sacrament and use it for prayer, healing and renewal. Their ceremonial use of peyote was in marked contrast to the explosion of drug and power plant use that had begun in the sixties. The goals of most of the people involved were recreational, although a few folks had had goals similar to those in the peyote church: deepened sense of community, enlightenment, and sometimes healing.

However, I sensed that even the most sincere generally failed to establish *will*ful relationships with the power plants they used. They simply didn't have the spiritual "technology" to do so, nor did they have the experienced guidance of a shaman. I was glad I'd had years of spiritual disciplines before my first encounter with peyote, and Sean's suggestions allowed me to take even fuller advantage of the ceremony.

Even now, the compelling beat of the water drum still echoed in my mind and began to carry me slowly into dreaming…

"Peoples' attitudes toward dreams and dreaming states play a major role in defining their cultures," announced Sean, cutting suddenly into my reverie. As my eyes startled open, I noticed the sky was now almost dark. "Have you ever thought about that?"

As I tried to clear my head and consider the statement and the question, I finally replied that no, I never had. Sean was picking up the thread of our earlier discussion.

"I'm going to say some more on what I've learned about *will*, and in the process we'll come back to this issue of dreams and culture," he said, touching my back for a moment as my awareness shifted to a clearer focus.

"Most people don't even realize they have a *will*, let alone consider how they might develop and strengthen it."

"Nonetheless," Sean assured me, "*will* functions not only to give us energetic and spiritual coherence, but, when strengthened by ongoing spiritual practices, *will* splits into three distinct functions. Two of these functions can be consciously directed and refined, but the third can't."

To understand the first aspect, Sean suggested I reflect on the many times he'd put one hand on my belly while directing my attention toward something outside of me, usually some manifestation of nature. He'd often make an additional gesture, such as grabbing one arm and getting me to point my straightened fingers toward the object of our attention.

"These have all been efforts to invite your *will* to join mine in touching and interacting with something out in the world, to act spiritually in your waking state. I've tried to demonstrate how you can unfold a luminous fiber of *will*—of your own spiritual energy—out into the world and to send and receive energy and information through it."

He then explained that this manner of using *will* in the waking state was relatively rare outside of a few sorcerers and shamans. The martial arts, where I'd had some training, did have a similar awareness of the *will* being centered in the belly, an area of the body sometimes referred to as the *hara*. However, the primary use of unfolding the *will* in the martial arts was to sense one's opponent's move or push him around with one's *chi* or *ki*, one's life force, rather than use it to establish spiritual communication. Sean said that for most people, it was quite a bit easier to gain awareness in the waking use of *will* he sometimes called *dancing*, than in the second facet or split of *will* which was experienced almost nightly by *all* humans. The latter was the *will*ful activity of dreaming, and Sean called the part of the *will* that accomplished it the "dreamer."

"Usually the 'dreamer' unfolds inward from the belly and then up and out the back or top of the head, rather than directly out the belly as in *dancing*. Dreaming then frees us from our dependence on physical perceptions and limitations. Contrary to the psychologists' theories that dreaming takes place inside the body in the brain, REM brainwaves simply register *will*ful activity going on partly *outside* the body."

Sean said it is possible to gain awareness of *will*'s passage into dreaming. One way is by consciously following its movement from the belly up and out, just before we go to sleep. That awareness can eventually be sustained right into sleep and then throughout a dream itself.

"Our efforts and success in remembering our dreams cause the *will* to flex and strengthen. Every aspect of dreaming is a spiritual event, regardless of the content of the dream. The *will* is further strengthened by awareness of going into and being in dreaming.

"Recalling our dreaming is also good practice for gaining awareness in other spiritual states and bringing them back to more normal awareness. For example, without the strength of *will* to remember power plant experiences, memories of them can be as elusive as dreams," Sean reflected, glancing at me out of the corner of his eye. He paused, and then said, "Even though you've been remembering many of your dreams for years, you already *don't* remember much of what's happened to you when you've been around me." and he broke into raucous laughter.

"What are you talking about?" I exclaimed, thinking at first he was just joking.

"I did amazing left-sided things with your *will* that day in the mountains a month or so ago, numerous times since on this trip, and you actually remember very little of it." He stared at me for a moment, and I couldn't muster a coherent response.

This was an entirely unsettling idea. To forget where I'd put my car keys five minutes earlier might be bothersome, but the possibility of losing track of spiritual experiences upset me a great deal more. Was my inability to recall some of the Mexican dreaming during the peyote ceremony but one example of what Sean was referring to? I didn't know what to think about this, or if I should even take him seriously on the subject of my awareness and memory.

"As you know, there's more to dreaming than the kinds that take place during sleep," he went on cheerfully, disregarding my current turmoil. "I've helped connect you to Emily, a powerful dreamer who made a commitment to teach you the intricacies of waking dream states. I can't even begin to fathom what this is going to mean in your world. Why, she might even be able to help you find those memories you've lost track of!" He briefly touched my dreaming point, and then stared toward the heavens.

Just then a large shooting star arced from the right to the left of our vision against the velvet sky. The passage of time slowed and the night sighed in the wake of trailing light. I held my breath in awe, and then I, like the night, also sighed.

"Can you guess what the third split of *will* does?" Sean asked a few minutes later.

Since I'd already been trying to figure that one out with no success, I said, "No."

"The third split is the part of *will* that is unobstructed by time, and can travel or see into the future. This is what accounts for deja vu, clairvoyance and some prophetic states."

He pointed out that, although there were many ways to strengthen the other two functions of *will*, this third aspect seemed to develop as an indirect result of strength and control in the first two. In other words, there were no specific practices he knew of for enhancing one's *will*ful ability to see the future. The only exceptions were deja vu experiences, which most people have at least once in their lives, no matter what condition their *will* is in. But aside from those inexplicable glimpses into the future, he felt one was either born with the gift of clairvoyance, or one waited patiently for its manifestations while tending to the dreaming and waking development of *will*.

"Now let's get back to how attitudes toward dreaming define a culture. Mainstream Western culture attaches virtually no spiritual significance to dreaming. In fact, as we grow up and our attitudes begin to be shaped by those around us, the main attention given to our dreams is when they are frightening. Then, our parents address our nightmare and tell us it was 'just' a dream, a bad dream, but 'just' a dream nonetheless. That it wasn't real.

"This is typical of a culture that assigns little value to spiritual qualities in human beings or anywhere else. Our culture has become trapped in a *real* nightmare, in a narrow corridor called reason. And what Western reason can't explain, perceive, or accommodate, simply does not exist."

"That's for sure," I interrupted. "Did you know that in the dictionary it defines 'visionary' as either 'characterized by impractical ideas,' or 'not real'? Where would every culture be without its visionaries, without people who can see potentials others can't? Talk about a Western bias!"

"Yep," said Sean, wiggling his eyebrows humorously. "Once again we're addressing the tendency of most aggregates to define and agree on what is real."

"We really do create our 'reality' to a great extent," I mused, not for the first time.

Soon we pulled off the road and parked at the edge of a small canyon. We'd been driving non-stop for a long time, and Sean walked off toward a nearby tree. I dashed off in the opposite direction, found a nice sheltering cluster of bushes, and relieved myself in the bitingly cold night air.

When I returned to the side of the car, I did some fast jumping jacks to warm up and a few quick stretches to get some of the road stiffness out of my muscles.

The air was quite still, the sky enormous, black, and strewn with brilliant swaths of celestial bodies. There were no city lights in sight; only an occasional faint and far-away glow from an isolated home here and there. Once again, the eerie sense of being suspended out of time came over me, and I shivered from the combination of that and the freezing high desert temperature.

A fragment of the Dineh Bahane, or Navajo creation story, passed through my mind. Black God, one of the main Holy People, had been carefully placing the stars and planets in various orderly patterns in the sky. Coyote, always jealous of Black God, had managed to get hold of

Black God's bag of stars, and in a fit of pique, had tossed them out willy-nilly in all directions.

As I surveyed the sky, Black God's handiwork was quite apparent, always drawing the eye to his ordered patterns. And yet, I was glad too for Coyote's gesture, for the scattered stars whose patterns cleverly evaded the mind. Black God and Coyote each had their place in the universe.

I finally succumbed to the pull of warmth, and got back in the car. As we sat gazing into infinity, we began to talk about the ways psychologists had replaced shamans in twentieth century Western society. The primary difference was that psychologists dealt with dreams like detectives on the trail of the fugitive subconscious, while shamans addressed dreams as being filled with spiritual import like the rest of the cosmos. This difference was indeed a difference in definition of cultures.

"Don't you think Jung had a more spiritual sense of what dreams are?" I said to Sean, curious about his viewpoint.

"Somewhat," said Sean. "It's vogue now to be infatuated with the idea of archetypes of one sort or another. As far as I'm concerned, however, archetypes are just another fancy way of trying to stuff the human spirit into manageable compartments where everyone can agree on meaning. And Freud's compartments were even more limiting to spirit. It's really a shame how Western psychology has flattened out dreaming," he added pensively.

"How do you see the results of that?"

"Think about how most people live their waking lives," he replied. "Even people who pride themselves on being rugged individualists or free spirits are for the most part still prisoners and slaves of one social agreement or another. Psychological analysis often brings dreams down to the same mental and emotional confinement. And yet, when we dream each night, our *wills* are let out of the cage and become the free and fluid vehicles they were designed to be.

"We can try out new behaviors, go flying, meet animals who speak our language, and be heroic. Our dominating mental and emotional processes often take much more of a back seat in dreaming.

"Dreaming provides the needed balance to the restrictions of waking life. Without it, people would go completely insane. Now researchers have even proven that in true Western fashion. Experiments have been done where they interrupt people who are sleeping every time they start to dream. Dreamus interruptus," he laughed. "In a few days these people start going nuts. It's not from sleep deprivation, because they do get adequate sleep. It's from dream deprivation. The *will* insists on getting its minimum quota of freedom through dreaming. If it doesn't get it while we're sleeping, it takes it while we're awake, and people call it hallucinating."

We sat in silence. The subject was dreams fascinated me, and for years I'd kept an almost daily journal of my dreams. But something was now distracting me. In the absence of talking, I was suddenly aware of what it was. The wind had begun to come up, and its initial whisper was now turning into a kind of ghostly wail, as if the spirits of the land were roaming the desert looking for company.

Although the night sky in front of us still looked clear, I turned to gaze behind us. Sure enough, ominous clouds were beginning to gather, and the prospect of being caught in a blizzard didn't much appeal to me.

"Sean."

"Yes?"

"Don't you think we should get going? It sounds like a big storm is brewing."

"I love storms. There's so much wild power in them."

"Sean. Please start the car." I couldn't believe how unconcerned he seemed, given the possibility of being stranded in below-freezing temperatures in the middle of nowhere. However, he did start the engine, and we were soon on our way.

"I'll give you another example of attitudes toward dreaming in a different culture," said Sean, as we set off again. He went on to describe an Indonesian fishing culture. Every year, the tribal shaman would officiate over a major ceremony in which the tribe's young women took the primary roles.

"These young women each hold a blunt wooden ceremonial knife for the occasion. Accompanied by local musicians, at a certain point in the village ceremony the young women begin to dance. As they dance, they repeatedly 'stab' toward their midsections, not to draw blood or cause injury, but to awaken their spiritual *will.*

"Over hours of ecstatic dancing, one by one the young women collapse into a dreaming trance. When they fall, the local shaman picks them up and carries them to the steps of the nearby temple where they continue to dream. The shaman is like the head fisherman, netting a bounty of fish that slowly piles up on the temple stairs. However, that's just the surface level of the catch. The real bounty is the young women's dreaming.

"As each woman surfaces out of her dreaming world, she describes her dreams in full detail to the shaman and the rest of the community: a distribution of the spiritual bounty. After the last reporting, then it's up to the shaman to process the entirety of the dreaming and extract the essential meaning for the tribe. The total dreaming 'catch' guides what decisions need to be made for the overall welfare of the community in the coming yearly cycle."

This was one of the more evocative stories I'd heard in some time. I could see the beautiful young women dancing, spinning, doubling over as they focused into their *wills* with the ceremonial knives; their delicate, exotic features glowing with exertion and smoothing out as they went into trance; drums and gongs pounding insistently, bright-colored fabrics shimmering and swirling in the golden southern light, the rhythms building, the heat building...

"Unh!" I gasped in surprise. A gust of wind slammed into the car, rudely jolting me out of my reverie and pushing the car over to the opposite lane. Luckily, there was no on-coming traffic, and we moved back to our own lane. Although Sean slowed down somewhat, he still appeared unruffled and relaxed. I had very little experience of snowstorms, and was growing increasingly nervous. It seemed like dramatic storms were becoming an inevitable part of this journey. Piles of fine snow rapidly accumulated at the base of the front window and by the sides of the road.

"Uh, do you have any idea how far we are from the nearest town?" I asked as wind and snow mounted moment by moment.

Sean glanced at me as if surprised by the nervous tremor and tone in my voice. "Don't worry," he said. "We'll be there soon."

Where is there, I wondered to myself. *In fact, where is here?* I once again had no idea where we were or in which direction we were headed. While the headlights bounced off the swirling snow, I peered into the night and realized the wind was doing something very strange.

"Look at that," said Sean, evidently noticing the same phenomena. Once again he pressed his hand against my back, causing another flare of energy from my belly up my spine, and a sharpening of vision.

The wind was blowing in all four directions at once, but not as a whirl-wind. It seemed to be divided in layers, with the bottom layer sweeping across the road in one direction and the next in another. Sporadically, one layer would turn and launch itself upward while another dove straight down. Then the layers would trade directions, in an ongoing, mind-bend-ing display. Although mesmerizing, this was finally so disorienting to watch that I became queasy and had to close my eyes and take some deep breaths. By the time I won the battle over nausea, I was exhausted.

"You're not very balanced yet," said Sean after noting my difficulties.

"Gee, thanks a lot," I mumbled, not yet daring to open my eyes and confront the snow again. "What's that supposed to mean?"

"Well, that wind had a lot of power," he replied. "It's dancing for you, trying to engage all four directions of your spirit. Evidently some of your aspects are weaker than others, and that's why you felt off balance. Also, you're not really solid yet."

"I'm not following you at all, Sean," I groaned. "What do you mean, I'm not really solid yet?"

"I mean from the peyote ceremony. Peyote is still causing your usual energy configuration to be in a different arrangement. You'd better center yourself even more strongly than usual in your belly and *will*, or in your fluid state, things like the wind might just carry you away," and he erupted with one of his more raucous laughs.

"Oh, shut up!" I snapped, my eyes popping open, irritated at being called unbalanced and in no mood for this brand of humor.

"Good!" he said. "Your anger will help you get more solid again. And don't worry about being unbalanced. Most of us are! Besides, even if you are a little flimsy here and there, you've got great potential," and he leaned my way in a caricature of a leer, raised eyebrows and all.

"Watch out or I might use some of that potential on you!" I growled.

In a pantomime of terror, Sean moved back and concentrated again on driving. I turned away and closed my eyes once more, determined to ignore him.

The next thing I knew, I awoke to an icy blast of wind. Sean was urging me to hurry out of the car before we froze, and as I groggily staggered into ankle-deep snow, I saw we were in front of a motel room door. Within a few minutes I was in bed falling asleep once again. Outside, the winds whistled and danced deep into the night.

***

The following morning I wondered at first if the storm had been a dream.

We both awoke late, and by the time we went outdoors the sun was high in a clear azure sky. There was no snow on the ground, and the air was as balmy as an early summer's day.

Far in the distance, as we gazed out to the edge of the horizon, the San Francisco Mountains jutted toward the heavens. Their peaks glistened with snow, and I felt the drama of contrasts in this part of the world. From what I'd already seen of Arizona, one could be in desert sand looking vainly for shade, an hour later be driving through thick juniper and pinion foothills, and an hour after that be skiing down mountain slopes.

Although it was almost lunchtime, I wasn't really hungry, so I stayed behind while Sean wandered off in search of food. I welcomed the chance to sit in the sun, and the relief of being alone for a while.

Since leaving my home several weeks earlier, I'd had almost no time to be by myself. In "normal" life I generally took some time to myself every day, sometimes for entire days, and found a certain deep enjoyment in solitude. I could read to my heart's content, sing or talk to myself or stare out into space. Mostly, I welcomed the break from the palpable force and pressure of social expectations. I sometimes wondered if I weren't cut out to be a recluse.

As I lay back on the hood of the car, soaking in the heat of the midday sun, eventually my thoughts wandered to something Sean had said on our drive east. "Meaning exists only in relationship. Meaning is held *between* things or beings."

Sean perceived connective strands of energy or power between himself and all things, so everything had meaning for him. He noticed so much at any moment in time, often including minute details most people would miss, that very little escaped his meaning-full grasp. His style of attentiveness was impressive, and I'd begun to improve my own concentration in response to his inspiring example. However, my recent efforts to join him in seeing meaning and connections everywhere were fatiguing, and for the moment I was relieved not to strive for cosmic consciousness for a little while! To just lay in the sun like a lizard and do little more than breathe, bake, and enjoy my meaningless solitude.

By the time Sean returned, I felt refreshed, strengthened, and ready for the next phase of our day. Sean handed me a cup of hot chocolate and some crisp apples and cheese he'd bought at a local grocery store. It all tasted heavenly.

I continued eating and sipping my chocolate as we once again headed down the road. Sean and I had hardly spoken to each other this day. I'd noticed he generally avoided engaging in conversation for its own sake, and today I was happy to be quiet together, and to try to integrate the myriad experiences I'd had on this journey.

I also thought about my long-time interest and studies in shamanism and of different shamans I'd met over the years. Sean seemed very shamanistic, and yet he also was very much an intellectual and felt that being spiritual *and* being well informed about the world's progress on all levels, past and present, was necessary.

One day Sean had remarked, "To be a man or woman of knowledge, it's essential to know the context in which you're operating, whether it be large or small, secular or spiritual. This is important because of the ways we are connected to our environments.

"Modern humans like to think they're so independent, so autonomous, and such masters at exercising their own free will. The fact is, we're very interdependent, very interconnected in a vast web of energy, and few humans exercise any free will at all. Our actions are usually the result of conditioning. And as for *will*, a developed *will* is very expensive, not free and definitely not cheap!

"And yet, neglecting our *will* is worse than having two perfectly healthy legs but never using them and relying on someone else to carry you from place to place. When we don't develop *will*, our emotions and mind have to do all the carrying. That makes us vulnerable to being pushed around by whatever human pressures are stronger than us at any point, without much awareness of what is effecting us."

I must need more strength of *will*, I thought, given my ongoing battles with social expectations. And maybe I also needed a break from city living to explore my connections with nature in more depth.

"If modern people were in a more grounded and balanced relationship to nature," I'd mused aloud, "then nature would be more of what was impacting our decisions, rather than just other humans. And if that were the case, the planet would probably be in much better shape than it is now." And maybe I would be as well.

Sean responded to my meanderings. "Many of the problems in the world have simple solutions, and many of these solutions have been available for a long time. It's mainly greed and a monstrous appetite to be in control of the many on the parts of a few that have caused solutions to either be ignored or deliberately sabotaged." He then launched into a long talk about many of the world's ills.

I wasn't sure in how many more directions I wanted to stretch at this time in my life, or how much attention I wanted to put on the world's "problems." In some ways, I felt I would have been relatively happy taking off with Sean for Mexico or some other exotic locale, trying to gather together a group of spiritually compatible people, and hoping others who were of a positive but more political bent would start making better choices out in the larger society. I'd had my fling with socio-political activism during the Vietnam war and civil rights movement, and had eventually withdrawn from it, sensing the same games, self-serving maneuvers and power plays among the supposedly politically enlightened that existed in mainstream structures. Since then I'd focused my actions in more individualized arenas of healing and teaching spirituality seminars where I felt I could have perceivable, positive impacts.

Now Sean was inviting me to expand on all horizons, while I pined for my Castaneda-influenced fantasy version of the sorcerer's life. It seemed on this trip like I'd just gotten a taste of the latter, only to be learn Sean's vision of the spiritual life was somewhat different than my own. I wanted a clear printout from Spirit describing my role in this world, my link to *intent* and power. In other words, where was a table of contents when I needed it!

All of this was churning around as we drove down the road. I already had difficulty imagining going back to my prior existence; in fact, I knew I *couldn't* go back. Not that I couldn't physically go home, but my recent experiences were drastically rearranging my perspectives on spiritual realities. How could I go back to teaching my seminars after what I'd recently been through? I needed time to integrate the deluge of new experiences first. Maybe I needed a sabbatical from my prior life.

I finally came out of my introspection enough to notice the scenery. We had evidently recently pulled off the highway and were headed toward what looked like a small town dotted with apple and ancient cottonwood trees and surrounded by desert.

"What's this place?" I asked, trying to orient myself.

"Oh, just a little ghost town I drove through years ago. Thought maybe there might be some abandoned building where I could set up an ashram or something." He looked at my face and burst out laughing. "You think I'm kidding, don't you?" Sean teased.

"Well, I must confess, the idea does seem a bit incongruous," I smiled, not really taking him seriously. "I mean, this place is *dead*, Sean."

"Oh ye of little faith," he said, shaking his head in mock sorrow.

We cruised down what appeared to be *the* main street. Most of the buildings were boarded up, and many of the few houses that were apparently still inhabited had "for sale" signs in front of them. We then turned off and meandered through the small residential area, finding more "for sale" signs and some evidence of local life: smoke coming out of the occasional chimney, a bike or car parked here and there by a house. As we paused at a corner, trying to decide which way to turn, a little green car pulled up beside us. An elderly woman leaned out the window and so Sean did likewise.

"Hi. I see you're from out of town," she said cheerfully.

"Yes ma'am," said Sean, the country gentleman.

"Might you be looking for a place to rent?" she inquired.

He glanced at me and raised an eyebrow. "We just might be," he replied agreeably to the woman.

I groaned silently, wondering what mischief he was up to now.

"Well, follow me," she said. "I live right near some rental property that just opened up, and I can get the landlady over in a couple of minutes."

"Yes ma'am, we'll just follow you then," and off we all raced at about 15mph.

Five minutes later we were at the edge of town, looking out for miles onto flat desert framed in the distance by shadowed mesas and isolated rock formations. It was a stark and slightly lunar vista.

Our guide was pulling in the driveway of one of the last, lone house before the desert took over. *What are we doing here*, I thought to myself once again. On the other hand, having this woman approach us at a crossroad in a ghost town and offer us accommodations was intriguingly bizarre. Was power or timing waiting for us here?

I looked around. The simple adobe house at the edge of the desert was surrounded with trees on all sides and set back from the road, giving it a certain privacy. I tried to imagine it from spring through fall. There appeared to be a small orchard of fruit trees as well as cottonwood, locust, and what looked like a profusion of wild rose all around the front and sides of the house. Set on several acres of land, there was more than adequate space for a vegetable garden as well.

"Go ahead and look inside," beamed the woman, nodding. "The front door is unlocked. I'll go get the landlady while you two have a look around." And off she went.

Once indoors, we realized the house had looked deceptively small from outside. There was a spacious kitchen/dining area, a living room with a modest but adequate fireplace, several smaller rooms for bedrooms or a study, and a large unfinished workshop. The house needed a little touching up here and there, but for a rental, I thought it was in remarkably good condition.

I found myself trying to imagine living here, and noticed how quiet the house and surroundings were.

Sean came up behind me. "If I were you, I'd write out a check as a deposit right away," he said, his eyes dancing with excitement. "This place would be ideal for you."

"And just what would I do out here by myself in the middle of nowhere?" I said, eyes darting around the house, feeling my grip on the future suddenly slipping away from me.

"Don't you think it would be the perfect place for you to strengthen your *will* and your dreaming?" Sean replied. "And that could be just for starters!"

"I don't know," I said nervously, amazed that I was even taking his suggestion seriously. "I have certain things I'd planned to do that I can't see getting free of for at least another half year. And I don't want to pay rent for two houses for that long on the chance that I *might* move here then. I'll have to think about this some more, Sean."

He nodded and pressed me no further. "Okay. Let's go back outside and wait for the landlady."

We walked out the front door and after a dozen paces turned back to face the house. As we surveyed it once again, I heard Sean take a deep breath and step up behind me. Suddenly his hands were holding my head, tilting it slowly back. *Now what*, I thought to myself, and then thinking ceased as I felt a tremor go through my *will*.

An enormous bald eagle floated into my field of vision from behind me. It was only a few hundred feet above us and clearly visible. The moment it was directly over the house, it suddenly dove straight down, wings tucked in tight. Part way down, the eagle abruptly snapped its wings fully extended, causing it to stop in mid-air with a sharp whooshing sound. Then it repeated the sequence, stopping the second time very close to the roof of the house before it wheeled around and headed north, as it had originally been doing before this breathtaking display.

When the great bird was out of sight, I finally turned and faced Sean. His eyes were blazing with an eagle-like quality that pierced my doubts and connected me with the inevitability of this moment.

I said nothing, and sighed as the winds of change blew through my soul. Then I turned toward the car to get my purse and checkbook as the landlady pulled into the driveway.

Nine

-- -- -- -- -- -- -- -- -- -- -- -- -- -- -- -- -- -- -- --

... Trail of power, flight of ecstasy,
We hunger for the truth, we must embrace what we see.
Heart for knowledge, transformation's child,
Pulling like a riptide, our spirit's deep and wild...

from "Trail of Power"

As soon as the eagle's house was secured in the net of intent, we chased the setting sun, two wild spirits headed toward southern California. This time Sean and I actually discussed our next destination. There was a power place he knew of that I was eager to see, and we were both in a buoyant mood. At least initially.

Following the flow of power, I'd given the rental deposit to my new landlady-to-be. All the events leading up to this action were so extraordinary that it was hard denying this was ordained. The meaning of the eagle vision I'd see in the sky after Castaneda's talk about escaping stagnating social aggregates had been clarified by today's eagle. I'd become convinced I should move to the adobe house in the desert. However, once we were on the road and the initial momentum and excitement began to subside, second thoughts, grave doubts, and finally deep anxiety set in as I questioned my action. The longer I ruminated, the greater the contrast between my mood and Sean's.

How could I be thinking of moving to a ghost town, of all things? There was no real city for at least a hundred miles, not even a grocery store for ten, no library, no theater. Just the formidable desert. And I had no idea how often I'd even see Sean, gypsy traveler that he seemed to be. As far as

I knew, he might be planning on enthusiastically helping deposit me there, and then disappearing for a few years while I baked in the desert dust.

So what that I already couldn't relate to the idea of returning to my former life, friends and co-workers? I could fake it for a while as I checked out my options a little further. And just because an eagle dove out of nowhere at that house twice in a row didn't mean I had to *move* there. It could have meant something completely different. Maybe the bird had just seen a rabbit nearby and wasn't really aiming at the house at all. *Yes, I* said reassuringly to myself, *that was probably the logical explanation behind its strange actions.* I bolted up out of my slumped position.

"You know, I was just thinking," I said brightly. "About that eagle, I—"

"Ah!" interrupted Sean. "Wasn't it magnificent? That was one of the most powerful gestures of *intent* I've ever witnessed."

I slid back down in the seat, my spirit silently agreeing with the truth of his statement. It was clear I wasn't off the hook so easily. I dipped compulsively into a bag of tortilla chips, nibbling nervously and wondering what the penalty was for ignoring omens and extravagant gestures of *intent*. Would I be permanently out of the loop, on some spiritual nosedive? Or would *intent* be insulted and never offer me another opportunity to align myself with power? My dry throat constricted as I swallowed a mouthful of chips, resulting in a coughing fit. Sean pounded me vigorously on the back as I gasped for air.

"I'm okay, I'm okay!" I finally spluttered, after managing to drink a few sips of water to wash down the offending crumbs. Actually, even though I was a bit embarrassed, somehow I didn't feel quite as nervous as I had before almost choking to death. There's nothing quite like a confrontation with mortality for its tonic benefits!

I decided to express my questions and concerns about the consequences of not following *intent*. This gave rise to a bout of mirth from Sean. Finally he explained his understanding was that *intent* wasn't so human in its characteristics. It didn't seek slaves, nor did it punish people for wasted opportunities.

"Just keep polishing your link to *intent*," he said, "and you will know where power is headed. or might even learn its purpose, which would clarify if and why you'd want to follow and utilize it. Maybe you need more awareness of your life goals. Then your link to *intent* will show you where the power is for accomplishing those goals. I'm confident you'll know soon enough if going to live in that house is appropriate for you. Worrying and tearing your hair about the issue is not going to help."

This discussion helped shed light on a key issue. Although I'd been raised by agnostic parents, I'd nonetheless assimilated the wrathful God or punishing afterlife concepts. I'd then neatly transposed them onto issues like following *intent*. But there was no external punishment for rejecting an opportunity. I could choose. It simply was more *practical* to use available power when it offered itself.

As we continued driving west through the Mojave Desert that afternoon, the air warmed and made me believe in spring again. The silhouetted sharp black points of the Sierras snapped toward the blue heavens as if to consume any passing cloud or bird. High above and out of their reach, an invisible hand was painting the turquoise sky with white, Chinese calligraphy, tracing obscure symbols with delicate wispy strokes. I wondered dreamily if my fate would be revealed to me if I could somehow decipher them.

"The power of this area is a challenge," Sean said suddenly, jarring me out of my reverie. "The land between the Colorado River and the coast of southern California has some unique spiritual properties. It is one of the starkest, most raw, dry terrains in the entire U.S. This dangerous place is populated with more scorpions than humans, and I've found it can be both demanding and threatening.

"The Mojave is like a stern finger thrust north from Sonora, the part of Mexico that was never conquered. This southern invasion dragged its jagged Sierra teeth up here, ready to devour anything that moves."

"What does that mean?" I asked him, feeling slightly intimidated.

"Driving through this area is a confrontation with power for us both. You could help me by holding your *will* hard and being ready to deal with it."

I gulped and began meditating with sincere determination.

Late in the afternoon we stopped off the highway to stretch and walk a bit. Before leaving the car, Sean sat and stared intently toward the south, and began to breathe heavily. He ended with some violent exhales through his nose that resembled a horse snorting through flared nostrils. After this startling performance he flung the door open and exploded out the door with long energetic strides as if determined to be in Sonora by dawn.

I raced after him across the parched and barren soil. Just as I was finally catching up, Sean stopped so suddenly I almost ran into him. He raised his left hand and pointed it southward, then grabbed his first two fingers and somehow managed to make them pop and crackle while extended straight.

The sound and the energy of his action caused my belly to jump as if a rubber band attached to my navel had been twanged. Immediately we were hit with a wild gust of wind from the south. Sean raised both hands as if in some kind of silent greeting or benediction, and I found myself doing likewise. The south wind continued to blow against us for another minute until Sean put one hand on his belly and the other on the top of his head, bowing it slightly into the wind. Then, just as suddenly as it had begun, the wind ceased, and we were left standing in an eerie, silent vacuum.

My mind was absolutely still, almost as if something had it in a vise so it couldn't move. As the minutes passed without being able to engage in a single thought, I felt my mind being gripped and held by an invisible force and began to panic. Just before fear completely engulfed me, I felt a pressure on my back, and heard Sean say, "Let's walk a little more, shall we?" Whatever it was let go of my mind and I popped into more normal awareness once again.

"I want to suggest a project for you," he said, shifting gears and deliberately not giving me space to talk about what we'd both just experienced.

This pattern took place regularly. Extraordinary events would occur, often involving some force of nature, and yet, Sean's air of nonchalance would lull my mind into accepting the unusual and inexplicable as normal.

Part of what was so strange about this pattern of unusual events stripped of question or comment, was that non-ordinary plus non-ordinary added up to the seemingly commonplace. This had been repeated so many times and so smoothly that it was only now that I was beginning to see it. Had Sean encouraged me to verbalize these myriad experiences, my mind not only would have tried to analyze and demand logical explanations, but also would have been stunned by the extraordinary nature of the events and possibly become unnerved. As it was, it had been soothed into accepting the inexplicable, the unknown.

By a certain osmotic quality of *will*, I was absorbing spiritual interrelationships without intellectually understanding them, and was then enticed into acting without a "reasonable" grasp of what I was doing. In this sense, Sean was a great role model to my *will* of a variety of options for action, often by modeling possibilities himself. He would touch the top of his head, sides of his neck, belly, popping joints and taking various postures while Spirit manifested in some new way. In this fashion my spirit could learn kinetically without needing verbal communication.

Sean had also been placing his hands on the same points on *my* body, or positioning my arms or entire body in a certain stance or gesture. By doing so, he invited my *will* to face and interface with power in various ways. And I was now beginning to take the initiative to act *will*fully on my own in new ways through creating gestures and stances of spiritual meaning and power. When I'd try to *think* what I could possibly be doing, I'd feel like an idiot. When I simply acted *will*fully *without* thought, power would move as a major character in this spiritual drama.

At this time of my life, Sean played the role of host to a world previously less tangible to me. He kept opening the door to a realm of power and mystery, and I was participating in it through actions that others might perceive as rather bizarre behaviors.

"What kind of project did you have in mind?" I finally replied, coming back to the present as we turned to head back toward the car.

Sean was silent for a few minutes, frowning slightly as if to gather him-self for a somewhat difficult task. Eventually, his brow smoothed again, and he told me it had to do with my more deeply understanding the nature of social aggregates: specifically, my circle of friends.

"Most human aggregates are relatively slow and resistant to change," he mused, glancing at me briefly before going on. "We're like dinosaurs lumbering along with a great deal of accumulated inertia. It takes quite a bit of energy or something momentous to get us to turn in a new direction. The aggregate shares beliefs, covert and overt agreements, pecking orders, vested interests, and an overall sense of security achieved through maintaining the status quo. Therefore, if any of its members change much, even if the change is positive, the stability of the aggre-gate is threatened and rumblings of resistance are quickly heard."

"This sounds familiar to me from theories of psychology, Sean, partic-ularly as a dynamic between couples. Often, if one of the two began to change, the other will try to squelch or sabotage the fledging tendency. It's an effort to pluck out the 'offending member', which is change itself!"

He nodded, saying, "We cling to the familiar, the known, as if it were the ultimate salvation of the soul, when often it's no more than a life-raft for the mind and emotions. Facing the *un*known is what's really strength-ening to the soul. Don't get me wrong. Stability and familiarity have their place. But change *is* sometimes needed and sometimes happens whether it's needed or not. So it's good to be prepared for its inevitability and to understand the dynamics of group response.

"Whenever you eventually return home, I think you are going to need to be *well*-prepared for encounters with your old friends and acquaintances. You've changed and been changed a great deal the past few weeks in ways you haven't really begun to inventory yet. Things have been sneaking up on you in more ways than one, and now you're drunk!" He turned again to look at me, and opened his eyes wide, as if suddenly amazed at my condition.

Once again, I found my emotions bouncing from one extreme to the other. As soon as Sean pronounced me drunk, I began to feel offended.

But before I could even begin to act out my feelings, his ridiculous facial expression sent me off into gales of laughter. The longer I laughed, the looser, and yes, somewhat drunk, I began to feel. I eventually was staggering and weaving as I tried to walk, which just made the analogy seem even more accurate and caused me to laugh harder. At last, I collapsed on the desert floor, holding my exhausted belly with my arms as I prayed I would stop laughing before it killed me.

"Did you check the area for scorpions or rattlers?" came Sean's voice from a slight distance. Immediately I was on my feet and had leaped several meters away without knowing quite how, shaking my clothes and trying to peer over my shoulders at my own back. "Help me! What did you see? Is there anything on me?!" I demanded frantically.

Sean came over and brushed off my backside briskly, as he responded, "Yes, I did see something."

"What was it? A scorpion? What did you see?" I exclaimed nervously, prancing in place in an effort to dislodge anything that might still be clinging to me.

"I saw you going off the deep end, and figured this was as good a way to save you as any."

I finally realized I was no longer laughing, for which I was relieved, but the tiny smile beginning on Sean's face set me off, and I turned and chased him with teasing threats most of the way back to the car. Finally I was too tired to do anything but walk. Being here in the Mojave was definitely a challenge, as Sean had predicted earlier, but I wasn't sure what was the most challenging element to deal with—the desert or Sean himself.

When I reached the car, he was standing off to one side, casting a wary eye as I stretched out and caught my breath. "Come over here for a minute," he said as I finished, and I followed him to a place about fifty feet away. "This is 'fresh' lava flow," he said, pointing to the dark pools of hardened lava. "You might find it interesting to lie down on it and check it out with your *will*."

Curious, I strolled over to a large area of the smooth volcanic rock, and lay upon it belly-down. As I unfolded my *will* into the frozen fire, I felt my awareness being carried downward toward the molten layer of the earth from which it had come. Here was power that was rarely recognized by humans, seething and barely contained. Only when this power launched itself toward the heavens, melting everything in its path as it surged for miles before erupting through the earth's surface, were we reminded of Pele, the fire goddess. Pele bides her time within the earth until she is ready to touch our spirit with her presence, bringing dangerous, awesome, and glorious power into our lives.

As I too surfaced from touching the earth's hidden depths of fire, I sat up and looked around for Sean. He was sitting on a nearby lava boulder. "Now I feel more at home here in the Mojave," he joked. He told me he'd spent varying periods of time in the Hawaiian Islands and loved their lush green sea-touched energy.

"I could have happily retired on those islands, but the power there kicked me out," he sighed morosely, to my amusement, "and told me I still had much too much work to do before considering a Hawaiian retirement. But before I left, I witnessed several of Pele's volcanic displays and often wandered through the eerie cinder landscapes and craters of her spent, fiery passions." He stretched, placed both palms affectionately on the lava, and then uncoiled and rose to his feet.

By the time we got back to the car, I felt ready to continue with our earlier conversation.

"Even though your mind may be lagging behind, I can tell your *will* is ecstatic about the various experiences it's been having," Sean continued, picking up on my mood. "This inner euphoria is going to pressure you to share your experiences with all your old friends. I'm trying warn to you that that probably won't work, for several reasons."

"Why not, Sean?" I asked, somewhat puzzled. "I think they'll be really interested."

"Because," he said, shaking his head, "most of what you've been experiencing has been very 'left-sided'. Your mind hasn't understood, let alone remembered all of it, and this will present communication problems. Even if you *could* be articulate about your experiences, my guess is your friends will have trouble making room for them in any useful manner, and your stories will most likely end up as fodder for your friends' gossip hot line. Some of this should sound familiar, if you'll remember our talk with Rose."

I wasn't at all sure this was the case in my situation. Sean didn't know my friends and might be underestimating them.

"To deal with the situation, I think you are going to need to apply the *art of stalking*," he continued, ignoring the vaguely skeptical expression on my face.

"Wait a minute," I interrupted, springing to my friends' defense, "the people I hang out with aren't superficial. We don't exactly sit around and talk about fashion, the weather, or who's dating whom, Sean. A lot of them are open and interested in spirituality. I think they'd sincerely like to know what I've been doing, and maybe even to meet you."

"I'm not criticizing your friends," responded Sean calmly. "What I'm trying to point out are issues of power and how to handle them. At this point, chattering about your travels with me would catapult you into a clash of power and differing worldviews. You don't realize how much power you're carrying right now. Remember how much you affected the people at the peyote ceremony when your *will* merged with the fire? Well, you could easily and unwittingly unleash enough of it to knock your friends' spirits way out of balance.

"I know more about your friends than you think," he added mysteriously. "I'm concerned for their well-being, just as I am for yours. But you also have to take into consideration where your friends' spiritual viewpoints may now differ from your own. After all, you've recently adopted some new perspectives yourself."

He paused to give me a few moments to reflect on talks we'd had about some of these issues. Sean was dubious about the spiritual value of some of my friends' obsessions with reincarnation, channeling, astrology, and other popular "new age" interests. And I'd begun shifting some of my own views, partly from the effect of Sean's perspective but also from taking a hard look at my own past and present experiences. I realized my altered viewpoints might not be met with total enthusiasm by my old friends.

As I nodded, he continued. "Now let's look at power. Your stories will carry some of their own spiritual power. If you go and reveal your recent experiences to people who are less serious about power themselves, several kinds of things are likely to happen. One is that they won't really be able to hear you and you'll end up disappointed and lose energy. A second is that they will become jealous and competitive, and try to divert your power into emotional exchanges. A third is that they'll include the information in story swapping without any serious spiritual goals. This will simply make them feel they own a part of you they can pass around whenever they like, and will serve neither you nor them.

"Somewhere there will undoubtedly be the occasional individual with whom you could share the story of your journey, one who has both enough spiritual commitment and openness that it would fit in his or her world. Your story and its power would enliven such a person's *will*, and rather than drain you, would benefit both of you."

"This all makes sense, but if I have to think about all these things every time I go to open my mouth, I'm going to end up permanently tongue-tied," I sighed. "Besides, all of this sounds so cold and calculating."

"It is," Sean replied quietly. "The mastery of awareness has to penetrate all aspects of our life. This isn't just some dilettante path for a weekend high, you know. It's our life and power at stake here. Either we're reckless, squander them, and end up spiritually bankrupt and ineffective, or we become sober—spiritual conservationists—and have reserves of power with which to act effectively in this world and elsewhere."

He paused to give me time to consider this perspective, and then continued.

"To learn to use our energy properly, we first have to realize we don't owe other people personal revelations as some kind of membership dues. *Choosing* to reveal aspects of our life for our own reasons and goals is something else. We need to be responsible to ourselves and to choose what we want to project into the world. This is part of the *art of stalking*."

"This sounds like an lifelong project," I said wearily, feeling overwhelmed.

"Oh, I haven't even given you my idea for the project yet," he said, "and of course it's up to you whether you want to do it or not. But the project has to do both with what I've been addressing and with rearranging your personal history, particularly vis a vis social aggregates.

"The first part of the project is to make a list of all the people you've been relatively close to the last few years. The next is to look at each one individually and to make a serious effort to determine who among them has been energetically draining, who has been empowering toward themselves and you, who has taught you anything spiritually effective and useful, who has demonstrated any real power in his or her own spiritual life and practices, and who has shown himself to be your adversary, spiritually speaking."

Once Sean had outlined this sufficiently, we decided we'd talked enough about serious matters for the evening and we should relax for the rest of the drive. Relief washed over me at the prospect of a break from the intensity of our conversation. In an increasingly buoyant mood, I began to entertain Sean by singing an international medley of songs and chants I'd learned from many cultures: Russian and Spanish gypsy songs, East Indian *bajans*, plaintive Mexican and French love songs, sweet Zimbabwean folk chants, peyote songs, and even an Italian aria thrown in for fun. Then I sang all that I could remember of an operetta by Menotti called "The Medium," which had haunted me as a child.

It was the story of a woman who made her living as a trance medium in order to support herself, her daughter and a young mute boy they'd taken in. Although she called herself a medium, she was actually a clever charlatan who preyed on the emotions of her customers in their search for contact with their beloved dead. Eventually, the story turned a strange corner as ghostly voices began to make themselves heard, voices she had not rigged up herself with hidden phonographs or other technical manipulations. Were they indeed the voices of the dead now come to haunt her? Were they a trick being played on her by her daughter and the boy, who'd fallen in love with each other despite the medium's disapproval? The drama of this operetta was backed by some of the most beautiful, powerful music and lyrics I'd ever heard as a young girl, and it was one of my favorite passages—drawn from ancient gypsy magic—that I sang as the sun set and the first stars appeared.

> *With silver needle and with silver thread*
> *The stars stitch a shroud for the dying sun.*
> *Oh, black swan, where oh where has my lover gone?*
> *I had given him a kiss of fire*
> *And a golden ring, and a golden ring...*

***

That night while Sean slept, I began to work on the project he'd described, and which I'd begun to be mildly enthused about. Perhaps it was the late dinner, or the desert winds, but sleep seemed far away and the night was waiting to be filled.

I thought of the people I'd known, not only recently but throughout my life. Like a silent parade of phantoms, their images floated across my inner field of vision. Some I'd called friends, enemies, family, teachers and co-adventurers. Each had left an imprint on my spirit, an invisible signature of sorts, and now it was time to look closer and discern the nature of the markings. This night was only a beginning, and part of me dreaded the task of sorting things out as methodically as Sean had suggested.

But the call of the hunt was in the air, urging me on. Somewhere nearby, coyotes were singing of it in the desert night, while rabbits and owls and other ears attended to the song, listening as the waxing crescent moon floated across the star-strewn sky. I too listened to the song...and immersed myself into the *art of stalking.*

By mid-morning we'd already hiked several miles in Joshua Tree Park, and the sun and exercise were finally removing the last of the morning chill from my slightly fatigued body. I found out later we could have driven to within a two-minute walk of our current destination, but we needed to prepare ourselves and gather some energy from the earth while walking to this spot, one of Sean's favorite power places.

He had wanted to approach it from the south, which initially involved hiking by the road, then cutting off and meandering up a dry arroyo. In silence, I feasted my eyes on the exotic terrain of purple-shadowed massive boulders, red-bark manzanita, silver-green olive leaves and cholla cactus, and especially on the distinct and unusual Joshua trees for which this enormous park was named.

After an hour, to my surprise Sean became loquacious and began telling stories of previous experiences he'd had here in the past. Sudden storms, giant tortoises, eerie pink snakes and double rainbows peopled his tales as we plodded up the sandy arroyo.

Finally I began to get thirsty and ready for a short rest. But when I suggested sitting and began to reach for my canteen, Sean stopped me and asked if I could postpone both just a little longer. Slightly bewildered by the nature of his odd request, I nonetheless agreed to wait, curious as to his reasons.

A few minutes later, as we came around a curve in the arroyo, my mind reeled at a stunning sight. An oasis! It seemed impossible, here in the midst of this arid and sandy landscape, but it was neither a mirage nor a metaphor. A few giant palms came first, lining the sides of the arroyo like ancient sentinels. As the arroyo ended, a cluster of the majestic beings created a fairly large, shaded cathedral.

As we approached this verdant mystery, birdsong exploded out of the trees, a concert of virtuosos proclaiming their talents to the morning breeze. We stopped for a while, absorbing this sudden new deluge to our senses. Two hummingbirds raced by off to our left, startling me by their closeness and intensity. Sean took hold of my *will* area as they disappeared into the oasis, and shook it briefly. As he did, the two aerial magicians reappeared, accompanied by a third, and shot over our heads, finally coming to rest for a while in some cottonwood trees behind us. My *will* felt electric and fully involved with their antics.

The momentary quieting of the hummingbirds seemed to be the signal for us to proceed once again, so we continued the final stretch up the arroyo. As we entered the shaded grotto of palms, the air was suddenly cool and damp, and above the din of birdsong, I heard yet another sound—that of trickling water. As I did, I understood why Sean had asked me to wait a bit longer before drinking. I felt a little of what the ancient travelers, desert nomads coming up from Mexico or heading west on a trading expedition, must have felt, knowing this place existed, hoping the underground spring was still alive and offering its moisture to parched bodies.

We found an area where the water pooled at the base of an ancient palm. Kneeling down to splash a bit on our faces, we silently expressed gratitude for the cool liquid dripping over the water-smoothed, slick and mossy rocks slightly above us and down to our feet. After refreshing ourselves with the sweet water and finally drinking from the canteen, we surveyed our surroundings.

Giant bumblebees, some as large as the hummingbirds, floated in and out of the oasis. Even in winter, several kinds of butterflies were about, including a swarm of tiny pale violet ones that captured my attention more than the larger ones with their dramatic markings. Like us, the butterflies were thirsty, and they fluttered from damp soil to wet stones, drinking and then dancing their contentment. I watched them for a while, trying to keep track of their intricate interplay through the greenery, until finally my vision grew blurred. I leaned against one of the palms and closed my eyes.

We stayed in the oasis without speaking for an hour or more, and I drifted in and out of a mosaic of brief dreams and meditative waking states. I felt overwhelmingly rich there amidst the giant palms. Somehow the totality of the environment, an emerald jewel set in the heart of the desert and lush with life and moisture, permeated my being from the skin to the soul and satiated me with contentment.

During one of the intervals between dreams, I thought how different the oasis was compared to another place in this same park where I'd spent an unusual night with a friend years earlier.

Kate was a woman who shared my interests in indigenous ceremonialism and the spiritual power of nature. Both of us were physically strong and avid hikers. Having lived much of her life near Joshua Tree Park, Kate had spent a great deal of time exploring it. One summer, she invited me to come out and accompany her to the park, to spend the night at a place she felt was special.

In the mood for an adventure, I joined her there a few days later on the opposite side of the park from the oasis.

We'd driven into the desert around ten at night to avoid the scorching summer heat and the park rangers who might not allow us to stay overnight at this particular place. At one point Kate guided me off the park highway onto a dirt road and several miles later directed me to pull over by some massive boulders. We quietly put on our backpacks, locked the car, and like furtive shadows slipped into the waiting desert.

The air was mild, but I'd shivered slightly to be in this strange place late at night. I followed close behind Kate, trudging through the silvery sands until finally she stopped.

"We're here," she said softly.

I looked around but didn't see anything different at first than what I'd already seen in abundance: the outline of yet another huge cluster of boulders. Kate shined her flashlight on a little path that we followed between numerous clusters of glowing cholla cacti until we were next to the lowest of the boulders. Following invisible toe and finger holes in its surface, Kate scrambled up to the top of it and gestured for me to follow.

Not to be disgraced by someone several decades my senior, I searched about for a starting point, found a niche for my first foot and a few more for my hands, took a deep breath, and began to climb. Although from the ground it had looked intimidatingly high, I found I was up level with Kate after only a few fairly simple maneuvers. I shrugged off my pack and sat down to catch my breath. Kate then took her flashlight and aimed it straight up, and I gasped in surprise at what was revealed.

We were beneath a curved expanse of carved out, cave-like rock, which extended behind us a little ways until it narrowed to a small opening. Scattered across the vaulted surface was a firmament of ancient painted petroglyphs, the silent language of another time and people. Even by dim flashlight, I could see there was still a bit of colored pigment left, some reddish, some black, and other faint colors that would reveal themselves more clearly in the morning.

I gawked for some time at the myriad symbols and pictures, trying to decipher the meaning and story of the serpent, lizard and geometric abstract forms. I scrambled all about, taking a fair amount of skin off various portions of my anatomy in an effort to discover and scrutinize every last drawing.

After Kate was satisfied that I was suitably impressed by this favorite spot of hers, she broke the silence and told me her theory about the place.

"I'm convinced that long ago the local Indians initiated their spiritually gifted young women into puberty here," she whispered. "From what I know of their power plant use, they probably used *datura* to help induce visionary and dreaming states. The last time I was here, I found several hollowed-out stones nearby that looked like they were once used for grinding the dried plants. I think this place was the ceremonial womb, and that eastern back passage was the birth canal."

Kate's theories were intriguing, but I was glad the womb didn't completely surround us. From where we sat, we could turn west and look out over the desert floor to cliffs and more boulders a good half mile away.

Loving ritual as well as wanting to be respectful toward any lingering spirits of the place, Kate reverently lifted some tobacco and corn meal to all directions, scattering it finally through her fingers. Then we each made ourselves comfortable, finding our own niches and padding them a bit for the night ahead, and sat to begin our all-night vigil. We were confident the power of the place would reward us with something unusual if we could just stay awake. Our faith was based on all-night experiences each of us had had in other powerful places.

Kate and I were only thirty or forty miles from the nearest town, but it felt like we were on another planet. As we gazed out into the night, hour after hour, the domed black sky would periodically expel a shooting star whose meteoric flight pulled my spirit along on its arcing, brilliant journey. No matter how many times I witnessed them, each was different, each a surprise and delight, a gift showering out of the heavens.

An owl kept up a steady monologue into the night, joined later by its mate for some unearthly duets. But despite all this engaging activity on the part of nature, hours after midnight fatigue and restlessness began to set in. I started to wonder how much longer I'd be able to maintain my enthusiasm and alertness. As I entertained the idea of curling up and taking a little nap, I remembered this familiar phase from prior vision quests and other all-night vigils I'd done, so I resisted the temptation. I tried to awaken my mind and body with some yogic fire breathing. Moments later, something out in the desert tugged at the corner of my vision. I shifted my gaze slightly, looked, blinked and looked again in astonishment.

There before me, midway between our shelter and the distant cliffs, was a massive white, barely translucent wall or curtain. It extended up into the sky, looked about two hundred feet wide, and had a soft glowing quality, like a two-dimensional, rectangular cloud illuminated by moonlight. But there was no moon this night, so the source of illumination was a mystery.

If this same shape had been suspended horizontally above the desert floor, I could have explained it to myself as condensation, a blanket of mist settling from the cooling temperatures. But a vertical mist? Every few seconds, I'd blink hard to make sure this wasn't eyestrain or fatigue-induced, but the glowing form remained constant. I finally whispered to Kate, who'd been facing away from the phenomenon.

"Psst! Hey Kate! What do you see out there?" I said, pointing toward the glowing wall.

After a brief silence, she whispered, "Wow! It's a wall of light! I've never seen anything like this."

We sat staring at it, intrigued both by its mysterious nature and staying power. Finally, prompted by curiosity and memories of Carlos Castaneda's descriptions of a wall of fog leading to other worlds, I boldly decided to walk out and approach it. Kate was warier but wasn't about to be left behind either, so down the boulder we slithered as I shed yet more skin.

Once on the desert floor, the wall loomed increasingly massive and overwhelming. We two humans were puny and insignificant in contrast. Keeping a wary eye on it, I also scanned the ground to avoid cholla and some of the other thorny desert scrub like devil's claw. Slender and strangely glowing trails kept revealing themselves for us to follow. Their iridescence was something I once again couldn't explain, but they stood out as if demanding to be used. Whatever they were, I followed those that meandered in the general direction of the ethereal wall, for I felt more sure-footed on these paths of light than on the "unmarked" areas. Kate followed close behind me.

As we walked, I became aware of a general pulsing going on. It was partly felt, partly heard and seen. As if a giant heart was pumping the night itself, all sounds would get louder, little lights that I'd seen dancing about earlier would get brighter, and the wall would seem to expand. There was an eerie bird-like screech that also echoed through the night at each pulse. Then, for a few seconds, all would be still, the lights would dim, and the wall would contract. Then the pulse would repeat.

The closer we got to the wall, the more intense each pulse became. Kate finally dropped behind and stopped, afraid of whatever it was. I was on my own. I ventured further for a few minutes until the wall was towering over me. Then suddenly, I too could go no further. My feet seemed rooted in the ground, and I heard a deafening roar as if a jet had just flown in one ear and out the other. My sinuses plugged up, and then popped and cleared again. The wall split open in the middle for a moment, revealing what appeared to be an empty frame hanging far in the distance, before it closed once again at the next pulse.

Anxiously turning my head to see if I could locate Kate, I was finally able to move my feet. I felt a surge of relief. Her silhouette was there in the distance, and farther behind her our petroglyph boulder loomed. It too was participating in the pulsing, and a ring of light at its center kept expanding and contracting. I immediately felt it was time to return there. I knew I had just been in the presence of something overwhelming and inexplicable, and it was time to back off from the wall of fog since I obviously wasn't able to step through it. I joined Kate and we returned to our lair, silently pondering our experiences.

As soon as we were back among the petroglyphs, I focused on the area where the ring of light had seemed centered. At the back of the rounded shelter where the narrow passageway began, the light expanded and contracted rhythmically. It drew me hypnotically forward and I began to crawl through the ring of light and the narrow opening. The pulsing seemed to be squeezing me through a sort of birth canal, and I started to believe in Kate's initiation theory.

I became increasingly anxious as I moved through the passageway, finally dropping out the other side into a small clearing. Although I knew intellectually I was still in the same desert, my birth process had expelled me into a strange, new world. It felt a good ten degrees colder here, and everything was quite a bit darker, more obscure and dense. I stayed for a while and tried to sense the spiritual energy until something began to make a rustling noise off to one side. That was enough for me. Heart racing,

I turned and scrambled back up through the passageway. I was ready to return to the womb! Once again, something inexplicable had happened. I felt as if I'd been born into a completely alien world, cold and uncompromising, and utterly devoid of comfort and nurturing. This was a side of the unknown to be confronted only with extra reserves of energy, I decided, and knew my reserves were too low to withstand it any longer this night.

Kate had lit a candle, and I sat and rested in the warm glow that I welcomed after the chill of the other side. The flickering candlelight also gave me another chance to enjoy the petroglyphs. A tortoise clung to the surface near another figure that looked like a stylized thunderbird or waterbird like the peyote bird symbol. But what was the fish doing here in the middle of the desert? Some time later when I'd had my fill of pondering these ancient mysteries, I saw that dawn was approaching. After having come through a most extraordinary night, we watched its pink and lavender tendrils reach through the grayness until light finally triumphed.

At length we packed our things and headed back toward the car, breathing deep of the fresh morning air. We meandered down the dawn-lit trail, passing through turbinella oak, smokebrush and creosote. Soon we passed through the final pair of boulders, which were like sentries marking the end of the magical realm. A large bush crouched next to one of them, displaying its luminous, trumpet-shaped white blossoms. I strolled over to look at it more closely and buried my nose in a flower, seeking its perfume. When I glanced up, Kate was surveying me, arms crossed and one eyebrow raised.

As we approached the car, I asked her if she knew what the unusual plant was. She acted surprised, as if she thought I already knew, but finally replied as she shrugged off her backpack and got into the car.

"Datura."

The initiation plant of the ancient people of this land.

Ten

...Another spirit dives through like a kite
Moving faster than the speed of light,
She tumbles through beginnings with no end
Linked to intent, the spirit's only friend...

from "Quatro Mas o Menos"

The oasis was drenched with the nectar of life, and we satiated ourselves in its lush greenery like beggars at a banquet. As we sat, I told Sean the story of the petroglyph cave.

"I once had a strange experience in this desert too," he said, "one that has to do with our present circumstances. But I'd rather leave the oasis and walk back down the arroyo a bit before I tell you about it."

We lingered there a few more minutes. I was reluctant to leave, enchanted as I was with this magic place and uncertain if I'd ever see it again. Finally, I managed to drag myself away. The afternoon was growing late and Sean had said he had business to take care of in Los Angeles that evening and the next day. As we walked, it was almost impossible to fathom that in just a few hours we'd be trading this serene and spacious environment for the teeming chaos of Los Angeles.

Before we rounded the curve that would block the oasis from sight, he gestured for me to sit down and face the greenery once more. He sat to my left, his wide-brimmed Western hat leaving his face in shadows, like the oasis.

"As a young man," he began, "I used to come to the oasis fairly regularly. Its calm tranquility helped me meditate and clear my mind of all the things constantly pressing on me.

"One day, from just about this place we're sitting now, I saw three figures emerge from the shadows of the oasis. I stopped in my tracks and stared at them. Their appearance had the quality of a mirage, and although the day was cool, the air around them shimmered in waves. I couldn't make out their features at first, but all three were dressed in some kind of purple garments. And even though there was a silvery, flashing quality emanating from them, at first I thought they were real physical people. They slid out of the oasis in a line, holding hands and dancing. Then I realized that none of their feet were touching the ground. Not only were they radiating light but they were floating!

"The three figures, who gradually became recognizably female, continued in their dance, flowing from a line to a circle and back, again and again. The dance was deceptively simple. Some of the movements were actually intricate and complex, but the women were intentionally disarming me through the charming outer simplicity of their movements. There was so much power being generated by both their dance and their beings that I might have become more guarded without this soothing effect. But they completely captivated me!

"Two of the women were older, with strikingly silver hair. I never could see their facial features, and kept wondering who they could be. The other woman finally appeared to be quite young with rainbow glints of color in her hair. Just before this vision faded, her face became momentarily clear. She was beaming, absolutely radiant, and glanced briefly my way before they all disappeared. In that one moment, after having struggled to perceive *any* of their features, I felt an incredible sense of intimacy with the young woman, as if we really did know each other through and through. Then all three were gone, and I was left with a puzzle.

"Over the years I felt an eerie connection with the younger woman, as if I were a part of her life and could sense different things going on in it.

Even though I'd seen her in a vision, I was quite convinced she existed as a real flesh and blood person somewhere here on earth.

"About five years ago, I was observing a large group of people at a spiritual gathering, and one woman caught my attention. She was a bit skinny and looked strained at the time, but there was a strong light and energy pouring out of her. I watched her for quite a while, wondering why she seemed so familiar. Finally, I realized it was the young woman from that vision many years ago."

"Wow!" I said, unable to restrain myself at this point. "Did you talk to her?"

"No. I simply watched her for a long time from the outside edge of the crowd until she disappeared, swallowed up in the activity."

I was amazed, absolutely floored. I couldn't imagine not approaching her in such circumstances.

"The timing wasn't right," said Sean simply.

"But you may never get another chance," I said.

"Oh, but I did meet her again. It *was* a matter of timing and power. Through various motions of circumstance, I met her again a few years ago and have had periodic contact with her since. Recently, in fact, our contact has become quite regular."

I suddenly experienced a surprising pang of jealousy. I sat for a while, trying to be happy for Sean and the mysterious woman but not totally succeeding.

"Would you like to meet her?" he asked, with a sideways glance in my direction.

"Uh, oh, of course," I replied stiffly, as we rose to our feet and headed back to the car. I became convinced this woman was probably the "business" Sean had in Los Angeles, and with each step I felt an increasing sense of gloom. After these wonderful few weeks, I'd probably meet this amazing woman, and then be abandoned in Los Angeles to fend for myself while she and my spiritual travelling companion disappeared together into the unknown.

The sense of peace and plenitude of the oasis now seemed light years away. I ducked into the car and slumped in the seat. Sean slipped behind the wheel, but instead of turning on the ignition he reached over and flipped my sun visor down. It had a small mirror attached to its underside, and I found myself staring into my own eyes. I flipped the visor back up, wondering why Sean put it down in the first place, since the sun was behind us, and I had no desire to stare at my own face.

"Hey," said Sean, "I thought you wanted to meet this woman."

"I did," I replied, confused as to what that had to do with anything, particularly the sun visor. Was this woman about to appear out of mid-air in a burst of blinding light?

"Then pull the visor back down," he said.

I looked over and glared at him, crossed my arms over my chest and got increasingly annoyed. I was in no mood for some cute Zen riddle. Sean reached over and flipped the visor down once again. "You certainly are in a stubborn mood. Go ahead, what are you waiting for?"

As I sat motionless, staring at him as if he were out of his mind, he gently but firmly reached out, took my head in his hands, and turned it forward till I was looking once again in the little mirror.

"Aren't you going to say hello to her?" he asked.

***

A good hour later, racing down the freeway toward Los Angeles., I was only beginning to come out of a state of intense and deeply spiritual shock and disorientation. As I'd looked again into my own eyes and the meaning of Sean's implication finally dawned on my obstinate mind, that *I* was the young woman of his vision, something swept through my body with the impact of a lightning bolt. As soon as it hit, my *will* began to convulse, shaking me from head to toe with the force of a hurricane. Vague images began pouring through my inner vision, quick and fleeting as wild gazelles: Sean's piercing blue eyes watching me from the edge of one crowd, then another, disappearing and reappearing in strobe-like flash-backs until he finally loomed close, slipped behind me with a nod and touched my back for the first time. Finally, when it felt like I'd be shattered by the intensity of the visions and convulsions, I heard myself, as if from far away, let out a small sound, and then I felt the presence of Emily, the moth lady, and her friend Constanza. My eyes shut of their own accord. I saw the two women, silver-haired, flanking me on either side, and then each grabbed an arm and pulled me out of my body.

We floated up from the car, traversing above the same route Sean and I had just walked, and soon were back at the oasis.

"Time for a review," I heard Emily whisper from my left, while to the right I heard the muffled laugh of her Mexican friend.

Each held one of my hands as we floated just off the ground in front of the oasis, and they began to lead me in a dance. Hauntingly familiar, like a long forgotten song, it was as Sean had described, both simple and intri-cate, sometimes a serpentine line, sometimes a circle. When I gave up try-ing to figure it out, I was finally able to simply absorb the dance as it happened and flow into it like a stream joining the river. I became charged with a buoyant, rejuvenating energy, and felt I could go on forever.

But eventually the dance ended. "This dreaming dance is going to be like a spiritual well for you to draw from in the future," whispered Emily. "You probably won't remember this dance when you return to your nor-mal awareness, but soon it will enable you to begin dreaming new dances that you will both remember and teach to others," she continued. "The human world waits, waits for their spirits to be suffused with new energy from your dreaming dances, waits to learn again to dance their *wills* through their bodies."

I felt her words move me to a barely contained excitement. Then once more I was grabbed from each side, lifted through the air, and guided to my body that had become calm at last. As my awareness shifted into it, I felt a slight tremor, and then I was in the physical realm.

I gazed out the window for a few minutes afterwards, feeling slightly disassociated, as if I was watching a movie of the landscape. Something floated in front of my face. I took the bottle of water Sean was offering and swallowed a few sips, sighed deeply, and suddenly the world clicked into its normal perspective.

"Thanks," I whispered.

"*De nada*," Sean whispered back. A few moments later he reached over and tapped me firmly on the sternum, at about heart level, and then dragged his fingers from that point down to my belly, causing my *will* to jump slightly and then settle down again. This gesture was based on spiritual systems that mapped the movement of energies in and out of the body. The tap was for sealing off the emotions and then dropping awareness into a non-thinking, non-emotional state of *will*.

"Three is one," said Sean.

"Huh?"

"Three is one. I've said this before and I'll probably repeat it one way or another again."

I shook my head, trying to rearrange myself to deal with this new shift, one of several in the past few hours. I vaguely remembered having heard him use that phrase in Arizona shortly before arriving at the third ceremony.

"The Taoists say 'sink into the belly'," he continued quietly. "*I* say depend on *will*. Drop down from the first point, which is thinking, and the second, which is emotional reaction of heart, into the belly where *will*, the third point, is centered. Then one and two drop into three, three focuses of attention are layered on top of each other and held by *will*." He closed his eyes for a moment, breathed deep into his belly as if to demonstrate, and then went on.

"This is a process for anyone can apply after intense spiritual and emotional experiences. Tapping the chest and then drawing not only one's hand but one's attention to the belly helps quiet the emotions and protect the spirit from going into overload. Later, after applying 'three is one,' people can take time to think and to choose which emotions you want to feel about a particular experience. Emotions *can* be a choice instead of a reaction that leaves one helplessly attached to events a haphazard manner.

"The whole key to everything is 'three is one': how to *see*, how to use your *will!* In the end, and preferably in the beginning, we just have to practice stopping thoughts and emotions so we can respond increasingly with *will*, with 'three is one.'"

As I listened, I thought about my many years of meditation, and told Sean I felt I already had some experience of what he was describing.

"You're right," he said. "You've had extensive practice doing what I've described with an inward focus. But you can balance your spirit by practicing dropping into *will* as you focus *outward* and aim yourself into the world. You can learn to sink into *will* and then explode out into the world while holding your thoughts and emotions with an iron grip. This is a dance of spiritual action!"

As he spoke with some passion on the subject, I had an image of starry galaxies swirling as they were sucked into a black hole by some invisible force, and then the process suddenly reversing with an explosion of light.

"Most people's thoughts and emotions aren't under their own control," Sean continued. "It is rare and unusual for them to stop their emotions altogether for the explicit purpose of sharpening perceptions, or to shift their attention dramatically so body and *will* can draw all available energy for an act of power.

"Despite the minimal control they exert over thinking and emotion, many people, including some who you know, have a heart and desire for spirituality, and have concepts that a human being can *be* spiritual. But the very way they cling to their concepts of spirituality becomes an obstacle to the actual unfoldment of *will*."

Sean took some deep breaths, and then turned his gaze on me for a moment, his eyes blazing with a sudden fire.

"*Will* demands respect and a hatching out of its own egg. It demands a heating up of powerful attention in order to break free. To heat the *will* and hatch it out, to break it loose to act requires *all* of our attention in a given circumstance. If most of our attention is habitually flowing into thinking and emotion, it will be difficult to rally enough heat to bring *will* fully to bear when an act of power is called for.

"People in the West crow like roosters over the great power of reason. We also pound our chests and fall in love or are passionate over emotional attachments. We become enraged, or controlled by our fears: we then *know* the heart exists!"

I burst out laughing. "Excuse me, Sean. Some of your descriptions are so colorful. This last part sounds like our whole culture is at war with itself. I wonder who's winning—reason or the primal scream."

After settling down again I said, "You know, some psychologists feel it's not healthy to stop the emotions from having their way. Are you differentiating between stopping and repressing the emotions?"

"Absolutely," nodded Sean. "It's good for the heart to rest by stopping the emotions temporarily or briefly, and it's also the deepest wisdom to *decide* on an emotional approach. The heart is a *truer* heart when you can choose its responses."

"Is that because most of the emotions we humans display are socially conditioned, and to *choose* an emotion is to free ourselves from conditioning? Is that why you say the heart is then a truer heart?"

"Partly, because then it's not mixed with others and *their* emotional expectations. Most of our emotions are not really our own, not the pure response of our own heart. They're trapped in some penny ante exchange that's usually about shallow events and is spiritually deadening. And that's where our poor heart is ensnared day in and day out, except during extremes like various catastrophes or falling in love.

"I'm not recommending cutting out the heart and throwing it away at all. I'm addressing a balance: spend some time stopping emotions and dropping into *will*. Choose your emotions when you're going to exercise them. And use wisdom to decide when to allow the heart to be spontaneous. The heart will be a healthier and deeper instrument when protected in these ways."

"I think what you're really talking about living with awareness," I commented, trying to extract the thread that would help hold everything together for my saturated mind.

"Essentially, yes. It's all about the mastery of awareness."

"Well, I'm aware of needing a roadside rest stop. And I don't think I can concentrate on anything else before we find one!"

With that, we drove in silence for about twenty minutes until we came to a freeway rest stop. After using the facilities, I ran once around the rest stop to clear my head from the intensive course in "three is one." Sean had gotten really cranked up on the subject, and I wasn't sure how much I'd absorbed. Somewhat refreshed, I re-entered the school-on-wheels, and westward bound we headed once again.

***

By the time we arrived at the outskirts of Los Angeles the sun had long set, and the city and surrounding areas created their own dull orange glow in the overcast night sky. Long before we reached the city proper, my eyes and lungs were burning. I was starting to get irritable and resentful toward this smoggy metropolis, and already pined for the clean sweet desert air in which I'd spent so much time lately. I was tired, my senses were being assaulted in a variety of unpleasant ways, and I wondered if these last few weeks had permanently ruined me for city living.

"Do you have anything with you that you could offer as a gift to someone?" asked Sean, as cars raced by in aggressive darting patterns. "It doesn't have to be fancy, but something with a nice energy."

I thought for a minute, trying to figure out what would serve as a gift for a total stranger, and why I was the one to be giving it instead of Sean. I had absolutely no desire to go rummaging through my suitcase at this point. As I sat brooding, suddenly an image surfaced of a small amethyst crystal I'd once slipped in my handbag long ago. I searched about for a few minutes, and then, in a little side pocket, I found it.

"Will this do?" I asked.

"Yes," he replied, "that's just right. We're going to go visit an old girl-friend of mine, and it's just the kind of thing she'd enjoy. She's quite special. I really wouldn't want you to meet her without bringing a gift, and it's much better that the gift come from you than from me."

Once again I felt an edge of resentment. I'd been right before. Sean's business here *was* an old girlfriend after all. He'd apparently brought me hundreds of miles into this exhausting city to meet her, and now wanted *me* to give her a present!

Then, before I could do or say something I might later regret, I heard the whisper of a faint inner voice say "Three is one. Drop into *will*. *You* can choose your emotions." For a few minutes, a battle raged as I stared stonily out the window, feeling the emotional time bomb ticking toward explosion, and the opposing force of a different option, the option of *will*. I chose *will*.

I wasn't about to show Sean my petty emotions nor my struggle to resolve them. Rather than reveal a clue by tapping my chest and dragging the energy down with my fingers as he'd shown me, I used my breathing and an image of the turbulent energy calming, condensing, and flowing downward to pool in my belly. This was just as effective as the physical gesture. After a few minutes of intense concentration, I accomplished my goal, and was relieved to be out of the emotional storm. I didn't know how I'd feel when face-to-face with Sean's old flame, but for the moment I was at peace.

As it turned out, Sean and I spent an enjoyable few hours with his girl-friend. And with her mother and father and baby brother. His delightful "girlfriend" received my gift with all the appreciation, surprise, and gratitude a precocious eight-year-old could bring to bear in such circumstances! Before the night was done, Jenna and I were fast friends.

When we first arrived at the modern ranch-style home, Sean greeted everyone with obvious familiarity, plopping down on the sofa like a family member. I heard his friend Jay—Jenna's father—asking who I was, but I couldn't hear Sean's reply. Jenna approached Sean like a favorite uncle, immediately demanding his undivided attention with great affection and excitement until she was satisfied. I was intrigued to see him in such a different role. Then Jenna insisted I come see her room, where we proceeded to enjoy each other and the crystalline mysteries of the amethyst in feminine peace and harmony.

More than once that evening, I internally shook my head over the turmoil I'd gone through earlier over this situation and was able to laugh at myself. I was glad I'd opted for *will* and hoped I'd get stronger in the "three-is-one" approach. And such was my last thought before falling asleep later that night.

***

The next day was sunny and mild, as southern California can be in mid-winter.

We set out late morning for the San Gabriel Crest where, according to Sean, we had some kind of appointment with power. Evidently he had taken care of some of his "business" the night before. He didn't really elaborate on its nature, except to tell me he made it a point to periodically make contact with Jenna's father Jay, a quiet-spoken Asian-American man he'd known for years. As we drove down the freeway, Sean regaled me with riotous stories of some of their youthful and hair-raising capers in Mexico and Guatemala. Although Jay was now a respectable professional in the film industry, he was still quite comfortable with some of Sean's wilder nature, and they apparently had a deep spiritual bond.

"Jay always expected something spiritually unusual to happen when we were together," Sean said, "and he was rarely disappointed. We'd look for the power we knew would be there, and when we found it, we enjoyed it immensely."

As we wove our way out of the traffic and up into the mountains, the smog fell below us, hanging like a pale yellow-grey shroud over the city below. My eyes and lungs responded happily to the fresh air. Near the crest two red-tail hawks spiraled up on invisible air currents. I watched enchanted, ever envious of those creatures that had the power of flight.

We pulled onto a dirt parking area, locked the car, and began walking down a gravel road. Except for the crunching sound of our feet on the gravel, the surroundings were intensely quiet, as if something was waiting for us around the curve of the road. Even the air was eerily still, save for an occasional short breeze that would shake the small feathers in Sean's hatband.

On the ride up, Sean had spoken briefly, mysteriously intimating we wouldn't be exactly alone at this place. He added that Jay had first brought him here one winter many years ago and they'd christened the spot with a long, exuberant snowball fight. Since then Sean came here from time to time by himself, and in the relative tranquility of the mountains, he'd sent out strands of energy from his *will*.

I glanced at Sean curiously a few times as we continued. He was emanating a calm exuberance. His long stride was bouncier than usual, and his face was both serene and alive with hidden purpose. Even the evergreen trees on all sides of us seemed to catch his mood, urging us silently toward our destination with their graceful branches.

As we rounded the curve in the road, Sean slowed his pace and finally came to a stop. *This must be the place*, I thought to myself, though it didn't look all that different from the rest of the scenery. We were standing on the side of a gently sloping foothill, the gravel road having ended just a few paces earlier. Greater Los Angeles shimmered worlds away through a hazy brown veil.

I looked around the immediate area, but could discern no sign of the mysterious company Sean had promised earlier. Perhaps they'd be joining us later. Meanwhile, the air, if anything, had become even more still. Its compressed, concentrated quality of stillness was like a pressure. Once again, my mind suddenly clicked to the "off" position, but this time it didn't frighten me. It was starting to feel normal.

I followed Sean down the slope a short way, my feet moving easily through the soft, dry earth and occasional scrub. Then he stopped and gestured politely for me to sit down. He remained standing, and a chorus of birdsong momentarily erupted, stopping abruptly as he removed his hat. I knew without words that baring the top of his head was an invitation to the spirit and to the realm of dreamers. The wind came up and hissed around him, becoming still as he dropped his hat to the ground.

After a few moments, he shifted behind me and placed one hand over the crown of my head. Then he moved away, and I could hear him walking about. A sudden cracking sound jerked my head around in time to see him drop a small piece of a longer branch he still held. I watched him calmly as he continued to break pieces off and cast them here and there, much like a farmer sowing seeds. Still, I had no thoughts, no wondering about his actions. I was the silent witness.

Having made a large circle, Sean ended up at my right side and squatted down on the earth. He pulled a pocketknife out of my daypack and began to whittle the remaining bit of the stick. Finally, a piece about the size of my little finger with a blunt point at one end remained. Somewhere in the process Sean had cut his hand slightly. He touched the tip of the wood to the tiny drop of blood sitting like a dark ruby in his palm.

We sat side by side in dreamy silence for hours as the winds encircled us in a magical cocoon. It felt like we were patiently waiting for something or someone. After a while, I sensed something moving slightly below me and to my left. I turned my head slowly, and there on the ground was a small lizard. It moved closer until it was just in front of us, then stopped and began to do rhythmic push-ups. The lizard performed a series of them while staring at us out of one eye, paused for a bit, and then repeated its exercises. On the third series, suddenly there was a hissing sound behind and above us up the hill about twenty feet. Sean and I turned and saw a miniature rockslide trickle downhill. Not seeing what had set it off, I turned back around. The lizard was still there. As it continued its periodic calisthenics, the sliding, hissing sounds from behind us were repeated, and then repeated again at irregular intervals. Each time I glanced around, I'd see another mini-avalanche a few feet over from the last, as if something invisible was walking haltingly along the ridge.

I finally stopped looking around, but as the eerie cascades continued I became increasingly convinced there was a crowd behind us, a row of beings playing an invisible pebble game I could almost, but not quite, perceive. Along with this conviction, a tremendous pressure was building up behind me. It resembled feelings I'd had when being watched from behind, but multiplied several times over.

As the experience became increasingly unnerving, a small black and orange butterfly—that suddenly reminded me of Constanza's dreaming form—floated slowly in front of us, the lizard turned, dashed down the mountain and disappeared, and the pressure suddenly was gone. Immediately, as if my ears had been plugged and were now abruptly unplugged, myriad bird songs exploded into the mountain air. Once again I grew calm, and laid against the mountainside, relaxing my back into the soft, warm earth. I stayed there for some time gazing up into the cerulean heavens, my awareness floating like a hawk on a thermal ride.

I returned to my body as Sean abruptly stood and lifted his hat from the ground, brushed the dust off, and placed it on his head. He reached out his hand and helped me to my feet, placing the little stick in my palm. We climbed slowly back up the mountain to the gravel path. Then Sean stopped and drew me belly to belly with him. He put one hand over the top of my head and the other over the dreaming points of my back, holding me firmly in this manner for several minutes. My *will* fluttered lightly in my belly and then quieted again.

We continued walking back to the car and Sean repeated the same embrace once more before we got in. We hadn't spoken the entire time since we'd left the car, and my mind had also remained silent. I felt calm in a rather blank, detached way.

However, as we began driving down the mountain, that changed abruptly and quite rudely. Sean had some music tapes in the car, and he put on some raucous, grating rock and roll at full volume. I was so shocked I couldn't say anything at first. However, after several minutes, my nerves were completely on edge and I was starting to get angry.

"Would you please turn that down!" I yelled over the din. He complied by twisting the volume knob a fraction of a turn. After a few more minutes, I grabbed the knob myself, flipped it off, ejected the tape, and snarled at Sean that the music was unbearably irritating.

"That's the most awful music I've ever heard!" I exclaimed, still feeling aggravated and indignant. "And you were playing it so loud. What's the matter with you?"

Sean stared at me, nodding his head solemnly, and patted me on the back rather maternally a few times. Then, without saying a word, he put another music tape on. Fortunately this one was mellower, and I settled back in my seat with a resigned sigh. Why we had to have any music on at all right now I didn't know, but I could at least put up with this kind.

Months later when the memory of that afternoon had almost faded from my mind, Sean gave me his perspective on what had happened, including his strange choice of music.

That day we had truly had an appointment with power, power wrapped and held deep within a mode of silence. The cumulative effect of being together for weeks, my own spirit, the power of the place itself and other mysterious forces all had added up to a monumental shift in our *wills*.

"At first I felt exuberant," Sean smiled. "Your spirit, Josie, which had been shaped over the years by thousands of hours of silent meditation and solitary vision quests, matched up to the silent power of my earlier actions there, including some I'd done with my hat."

On that afternoon together, Sean again used his hat in a specific spiritual maneuver. He had placed the little stick with his blood on it under one side of the crown, which balanced the hat upright on the edge of its brim. Although the stick looked much to small and flimsy to hold the hat up against the winds that blew capriciously off and on, it did its job. Sean's hat was a power object, one he'd used repeatedly for a variety of spiritual purposes. That particular day, he'd set it up to act as a shield against the battering power of the many forces blowing around us.

He explained further. "Your presence there grounded me even more deeply to that power place, and as the hours passed, your spirit harmonized with some of the weirdest, most isolated parts of my own. This was deeply bonding," he admitted frankly, "and since that day I've never felt quite so alone again.

"But I also could *see* that you were so open that more than once, I had to place my hand over the top of your head to protect you from the intensity of multiple forces swirling about. And there was a *lot* going on there that day! Left on your own, you might have blithely absorbed everything and been completely carried away."

I had to acknowledge in retrospect that he'd acted prudently. It did not occur to me, except dimly when the rockslides mounted up, that I might be on the verge of being overwhelmed by forces I couldn't identify. It later took me some effort through the *art of dreaming* and certain kinds of recapitulation, to remember some of the things my mind wasn't registering at the time. The clearest image I retrieved from that unusual afternoon was from the period of those little rockslides. I finally *saw* a row of people, most of who appeared to be Mexican and slightly younger than myself. All of them, male and female, exuded a vibrancy, an intense vitality that seemed to make them glow as one by one they tossed a pebble down the hill in our direction.

Their presence and the other forces there enlivened my *will* to an extreme degree. As Sean and I finally prepared to leave the area, he had drawn me belly-to-belly with him several times, as I'd remembered. My own spirit and *will* had absorbed vast power that afternoon and were vibrating at high frequency. Over the prior few weeks, Sean had been inviting both into various activities, and was, in one sense, in control. He'd also been very actively engaged with the various energies swirling about the power place. Now, slightly fatigued from his efforts, he was confronted with the possibility that my *will* was suddenly capable of carrying us both off, and he was in a real struggle to ground us. Part of him was tempted to just go with it, but he knew we had to tie things off spiritually before leaving. It would have been folly to go floating down to Los Angeles in the open state we were in. And his assessment was that we'd both had enough—and maybe even too much—of other realities for the moment.

"Each time I held you belly-to-belly, I tried again to ground you. But as time went on, I became increasingly anxious about your condition," he said, shaking his head at the memory. "You were like a balloon about to float away on currents of eerie forces. And I couldn't express my concerns to you since your *will* was in a precarious balance, so I was on my own and taxed to the edge of my reserves.

"All the way back to the car, I bounced back and forth between feeling ecstatic about the impact of power on your *will*, and consumed with concern that I'd helped get you into a spiritual state I now couldn't help you out of. Meanwhile, you continued on oblivious to your spiritual state, having a lovely stroll at one of your good buddy Sean's power places."

I broke into laughter at this point in his narrative. I empathized with Sean's difficulties that day, and it was clear he'd felt things were quite serious. But I couldn't shake off the humorous image of Sean as an anxious mother hen nervously clucking over a wayward chick.

"Easy for you to laugh now," he said with a mock scowl. "Anyway, as we drove down the mountain I tried one final tactic in a last-ditch effort to ground you. I put on the loud and grating music in hope you would get angry enough to become solid once again."

I nodded. Since I have always been hypersensitive to music, this was probably one of the most effective tactics he could have employed. I became irritated, then angry, indignant, and finally verbal. All had a solidifying effect, and my frazzled friend could at last breathe a sigh of relief. Paradoxically, I'd thought I was doing just fine *until* then.

Sean concluded his review by saying that one result of that afternoon was his deeper commitment to—and healthier respect for—my *will* as well as his own. For me, the afternoon was a mystery I contemplated for many years.

Eleven

...An empty picture frame hangs from the stars,
Travelers come to gaze from near and far,
Strands of light pass through from east to west
And magic from the south holds up the rest...

from "Quatro Mas o Menos"

My life became an accelerating kaleidoscope of changes shifting from one color and pattern to the next with dazzling and meteoric velocity.

After that day at his power place, we departed for my home. When we finally arrived, even though everything was still in its proper place, my house felt empty, as if all the energy had been drained out of it. I'd noticed this feeling several times before in my life, inevitably prior to moving to a new environment. It was as if the *energy* that created the atmosphere of "home" moved to its next location before my belongings and I did.

When we first walked in, Sean looked around and commented, "Looks like we're back at Josie's curio shop."

I had to laugh. It suddenly *did* look rather like a curio shop to me, and I squirmed inside with slight embarrassment as I thought about the boxes and trunks of collected objects that weren't even out on display. I saw my home from a new perspective. These numerous objects placed in their niches held memories of decades of travel, experiences, hopes and fantasies. And yet they now all seemed almost unreal compared to what I'd recently lived through, as if my entire life's experiences up to a few weeks ago occupied a thimble, and the past few weeks an ocean.

Oddly enough, one of the first things Sean did after we arrived was to give me yet another object, one I treasured and whose energy subtly pulled on my attention for some weeks. The gift was a delicate ear of corn, Pueblo Indian corn that Sean said was sacred to their women. It was a color I'd never seen before in corn, a deep rose pink that made the kernels appear as rows of softly glowing pearls. I was so taken with this corn, I secretly plucked out one of the kernels and placed it under my tongue. Except for when I was eating, it remained in my mouth for weeks. Somehow I felt I could get it to sprout in my mouth. I could not explain to myself why this seemed so important, and therefore did not speak of my efforts to Sean or anyone else. I was content to simply hold this feminine power in my mouth, to give it my own body's moisture, and to wait like the earth to see what life would come forth.

Meanwhile, the emptied-of-energy phenomenon in my house created a strange tension in me, particularly as I was not yet reconciled about moving to Arizona. In a last-ditch effort to ground myself in what had been home for some years, I began to introduce Sean to friends I felt might be interested in meeting him. My friends themselves had provided a natural opening for this project. On arriving home, I'd found numerous messages left by them on my answering machine, with the dominant theme being "Where are you, what are you doing?" and "Are you ever coming back?" As I began to return calls, their curiosity often led me to invite them to get together with me and "a new acquaintance I'd recently spent some time with in Arizona."

Over the next few weeks, I watched my mystified friends meet Sean as if in some eerie reception line. I'd casually invite a friend over to my home, or take Sean to theirs. I tried to hold my power and be careful not to spill over with my experiences. I was slightly anxious that—as with my house—the energy of connectedness between my friends and I might also have disappeared, but I was soon relieved of this concern. In fact, each person was more intriguing than ever.

Sean' energy brought out the best in many of them, and highlighted the worst in a few. The majority became livelier, or wittier, and at some point, spiritually deep. Even friends I'd known for many years became both more mysterious and more interesting to me, and apparently to themselves as well. I was spared the necessity of relating the travel itinerary of my past few weeks because real power—power many of them had searched for high and low over the years—unfolded faster than any of us could keep track of.

I was thrilled to be both witness and part of this collective spiritual explosion. In my initial excitement I envisioned a future community of devoted practitioners of the mastery of awareness, all moving out to Arizona with me. I saw each of us urging one another to greater and greater manifestations of our spiritual potential until finally we would return to the larger human community bearing wonderful gifts of spirit. My vision of this ideal future lasted until the real struggles between spirit and the crushing inertia of habit became more obvious. Meanwhile I enjoyed myself.

Each interaction between Sean and my friends had its own unique tone and dynamic. One evening, he and I went to visit Tess, a generally quiet, introspective and self-effacing woman who—like many of us—frequently battled with a host of personal insecurities. Over a period of about four or five hours, this woman went through an amazing transformation.

Before going to meet Tess, Sean requested that I introduce him as my student partly as an exercise in *stalking*. Early on in the evening he regaled Tess with lavish praises of me and my spiritual activities of recent weeks. "I still can't believe my good fortune," he told Tess, "that someone of Josie's power would drag a worn-out tumbleweed like myself out of the desert and start training me in the mysteries of spirit! And her knowledge is so vast. She knows about energy and omens and power plants, and I'm sure there are a lot of things she's still hiding from me, until I'm worthy of learning." I gazed inscrutably at Sean, playing my part.

The whole situation was a real turn-around, one that surprised and greatly amused me. Sean's modus operandi was so different than anyone else I'd ever met. Many male—and some female—teachers I'd met would have expected me to put them up on a pedestal of some sort. And in some ways Sean *was* my teacher, although in truth it was Spirit teaching both of us. Sean's claim that I was *his* teacher was a unique way of treating me as well as himself, and was sincere in that he *was* learning from my spirit along with teaching me. Usually when strangers meet, they like to brag about themselves, either subtly or more overtly, pulling out their best stories to share. But Sean was bragging about what a great master *I* was.

One of the results of our evening was to allow me, then Tess, and finally even Sean to display new sides of ourselves. His tactic of shifting the initial focus onto me also helped Tess from being overwhelmed by his intensity and enabled him to remain cloaked in mystery.

As the hours passed, at a certain point he began to beg Tess if she too would accept him as a student. As with his earlier claims about me as his teacher, this request was not just joking around, for Sean was well aware that he had something to learn from every person's *will*. But his supplicant's attitude set off waves of riotous hilarity, with Tess suddenly becoming not only extremely funny, but very demanding and spiritually powerful as she entered into the role of being his teacher. I was flabbergasted by the transformation, and alternated between trying to keep my jaw from dropping and restraining myself from falling on the floor with laughter. The witticisms that began flying back and forth between Tess and Sean bounced from the intellectual to the mystical in short order, with me chiming in occasionally. Much of the time I don't think it was even what we were saying that carried the conversations. It was more like a force was blowing through us, transporting all of us to realms of delight in each others' spirits; a force that was merely using conversation to express that delight.

I talked to Sean for a while after our first meeting with Tess, partly to ground myself from the hours of spiritual intoxication.

"You know, in all the time I've known her, I never saw Tess the way I experienced her tonight. She amazed me, Sean."

"I'll let you in on a secret," he replied.

"Okay. What is it?"

"You think you're introducing me to friends of yours whom you know. But what's really happening is that I'm introducing you to your friends that you don't really know. And you're seeing that everyone's *will*—including Tess's—leaps at the chance to touch and interact with power, and enjoys the opportunity immensely."

Selena was another such friend, a spiritually confident woman with a predilection for dreaming. I had consulted her on occasion for suggestions on strengthening my nighttime dreaming, and the two of us had spent many enjoyable hours as mystic detectives tracking down various clues given to us in our dreams.

Selena almost always projected an aura of assurance about any manner of spiritual realms, with dreaming being her specialty. She'd bring up a dream, either her own or someone else's, and speak with emphatic certainty about its meaning, eyes flashing with the intensity of her conviction.

Our meeting with Selena took place in an immense public park. The three of us spoke a bit as we strolled through the grass. The subject meandered onto the topic of dreams and dreaming. Selena was accustomed to sharing the content of her dreams with any and everyone who displayed any interest. I sensed she felt this was a benevolent action on her part, like the distribution of valuable gifts. Sean came from a very different perspective, and began quietly but determinedly to caution her against this practice.

"Every time you think about revealing the content of your dreaming," he said, "you need to be more discerning about your potential audience."

"Why, what's the problem?" asked Selena, mildly miffed that anyone might challenge her in her personal area of expertise. I was immediately certain that this encounter was going to be very different than the one with Tess.

"Because," Sean said patiently, "it's like talking about any other deeply spiritual event. You can dissipate all the power of the dream in telling it too soon, particularly if your audience is not going to do anything more constructive than be impressed or tell your dream to yet another person as a form of spiritual gossip. That practice can actually weaken your spirit over time, even though it may not be apparent to you."

I could see Selena weighing the value of this new perspective. Finally she said she'd consider his suggestion but didn't look convinced. Why should she be, I thought. She had no basis at the time for giving more weight to the advice of a stranger than to her own past patterns.

We strolled further through the park, passing food vendors hawking international fare: hot dogs, tacos, pizza, and egg rolls. Sean pointed through the small crowds, and suggested we should head that way, to a nearby power spot. Its existence was a little hard to relate to in the moment, surrounded as we were with such mundane activities, but Selena and I followed him anyway. Sean then asked us both to be quiet, to get ready for the power in silence. I was by now quite used to this, but Selena began bristling again. I thought again how very different Selena and Tess were and how differently Sean behaved with each of them. He was definitely putting on a much more forceful face with Selena, and was encountering obvious resistance.

After traipsing through the clusters of people, we came to the edge of a modest-sized clearing, which I began to sense was the power spot. Sean strode ahead of us to the other side of it, then stopped and waited for us to join him. He placed himself between Selena and me, and gestured for us all to sit in a slight semi-circle facing the clearing.

Sean then began to display his *will* in a particular way for the benefit of my friend and me. He would touch my back or the top of my head, and my body and spirit would respond with the now-familiar surges of energy. Sometimes my belly would get hard or jerk, sometimes I would be drawn toward a dreaming state and I would drop over into a posture like Emily's "fire yoga." My body trusted Sean's *will*ful touch. I was quite happy to have him enlivening my own *will* in these ways, and not in the least bit self-conscious that Selena was a witness.

But Selena was understandably unnerved, for I must have appeared an eerie puppet, slumping over, then spine jerking up with energy as my eyes snapped with power. Actually, my *will* and spirit were contributing their own energy to the situation. But the deepest truth was that all three of us were puppets of Spirit.

Selena found herself in a steadily intensifying dilemma. I sensed that she could feel part of what was going on and was torn between wanting to experience what Sean's energetic touch might have to offer her and her own need to be in control. And Sean was enjoying amping up her conflict. He would touch me with one finger and I would respond. Then he would temptingly hold up a finger on his other hand and glance at Selena as if to say "are you ready yet?" He probably had driven his older sister crazy when he was a kid: the consummate mischievous little brother.

Finally, speaking for the first time since we'd entered the clearing, he said, "Josie, that tree across the clearing has some very unusual markings. I think you might enjoy looking at them." I got up and on slightly unsteady feet began wandering my way toward the tree he was pointing at. I felt light as a feather and in a deeply ecstatic mood.

Although Sean was behind me and I couldn't see him, he told me afterwards that he would periodically gesture toward me, sending some of his energy in my direction. My body continued in its *will*ful responses to his actions, making our spiritual connection obvious even without physical contact.

An unusually large yellow butterfly with black markings flitted at the edge of the clearing, and Sean began to unfold his *will* to cajole it further into the power spot. His body stiffened as he placed one hand over his navel and extended the other one in the creature's direction.

I saw the butterfly at about that time, and began to extend my *will* toward it as well while walking slowly in the direction where it lightly hovered. I stopped about twenty feet away, shifted my weight onto my left leg and raised my right till I was standing crane-style. Then I placed my left hand on the top of my head, covering that dreaming point, and extended the other toward the butterfly.

The butterfly began to circle and dive more energetically. Abruptly it dropped to the ground, and did several leapfrog maneuvers up and down along the grass before attaching itself to the side of a tree midway between Sean and myself. For several minutes we all remained motionless. Suddenly Sean lifted his head, I set my right foot down and spun once around, and the butterfly let go of its perch, circled the tree, and spiraled up until we could no longer see it.

After the butterfly disappeared, I turned around to look for Selena. She was standing on a low hill at the edge of the clearing, from where she'd apparently witnessed our dance. Her expression was difficult to read, but for the first time since I'd known her, she looked somewhat disconcerted, and something else a bit harder to identify.

Sean told me later that immediately after the first butterfly left, a second smaller one appeared, moving fast and in jagged patterns. It dived past Selena, coming in fast and low, and then turned and raced around Sean and Selena before disappearing into the trees. Sean collapsed onto the ground, pretending to have been overwhelmed by the butterfly's power. He remained there flat on his back, eyes closed, as if in a deep dreaming state. Selena, who minutes earlier had distanced herself, began to walk slowly toward him. Sean felt that she was quite drawn by the idea that he had entered into dreaming, which would have placed her on more familiar ground at last. Finally he sat up, acting dazed and looking vulnerable. He thought she was practically rubbing her hands as she observed his dreamy appearance.

At that point I returned from examining the tree with the unusual markings. Sean mumbled softly, "None of us should speak of what had happened here in the power spot for a good four days or more. We need to let what happened here settle for a while." Before Selena could become offended by another suggestion that ran contrary to her usual patterns,

Sean quickly drew her into conversations on her own spiritual turf—why and when she'd become so interested in dreams and dreaming. When we finally said good-bye, Selena was calm and seemed to be looking forward to further encounters with us in the future.

There were a variety of milder meetings between Sean and my friends. My male friends generally seemed more closed and competitive with him, while my women friends were more openly curious even when, like Selena, they might have been confronted with different points of view from their own.

One afternoon we were sitting in my living room listening to a sudden burst of calls from nearby crows outside the window. Sean reached over to a nearby table and picked up an object, cradling it gently in his hands for a few minutes before putting it back down. A few days earlier we'd taken a walk through an arboretum that featured trees from many parts of the world. Sean had picked up an unusual seedpod from beneath one of these foreign trees. It was dry and split open in such a way that its shape resembled a beautifully curved boat. Inside was a double row of golden seeds: the boat's passengers ready to sail to distant shores. He brought the little "boat" to my house and placed the small stick that he'd used for balancing his hat at the San Gabriel Crest in one end of it. It was a perfect mast, and day after day he would add or remove various other objects from the boat.

Sean had also begun making comments focused on the humble little boat, including one day's comment that "we're all in the same boat." Later he told me that for him, the rows of seeds partly represented both of us plus the people in my circle, and that we were being cast onto stormy seas by a mysterious force. He'd even placed a mini-roll of candy Lifesavers in the boat. "Some of the passengers might need these," he said gravely, "because sometimes the wind can come up strong." From my own years of past experiences, I already knew the spiritual journey could be challenging, and quickly said a silent prayer for all of us in the boat of life.

Over two weeks, I invited close to two dozen people to meet Sean and to share, without going into too many specifics, some of the excitement and power I'd felt in my recent spiritual interactions both in nature and in the newly expanding potentials of *will*. In time, I became baffled and sometimes frustrated with the variety of my friends' responses and seeming resistances. I expressed my confusion to Sean one evening, and he gave me his analysis of the situation. As I listened, I moved the little kernel of sacred corn from between my cheek and gum where I held it when I talked, back to its moist niche under my tongue.

"What you've been witnessing, both in your own life and those of your friends, is the motion of a powerful spiritual wind. A few times in the past I've experienced this same force blow through me and touch an entire group of people, just as it's doing now. It's always overwhelming. And it has the potential to free people from *all* the results of the social fixations of *all* their prior history. We could then redefine ourselves and actually *have* our *will*, consistently act with *will*, could be totally present with Spirit. But dealing with this force isn't easy. It's a massive pressure that puts intense strains on everyone encountering it. The power that's released needs great care. No one we've been dealing with has a *will* groomed enough to deal with the power very well. I'm a little more prepared, having gone through this before several times, but you've seen some of the repercussions already in yourself and your friends. The emotional explosions, anxieties, sometimes overwhelming fatigue and other somatic symptoms, all are fairly typical.

"But the spirit wind *is* capable of rearranging a person's spirit very deeply. Either one adjusts to this or one gets torn to pieces. And most people, if they can't adjust, turn tail and run early in the game before they feel its full benefits *or* get blown to pieces. The longer one stays with it, the greater the potential benefits and the greater the risks."

I shivered. *Well*, I thought to myself, *I guess I've been warned*, and rolled my little corn kernel nervously around my mouth. I wondered how far gone I was at this stage. Would my spiritual life be blown to smithereens if I tried to bow out now, or could I still escape relatively intact? This spirit wind or force was intriguing and exciting, but its potentials partly intimidated me. What stuck in my mind the most at the moment was the fact that, according to Sean, even years of strict training and commitment didn't begin to prepare one to take advantage of this force. If that was so, what was happening with me and my friends, including Rose who'd been the first to meet Sean? None of us were in that ideal state of readiness, and yet the spirit wind was now blowing through all our lives.

When I voiced this question to him, he said simply, "Power is giving all of us a chance to take Spirit up on its offer."

My expectations about how fast we could all embrace a life dedicated to the mastery of awareness slowly became more tempered with perspectives of timing and patience. And Spirit continued to reach out to us all, as it always has and always will.

Among the friends I saw during that time was Lisa, who'd visited us one afternoon.

"Lisa actually met me about a year ago," Sean said to my surprise.

"Really? How did that happen?"

"Colette introduced us. She told Lisa I was a shaman. Lisa's been trying to pump Colette for more information about me ever since, so she may try to grill you too. Be forewarned."

"Don't worry. Your secrets are safe with me," I joked.

When Lisa arrived, Sean assumed a very subdued, almost passive role as he lounged silently on the floor in one corner of the room. I tried to project a calm, quiet energy myself, partly to discourage a possible interrogation but also because I was concerned about Lisa, who seemed particularly anxious and tense that day. She soon began to talk about herself and some of the reasons became clear. She expressed various frustrations about her life, many of which had to do with her mounting disappointments with spiritual teachers she'd encountered. She complained to Sean and me that she was getting tired of too many wild claims and not enough coming through with the goods. "I don't know if I believe any of these teachers any more! I'm beginning to wonder if there are any real powerhouse spiritual teachers anywhere in the new age," she sighed wearily. "Or even any real power anywhere."

"Me too," Sean piped up from the shadows. "I've been looking all over for some myself."

I almost choked on my tea at that point. However, I regained my composure and nodded at Lisa in understanding. Because some of what she was going through was so familiar, not only was I truly empathetic, but in view of the last few startlingly different weeks, I wanted to offer her hope. I assured her that there were authentic teachers as well as other powerful forces in the world that weren't human, such as peyote and the wind.

The situation was somewhat ironic. The room was fairly dancing with power, some of which was emanating from Sean, and Lisa—for all her former curiosity about him and current desire for powerful teachers— seemed unaware.

Nevertheless, the power was affecting her, and she slowly began looking more hopeful about life's possibilities.

"Maybe I'll find a wise spiritual grandmother some day," she said, a bit of light sparkling in her eyes.

I thought of Emily and said, "I'll keep my eyes out for one. You just never know…"

Just then her boyfriend Jerry arrived, and he slowly began to dominate Lisa and the general tone of our gathering. Lisa, who had been opening like a flower just minutes earlier, could no longer speak her true heart in Jerry's presence.

Later that night, I was reflecting on couples' dynamics and telling Sean how, besides with Lisa and Jerry, it seemed like similar tensions existed in many of the couples I'd known over the years. It was very rare to find two people who truly supported each other in becoming as powerful, spiritually or otherwise, as they could be.

"It's part of that issue of change and the unknown you're seeing again," said Sean. "When one person starts to stretch his or her wings and fly, even if it's only to a short distance away, the balance of the relationship is temporarily upset and the other person rushes in to try to pull the partner back out of the air before he or she can go much further."

"We humans are pretty strange creatures," I mused.

Sean smiled and picked up the little seed-boat again, moving it gently from side to side. "No one wants the other person to rock the boat, Josie. It feels threatening, even when it might be the best thing for both of them. In a way, Jerry is Lisa's spiritual tyrant. Neither of them will ever see the situation in that way, but despite talking a good line, he doesn't really want her to become more spiritually powerful. What he really wants is to continue the status quo that, from what I've seen, won't leave much room for either of their spirits to grow. And that's part of a more general issue we're both witnessing at this time: who is going to make any room at all in their lives for the presence of Spirit."

Something very powerful was obviously taking place as one by one, each person from my circle—including myself—was being confronted with a new evaluation of our inner and outer worlds. The wind of change was cleaning the slate, stopping our worlds long enough for all of us to feel something fresh and new. After each encounter with my friends, Sean would caution me to be sober, to suspend judgment and to delay jumping to conclusions about the person's future.

"Power is pushing conflicts, weaknesses, and other enemies to the surface, and will challenge everyone," he said one day, "and the boat is still floating, but keep those lifesavers handy."

I tried to follow Sean's suggestions and be realistic about the near future. After several weeks, although my friends' lives were being deeply affected, they weren't ready for major life style changes at this time. I found myself becoming oddly detached from this group of people. During my travels, something irrevocable had happened to me, something I was barely able to assess at the time. Now that I was back on my familiar turf, not only could I see the "juice" had already left my house, but was apparently leaving other parts of my old life. I could no longer imagine going back to my job or maintaining the same kinds of social interactions that I had in the past.

Part of me knew it really was time for me to leave. I'd brought what love and power I could to my friends from my recent journeys, and it was looking as if this gesture might be—for now—my farewell gift to them. My anxieties over the dramatic change of moving to Arizona were still there, but Spirit power was inexorably shifting the balance.

***

I'd been asked to take a group of thousands of people through a sacred ceremony. Now I stood before them, praying to Creator to bless and guide everyone through the difficult times to come. The masses stretched their arms toward the heavens as I too raised my own. My hands began to tingle with power. Suddenly a long and graceful medicine pipe lay in them. A bald eagle feather fluttered from the stem and the soft red stone of the bowl glowed in the light of the setting sun. I offered the pipe to the sky, the earth, the four directions, to the mystery from which it had come, and the crowd sighed as a wind blew through it.

Dusk fell. I left the podium and slipped away into the shadows. I walked through the forest, hearing the muted footsteps of the few people who had chosen to follow me. When we arrived at a large clearing, we stopped and waited in silence.

Moments later, a large glowing craft descended from the sky until it rested in the clearing. I lingered as the others boarded the craft, disappearing from sight. Then I too began my ascent. But halfway up, I stopped as a force gripped my entire being with searing anguish. I turned, rushed back down and threw myself onto the waiting earth.

"Mother Earth, Mother Earth," I wept into the warm soil. "I love you so. I cannot bear to leave you." My heart felt like it would break with love and grief...

...and awoke from the dream still sobbing in gut-wrenching heaves, my pillow soaked with tears.

It was time to go. I'd done the "sacred ceremony" for my circle of friends, offering the best I had at the time—a new connection to Spirit. On the surface, a few friends seemed like they wanted to take the journey with me, but I'd slowly realized their idea of the journey was different than mine. They were more interested in travel to the "outer space" of spiritual concepts. But at this time of my life, I needed to be more spiritually active, to find more *will* and to explore the rich spiritual connections to nature, to Mother Earth. I needed to go to the desert where every expression of life stood out against the stark landscape, waiting to be valued, as precious as every drop of rain.

I began to pull up my roots and prepare to move to Arizona. Ironically, as soon as I came to that resolution, without even telling anyone of my decision, there was a sudden flurry of tempting offers enticing me to stay put. Someone I hadn't seen in five years called me to tell me about a great *ayahuasca* shaman from South America he was now working with, and that I really must meet this shaman and get involved in his special group. Someone else hinted strongly there was an opportunity for me to get involved in a documentary film on spiritual practices, and there were several other semi-tempting job offers. It felt like Spirit was testing my clarity so I could see the choices available and decide what I really wanted once I had the whole menu.

I carefully picked my way through this minefield of "golden opportunities," reaffirmed my decision, packed my bags, and Sean and I headed for Arizona, both our cars and a small trailer filled with my worldly possessions. But just before we left, I took out the as yet un-sprouted corn kernel and placed it in the earth outside my now former house. Perhaps some of its energy would grow here and continue to touch those I was leaving behind. I resolved this spring that I'd plant some of the other kernels at my new home.

We pulled into the ghost town several days later. The adobe "eagle's house" was glowing in the late afternoon sun, and as I drove up, I was filled with nervous anticipation and excitement. Here was a doorway to the unknown, a whole new chapter of my life.

I spent part of the first few days unpacking and trying to make the place begin to feel like home, while Sean contributed various spiritual focuses and experiences. As the house began to shape up, he and I spent more and more of that first week taking long walks in the desert and exploring the little ghost town. Sean was clearly delighted for me that I'd decided to live there, and we mapped out extensive plans for future spiritual activities.

Then one day, to my dismay, he announced he had some other pressing obligations to attend to, and the next day he was gone. Perhaps I shouldn't have been surprised, as I already knew Sean followed his own invisible drummer. But I'd begun to take his daily presence partly for granted and was having to face the inevitable reality of being left mostly on my own. I was glad that I had scheduled a number of seminars to teach over the year to break up what looked like was going to be a fairly hermit-like future.

Before leaving, Sean gave me a number of suggestions of things to do to stay occupied and balanced spiritually, mentally, physically and emotionally. This plan included devoting attention to nighttime and awake dreaming with Emily and her friend, continuing to work on new aspects of the *stalking* project he'd given me on the way to Joshua Tree, hunting for power and power places in the desert, paying attention to the wind, fasting occasionally for physical and spiritual purification, and recollecting everything I could of our spiritual actions since we'd met.

During the last hours before Sean left, I tried valiantly to combat my dismay at the thought of being alone in this remote place for some unknown period of time. I kept reciting a rather anxious mantra about what a wonderful opportunity this was going to be: I'd really been needing peace and quiet and time to sort out the recent weeks of my life, to get to know myself better, to work on some creative projects I'd been wanting to get to, to read, walk, dream. To connect with nature. I was going to become stronger, full of *will*, more tough and independent, a real desert woman. This was my lengthy but purposeful mantra.

Just before he walked out the door, Sean gripped my belly and back fiercely, then rubbed the top of my head, murmuring something in a language I didn't recognize but that seemed reminiscent of some ancient meso-american tongue. I felt a shiver ripple through me, and then heard peyote's faint rumble as Sean turned and walked away. Just before he started his car, power surged through me and I flung myself into a brief but wild dance there on my front porch. Sean smiled, drove down the long dirt driveway, glanced back once more and raised his left hand toward the heavens before he disappeared into the bright desert morning.

Twelve

...La soledad me sigue en los arroyos
Donde bailan las ombras con el viento.
Siguame, siguame, eres mi companera,
Siguame, siguame por la ilusion de muerte...

(...Solitude follows me through the arroyos
Where shadows dance with the wind.
Follow me, follow me, you are my companion,
Follow me, follow me through the illusion of death...)

from "Verses of Twilight Meditations"

After some momentary pangs resulting from Sean's sudden absence, I became filled with a sudden buoyant confidence that my time alone really was going to be a wonderful adventure.

The first week passed relatively smoothly. I began to develop a loosely structured routine, spending part of the day in domestic projects, and the rest divided into the tasks Sean had recommended as well as some of my own. I wrote some poetry and songs, did some dance and martial arts workouts, and spent time outside when the weather permitted.

Around noon, when the day was at its warmest, I often went out to the easternmost part of the grounds, to a spot Sean had touched with his power.

A few days before he left, he'd spent hours there while I was cooking a fancy meal. My curiosity eventually overwhelmed me, and I moved stealthily to a window at the back of the house and peered between the curtains to try to spy on him. Much to my disappointment, he was behind some trees so I couldn't see his acts of power, but when he finally came back to the house, he'd led me outdoors to this particular place. He said it would be a good place for me to ground myself and gather energy. Then he moved behind me, held my belly with one hand and pressed my back with the other, and once again turned me slowly to face each of the four directions. Although the air was completely still at the time, he told me later that he felt this would also be an excellent place to come and pay attention to the wind.

When I asked if there was anything else about the spot that I should know, he replied briefly, "I've made you a nest in the earth where new aspects of your own power can hatch."

I was intrigued and went to that power place fairly regularly. The first few times were undramatic. I would tromp out through the forest of high dried grasses and weeds carrying a large thick quilt for padding and warmth. When I got to the round, slightly indented area in the earth, I'd place my quilt on the increasingly flattened grasses, lay down on my side, and roll myself in the remainder of the quilt. Indeed it felt like a nest in the earth, cozy and protected. Following Sean's suggestion, one day I would lay on my right side, the next on my left and would pay attention to any differences in my state of awareness or energy that were consistent with which side I was on.

Mostly, those first days, I'd become warm and slightly drowsy from the mid-day sun, and then slide in and out of half-sleep states for the duration. Eventually the firmness of the ground would rouse me, but despite being slightly stiff, I'd have a strong sense of wellbeing and comfort. I'd go indoors energized and ready for whatever was next on my agenda, but wondering vaguely if I was missing the point of my nest experiences.

The fourth time began as before. But as I started to drift into my typical dreamy state, Sean's image appeared before me. Next to him was a woman whose features I couldn't identify. She began to blow her breath toward me, and it wrapped around my body like a silvery mist. The mist turned me a quarter turn so I could no longer see them. Then Sean appeared again, this time with a different unknown woman, who also breathed a visible silver mist that encircled me. I could feel its soft motion on my skin. This repeated two more times, always with a different woman. Finally, I'd been turned to all four directions and was completely wrapped in this misty cocoon, suspended without weight in the air. Although I could not see through the mist, I began to hear something, faintly at first and then a bit louder. The sounds were pure, pristine harmonies ringing out from an invisible, celestial chorus. I felt the harmonies fill my entire being, vibrating through skin and bones and spirit. They faded so slowly and subtly I couldn't say when they stopped, because the feeling of them in my body continued and became a part of me forever.

I awoke gradually and lay there a long time on my back, gazing into the endless blue heavens as the winds danced softly around me. Sean had woven strands of power from all four directions around my home, and here at the center of the "god's-eye," he'd heated up this nest with some of his own energy before he left. My spirit was being enlivened and hatched out of the mysterious cocoon that still surrounded me, and today it had met and been blessed by the spirits of the four winds.

***

The days rolled along toward early spring, the high desert air warming steadily while the nights still held the frosty tail of winter in their crystalline grasp. Sometimes I ventured out for a few minutes late at night to take in the dazzling brilliance of those amazing starry skies. I was falling in love with my new world. Its very strangeness was alluring to my spirit.

One warm day I felt in the mood for a modest hike. I filled my daypack with water bottle and snacks, donned denim jacket, jeans, and my favorite walking shoes, and headed out into the desert. I let my feet and *will* guide me down a wide and dry riverbed, turning off into a shallow arroyo which became deeper as I strode along.

There was just a hint of green beginning to show in the winter-grayed grasses, sagebrush and ephedra shrubs, life singing its subterranean melodies into the dormant desert flora. Far in the distance, a raven called out to even more distant comrades, and I sang my own songs in rhythm to my sandy footsteps.

Something glittered ahead at the next curve of the arroyo, and as I reached it I bent over to gaze at my first desert crystal. Geologists must have given them a name, but in all my rock-collecting days, I had never heard it. The crystal was flat and shaped like a spearhead, colored a silvery gray and layered a bit like mica, but with much more uneven edges. I picked it up gently, brushing the sandy soil off its underside with great care. As it turned out, it was not that fragile, although it wasn't anywhere near as strong as the more common quartz crystal.

The strange mineral content that had created it was evident all around me. The sides of the arroyo and the distant rounded hills had a wide spectrum of colors in their make-up, ranging from pale gray and yellow to brighter reds, slatey blues, subtle mauve and deeper purples. I recognized them as the color themes used in many of the lovely Dineh weavings so abundant here in the Southwest. I wrapped the crystal carefully in some tissue paper and set it gently in one of the side pockets of my daypack.

A little while later, I enjoyed a second rocky discovery. As I climbed out of the arroyo to seek the wide panorama of higher ground, a hilltop strewn with thousands of what first appeared to be red pebbles pulled on me. Arriving at the site, to my delight I discovered them to be various size chunks of petrified wood. Many of them were solid rusty-red in color, but some had shades of yellow and purple and black painted through them. A few rare ones had, at their center, tiny crystals sparkling like diamonds in the desert sun. I was in rock-hound heaven!

The hill where they lay reminded me of some animal burial ground, like the places elephants went to die. Some of the petrified wood was still in huge, log-size pieces, and I could see where the ancient trees had fallen, eventually breaking into these large pieces, still in lines suggestive of the original whole. Most were smaller, but from a slight distance they looked like a mound of skeletal remains of some lost specie of prehistoric animals.

After exploring the site to my satisfaction and choosing several small stones to add to my new collection, I wandered further up into the painted hills. The eerie landscape I traversed lay utterly silent save for the occasional raven in the distance or rustling of wind through the dry grass and scrub. I'd been given my own vast and enchanting playground and turned loose in this land that called to my spirit like no other.

After several hours, I was tired and hungry enough to need a break. I found a flat, sunny and secluded area between some of the large hills, drank my chilled water, and ate a simple lunch of apple, raisins and almonds. Pleasantly filled and quite warm, I lay down on my back. It was still too early in the year for insects, and no humans were remotely near, so I relaxed undisturbed in the sandy soil's embrace.

As my muscles started to melt under the sun's warmth, my mind began to wander through the many experiences and discussions I'd had with Sean. I'd been making some daily effort at recollection as he'd suggested before leaving, but not in a normally organized fashion. Rather, I would relax, holding an intention to recollect something, and then I'd let my memory push to the surface whatever most demanded my attention.

This time, what floated up was a talk during which Sean looked into my soul and reflected me back to myself.

"I've mentioned before that I've *seen* you have four faces," he began as we sat on the porch watching a spectacular sunset. Sean often was inspired to speak of spirit at this time of day and entered what I thought of as his mystical shaman mode. "These faces reflect each of the four directions, or four winds. They *can* give you a certain unusual fluidity, allowing you the ability to quickly change spiritual and even emotional temperament from one moment to the next. Other people can see this and think you mercurial as you shift from one stance to another. As a result of your make-up, both you and others may wonder at times if you have a mind of your own, since you see any situation or person from a variety of perspectives.

"From birth, part of your spirit has remained free, unfettered by social conditioning and pressures. The intensity of your early childhood visions accounts for some of your spirit's strength, and has given you a sense there is something in you more powerful than many people, or than what normal social interactions define you to be. The part of you that senses this waited, always hoping some day someone would recognize your spiritual qualities and help you find a place for them.

"Until now, you've had certain identity problems as a result of your spiritual make-up. Most people, upon looking to define their identity, will focus on their social self, their mental-emotional body, and can say 'I'm like this and that and so forth' to themselves. But when you've looked deep into your being, you've found something that feels like emptiness, or a lack of core identity. That is because your core identity is your spirit, which defies thinking and has no personality. When you confront that core and its accompanying sense of emptiness, you can become intensely angry about this seeming lack of self-definition."

By this point in his talk, I was already reeling from the accuracy of these descriptions of my life and was filled with a combination of excitement, self-recognition, and something undefinable.

"Strangely enough," Sean continued, "this lack of core personality has certain odd advantages. Your fluid nature can be a powerful quality that allows you to merge with and become harmonic with others; to be supportive of their growth in a very empathetic way. Depending on the situation and how much positive feedback you get from others for your support, this chameleon-like, merging quality *can* be a source of joy for you. On the other hand, it can potentially make you angry once again, feeling that you have no identity of your own.

"Normal interaction aside, in a spiritually oriented group of people, this ability of yours to become harmonic with anyone can be invaluable. In a certain way, I perceive your essence to be like a subtle, inaudible hum or harmonic. This harmonic can resonate through such a group and help integrate them into a left-sided whole. You can help them become more open, cradling their awareness as your spiritual harmonic sings through their *wills.*"

By the end of Sean's talk, I was suffused with a sense of being more complete than I had ever felt and was filled with appreciation for his gift of reflection. Even if, after later consideration I began to wonder if the essence of what he'd said about me wasn't actually true of everyone, it had still felt very personal at the time. As I now lay absorbing the desert colors around me and recalling that conversation as best I could, I wondered if there would ever be an opportunity to serve a group in the manner Sean had described. I was so far away from all the people I'd once known.

When I'd finally decided to move to Arizona, I was packed and on my way within a few days. Just as Sean had foreseen, the place where I now belonged had been pointed out clearly by *intent.* No one knew I was leaving. I wanted this to be a unique act of power in my life, to completely sidestep typical good-byes or advice from friends, and to set out into the unknown leaving mystery in my wake.

Once I'd settled into my new home, I wrote a few notes and made some calls about my change of locale. My friends were slightly baffled by the suddenness of my actions. I didn't really want to tell them their possible reactions might have delayed or drained me of resolve, so I just said the Spirit moved me and I had to follow, which was the truth. I sensed a blend of curiosity, envy and admiration, and warmly invited them to visit if they wished. To my delight, this was met with interest and enthusiasm by most. I even joked with some, telling them there was still most of a ghost town to choose from for habitation, if they ever felt the urge to move.

Nonetheless, I was surprised when one of these possible future guests called me later the afternoon of my desert hike, saying she was in a nearby town and en route to my doorstep!

"What on earth is going on, Rose?" I exclaimed. "What are you doing out here?"

"I really need to see you, Josie. Can I just come by and explain things when I get there?" she replied. "I know I didn't give y'all much notice or anything, but it was kind of spur of the moment for me."

"Well sure, Rose, come on by. After all, Sean and I didn't give you much notice last time we dropped in on you." I gave her directions to the house and put on a pot of mint and chamomile tea, an herbal combination she had often found soothing.

Rose was the first of my friends to be brushed by the spirit wind that had swept through all the others, but the Rose that arrived on my doorstep was not the same Rose we'd left. She collapsed into my arms briefly like some disheveled war refugee, and I led her into the house. Rather than start questioning her right away as to how she'd gotten herself into this fragile state after having been so full of confidence just weeks earlier, I sat her down and served her some tea in relative silence. I quietly suggested she relax for a while before we started talking.

We sat in the twilight without turning on the house lights. The last shades of pale gold and tourmaline pink faded into the vibrant evening blue that always both stirred and soothed my spirit. The shadows outdoors lengthened and merged like smoky moths into the gathering darkness, and the world became still, hovering at the edge of night.

I thought of the beautiful Spanish term for twilight—*entre dos luces*— between two lights.

Sean once described twilight as a unique energetic transition. "From dawn to dusk, the sun's energy dominates the Earth's, making her energy more difficult to discern. But as the sun sets, there is a distinct shift, as if the Earth's spirit suddenly rises out of the soil and begins to take over. The night belongs to Mother Earth. She embraces us most strongly just as we begin to slow down from our day's activities and move steadily toward sleep and dreaming. As the surface of her body cools from the sun's lingering touch, her own emanations can be felt more clearly—deep, primordial, and mysterious as the night itself."

Sean's comments had given me a new perspective on the spiritual qualities of day and night, and I felt drawn to explore the night's energies with
this in mind. I began to take some of my walks at twilight, and occasionally
had ventured out for short walks alone even later. The nights were still quite
cold, and I was looking forward to extending these starlight journeys when
summer arrived. Nevertheless, I already was quite enjoying my nighttime
explorations at the edge of the desert. They were just spooky enough to keep
me alert and on my toes, and I'd begun to see strange shimmering forms and
glowing energies rising from the earth as my spiritual awareness and perceptions became sensitized to this new landscape I was calling home.

I came back from my reflections as I heard Rose begin to shift about on
the couch and immediately got up and turned on a few lights.

"Well, Rose, what brings you to the desert?" I asked with concern.

She wrapped her arms around herself, sighed tragically, and said, "I
think I made a really big mistake."

"I hope it wasn't fatal," I commented wryly, trying to ease her out of
this melodramatic mood.

"Sean is going to kill me," she said. "I did everything all wrong, despite
his advice."

"Come on, Rose. Whatever happened, I'm sure you've learned something, and I seriously doubt that your actions, whatever they were, will
even cause Sean any anger."

"You're probably right. But I feel terrible, because I could have so easily avoided this whole mess."

"Why don't you just start from the beginning and tell me what this is
all about."

Rose took another deep breath, and then launched into her story. And
as I listened, I realized how accurate Sean's interpretations of the Texas ice
storm omen had been.

***

I was up with Rose almost till dawn. We slept in until noon and spent the afternoon walking as I tried to help her get more grounded in her body. I took her behind the house and into an arroyo Sean and I had explored. The arroyo was almost hidden with the overgrowth of river willow and salt cedar on its banks, and it meandered its secret way like a snake until eventually running into the Little Colorado River. Sean had told me it was the Little Colorado that separated the Dineh from the Dineh as it flowed west toward the larger Colorado. North of it were the Navajo/Dineh, and south, as the land rose to the pine forest mountains, were several tribes of Apache/Dineh. I told Rose about this as we walked. She had some Indian ancestry herself, and had been developing a growing interest in Native American history and spirituality for some time.

At one point during our walk, I saw a hawk floating off to the south. I immediately pointed it out to Rose, and then placed one hand over my belly and extended the other in the direction of the hawk. I quickly gathered my power together and started unfolding my *will* out through my extended arm toward the hawk. Then I began to move my arm in large circles, trying to make a lariat out of my *will* to encircle the bird with my energy. Once I felt I'd accomplished this, I began slowly shifting the angle of my arm, drawing the circles closer and closer and pulling with my *will*. The hawk moved with me, bringing its spiraling flight nearer until finally it was right over our heads. There it stayed for a good five minutes. Finally I dropped my arm and attention, and the red-tail broke out of its circling and flew directly west. Rose looked at me wide-eyed, but we continued on our walk in silence.

The kind of *will*ful act I'd done with the hawk was both new and yet familiar to me. I'd done a great deal of energy-based, hands-on healing work in the past, and had become accustomed to sending energy through my body and intending it to flow through my hands into my "patients'" energy fields and bodies. Now I was getting a chance to explore sending out energy for a different purpose which Sean had introduced me to: *dancing* with nature.

Rose and I spent a tranquil evening and were asleep by midnight.

The next day to my delight, with impeccable timing Sean dropped in out of the blue, and that evening he asked Rose to tell her story to him.

As she'd already told me, Rose now explained to him how, after we'd left her in Texas, she'd spent several days by herself in a rare mood of emotional equanimity and deep contemplation, allowing the reverberations of her experiences to continue rippling through her, writing her thoughts in her journal, and being quite content to be alone.

"Finally," she said, "I was so excited about my spiritual rebirth I just couldn't contain myself. I started calling a few close friends and Robert, my sort-of 'ex'. And that's when I blew it even worse, y'all. I couldn't just shut my mouth after telling everyone about my week alone. Nope. I had to go and blab about your visit and Sean's hawk dance. And the feather gift he left me."

I glanced at Sean. *You were right*, I acknowledged silently.

Rose's actions had catalyzed a personal disaster. Although at first her "friends" had listened to her with apparent openness, she described how their spiritual jealousy and self-importance came together in a deadly combination. Slowly and insidiously they began creating doubts in Rose's mind about what she'd really experienced and about Sean. Robert, her separated husband, had contributed to her turmoil.

The cumulative result of the interactions threw Rose into an intense state of anxiety. "I didn't know whether to trust my guts, which believed in my experiences that week, or my mind, which was trying to deny them. Finally, I hopped on the next plane out and headed for Arizona. Even though my friends were trying to shake me up, some part of me still trusted you and Sean enough that I felt seeing y'all again would help return me to sanity, and maybe to my own spirit. I guess Lady Luck was with me, since both of you are here and I'm already feeling better.

"Rose, do you remember what I suggested at the end of the time we spent together last month?" Sean asked after listening to her emotional tale of woe. His manner was mild, but his eyes glittered with intensity.

She considered his question for a few minutes, her brow slightly furrowed. Then she nodded, her forehead clearing, and said, "Oh. I know what you're talking about. You said it was important how we dealt with power, and particularly how we spoke about it and to whom. And even how we organized powerful events in the privacy of our own thoughts."

"That's right," said Sean. "Most people aren't trained to contain power for very long, should they experience it awake or in dreams, without immediately retelling their experiences in any receptive ears. The events most people share with each other—the details of their daily lives—hold minimal power so it's not quite so critical. Talking is mainly a habit, and if that habit carries over into making one's spiritual experiences fodder for the gossip mill, the result can be wasteful and even dangerous. What does this mean to you at this point?"

"I'm sure you already know," she said wryly, shaking her head. "You told me, you warned me, I understood, I even made notes to myself about it, and I still screwed up."

"Don't beat yourself to a pulp or there won't be anything left of you," laughed Sean, lightening the mood somewhat. "Let's try to move forward in a practical manner. We all make mistakes, and sometimes that's where we get some of our deepest learning.

"One of the things I described during our visit was the kind of control people try to exert over each other. Most people are more concerned with controlling others in a variety of ways than they are about gaining control of themselves. I tried to give you a way to exert positive control over the bad habits of yourself and others when I suggested you keep the details of our visit to yourself, especially those of my 'dance.' A great deal of mysterious power was left in that feather I gave you, and I knew that power would have explosive results if you didn't take care of it. During our Dallas visit, didn't you feel that Spirit touched you deeply?"

"Yes, Sean," answered Rose in a slightly irritated tone, "I was quite aware of that at the time, as you well know."

"Just checking," he smiled, delighted to see a spark of feistiness surfacing in her. "It's just that memory can be elusive and subject to a variety of forces. Well, your intensified spiritual power was then felt by your husband and friends. Since it was a new element of unknown origins, they immediately felt a need to try and control it, and by association, you. This took the form, according to your account, of a rather thorough grilling on your recent activities. But this was after you'd already chosen to open the conversation up yourself."

Rose nodded, now more curious than apologetic.

"Sadly, their goal in questioning you was not very constructive," Sean continued. "There was too much ego floating around masked as concern for your welfare. Those people exerted pressure to get you to reveal even more about our interactions with the hope that the information could then be manipulated. The goal was to shake you up enough to get you to begin to doubt your own experiences. Does that sound like an accurate enough description of what occurred?"

"Yes again. And I capitulated to the pressure and did exactly what you said I didn't have to do. You told me I didn't owe anyone the details of my personal life. But this was all so new to me that I fell right back into those old patterns just days after you left. Not only did that cause me problems, the worst being losing sight of my experiences with you, but now I may have caused problems for you and Josie as well.

"What do you mean?" I asked with some alarm.

"This was probably a mistake, but I told Robert where I was going, and now it looks like he's on his way out here too," Rose said with an anxious look.

"He's not on his way with some lynch mob, is he?" Sean joked.

"No, of course not. He's just a little overprotective. Or something," said Rose.

"I'm sure we can all enjoy each other," I said. "You can stop beating yourself now."

"Okay," she sighed. "But you know, what really bothers me now is that, even though I see and understand all this, if I were put under pressure again in similar circumstances tomorrow, I don't know if I'd do any better. It just seems like those social patterns are so ingrained, I don't know how I'll overcome them."

"It takes time, understanding, and clear goals and intentions. And most of us have to keep re-clarifying our goals over and over so that our actions will be in harmony with them," said Sean, his eyes softening in empathy.

By the time Robert arrived a few days later, Rose was back on an even keel again, and was once more filling up with power and increasingly delighted to be with us and with her own spirit.

Robert was a gregarious and congenial man, with a good sense of humor and a slight spiritual openness. However, at this time in his life he was not very interested in letting go of his social habits to step into a non-mental realm of direct spiritual experience. At first he seemed to have come partly out of concern for Rose and partly out of spiritual curiosity, but most of Sean's efforts to help him open his own spirit were met with stiff resistance. Eventually it became apparent, as with Lisa and Jerry, that in both subtle and more overt ways, Robert was in fact trying to sabotage Rose's spiritual life. He wasn't outwardly hostile. Rather, he would downplay or try to distract her from any spiritual action, event, or discussion going on. And he had big problems with being silent for any length of time, repeatedly trying to draw Rose, Sean and myself into constant conversation. Since Rose had her own struggles with almost compulsive talking, Robert's influence in this area was particularly undermining her efforts.

One afternoon, the four of us went walking in the desert. Before Robert arrived, Rose had been on several desert walks with me, and then with Sean and I. We'd almost always walked in silence, trying to encourage her to pay attention to the wind or birds or whatever was there to experience. Rose had controlled her usual tendency to chatter, and was beginning to enjoy the benefits of silence. However, her husband's presence threw her back into her old patterns. Even though we'd invited

Robert to join us in a silent walk, he was not able to do so and repeatedly drew Rose into conversation until finally Sean and I dropped back a ways in order to have some peace and quiet.

Just before we were about to turn around and head back to the house, Sean and I saw an unusual sight in the sky. We raced to catch up with Robert and Rose so we could bring their attention to it. For a few moments we all stood and stared.

The late afternoon sun was surrounded by a glowing halo that had a piece missing from the bottom of it. Off to its left was a brilliant white sun dog. Just below and over to one side of where the halo's circle was broken was a long, slender white cloud. It looked like a finger pointing toward the empty space. If the cloud would just move to the left a bit it could patch up the broken circle, but it never did.

Rose was quite focused on the phenomenon until Robert broke the brief silence by saying, "Oh, yeah, we get those sun dogs all the time out in Texas, don't we, honey?"

With that casual comment, he dragged Rose right out of the power of the moment. Sean told me afterwards he felt they'd both missed seeing the message in the sky which was for them: an omen of their future. Their own circle was broken—the circle of their relationship. Within a few months Rose had begun divorce proceedings and was involved with another man. And finally, the sky had painted a picture of power off to the left, spirit power that Rose was struggling to find a place for in her life.

Shortly after Rose and Robert left, I asked Sean if he had any new predictions about Rose keeping herself together now.

"I'm not sure," he replied. "As you told me yourself, when she was alone with you and 'Mother'—Mother Nature—she had a much freer space and started pulling her power tighter. But as soon as Robert arrived, she quickly started slipping backward again. My guess—not a prediction—is that as soon as she's back in the clutches of her 'friends', she's going to revert back to her old patterns again and give away her power. She'll probably need all the support you can give her."

Seeing Rose and Robert together, and thinking back on Lisa and Jerry's interactions and those of other couples I knew, I considered how rarely men throughout history had encouraged women to become spiritually powerful.

Sean was a unique exception in my own experience, and in that of the other women I knew, some of whom he had now met: Lisa, Rose, Tess and Selena. There were also some women I'd known whose lives he'd already touched in the past without my being aware of it earlier. Colette was one. Then there was Brooke Medicine Eagle, who'd been a student of his for some time, and Joan, an anthropologist who I'd had contact with off and on since the mid-seventies. And there was a part-Cherokee woman who I'd not yet met, but Sean referred to her as a powerful woman with a strong dreaming predilection who he'd influenced considerably. He had made connections to all their *wills*, some deeper than others. Each of these women were in the so-called New Age seeking spiritual knowledge, and all had been dissatisfied to varying degrees with many of the teachers—especially the male teachers—they'd encountered. Sean told me a little about Colette, Brooke, Joan, and the Cherokee woman, and it was clear that he supported and took each of their spirits seriously, as he did mine.

These mysterious women varied in age, temperament and profession, but all were interested in their own spiritual growth. I was strangely comforted and delighted to have this etherically connected group of women accompanying my own spirit's journey.

Many of the spiritually adventurous women I knew had encountered their share of male teachers. And all too often their male teachers were more interested in sex than anything else. Brooke, part Nez Perce and Sioux, had been unable to get one single male Indian teacher to get serious about teaching her anything. They had routinely put off teaching her sweat lodge songs, pipe ritual, or anything else. And yet they had tried persistently to have sex with her, sometimes even chasing her around sweat lodges or luring her into sacred tipis with lies as a part of their sexual "hunting" tactics. She had complained bitterly and sometimes humorously to Sean about this situation. Unfortunately, this was nowhere near an isolated example.

Between all my women friends and I, we knew most of the male spiritual teachers on the New Age circuit. All of us had read many books on shamanism and spiritual development, all of us had high expectations, and all of us had been frequently disappointed in the behavior of many of these male teachers.

Oddly enough, the situation was debilitating for the male teachers as well. Men who had started out their teaching "careers" with some personal power, visions and inspiration had often expended much of their power into seeking sex. The situation wasn't only limited to new-age figureheads, but spanned many paths and included some Eastern gurus, Western preachers, and shamans from many cultures. Many women I knew had either given up on spirituality teachers or had decided to seek out only women teachers in order to avoid some of the sexual games.

I was trying to learn as much about the human spirit, both for my own growth and in the hopes that I would have increasingly more to offer to others who were on the spiritual journey. People, including Sean, could teach me some things. Nature was fast becoming my most consistent mentor. And death was my advisor in this venture. It waited somewhere in the shadows of the future and whispered that time was trickling through my fingers like the desert sand. I listened and unfurled my *will* into the wind.

Thirteen

... Women of darkness and women of light,
Women of daytime and women of night,
I reach out to you with my spirit and song
Will our dance be short now or will it be long...

from "Pool of Reflections"

Sean stayed for about a week after Rose and Robert left. During that time, we discussed my process of recollection, dreaming and power-gathering. One evening, he asked me to lay down on my side, and from behind me he placed his hands on my back and the top of my head.

"I want you to practice some awake dreaming with me," he said softly. "I'll help you find Emily. When you do, ask her if she would show you Colette's spirit and how to help heal her. Colette's got some serious problems, and long ago I took on a role in her spiritual life that hasn't ended even though we rarely even speak any more. Maybe the three of us working as a team will be helpful to her."

I nodded and began to prepare myself. I was happy to support my friend and intrigued about the possibilities of doing so through awake dreaming. After a brief meditation to silence the internal chatter and free my energy for absolute concentration, I focused my *will* toward Emily, and unfolded my *dreamer* out toward hers. We made contact more quickly and easily than the times I'd tried while Sean was away. As always, a wave of deep pleasure and a slight tremor of nervousness swept over me as soon as I saw Emily. Though frail in outward appearance, her spirit and *will* made her the most powerful and formidable woman I knew.

I'd always believed in the potentials of women's spirit and power. I was also aware of the difficulty in finding strong and balanced female role models for women. When I was a young girl, the only powerful spiritual female figure ever taught about in school was Joan of Arc. I became utterly obsessed with finding out more about her, reading every book available in our little library. Intense drives that I didn't fully understand as a ten-year-old compelled me to know this woman who actually heard voices, talked to God, received divine guidance, and was a powerful warrior. The circumstances of her death appalled me, but she was all I had at the time, so I clung to St. Joan's burning skirts for years. By my late teens a few *living* women had been added to the list including my shamanistic dance teacher, a creative writing teacher and a gifted painter.

However, I knew that there were many other women still looking for a new and improved vision of our potential. In the mid-seventies I started one of the first women's groups in my city for the purpose of exploring the barriers and solutions to our spiritual and social development. Over the course of the group's evolution, I became increasingly clear that we *ourselves* would need to be the new role models. Since we had few historic spiritual figures we could read about as examples, we were going to have to be creative. The images of the ancient goddesses were coming into a popular renaissance at the time, but again, they weren't alive, nor were they even human. I felt what many of us needed to see was flesh and blood women who'd struggled for spiritual authority and originality and been victorious. Since there weren't many in the history books, it was up to those of us living now to plumb the depths of our souls and pull out some new material, some fresh images. Not only did we need to do this for ourselves, but my feeling was that it was our duty to do so for the future generations of women. I was on fire myself!

The women's group itself was a modest success. One of its best features was that it provided the first all-female spiritual environment I'd ever experienced. Away from male pressures, we were quite supportive of one another. The competition and jealousies so often present in other circumstances had been magically banished by our intention to bring out the best in ourselves and in each other. I was so delighted with this result, and so inspired to try to take the goals farther, I went on to develop seminars for women that I'd been teaching on request ever since. Over the years I continued to synthesize everything I could learn on women's spiritual health and growth into these rewarding trainings.

Now the issue of women and spiritual power was alive in my life in a new and deeper manner than ever before. I was living out the unfolding of my own spirit and watching my women friends as their *wills* faced the winds of spirit in a variety of ways. And finally, after years of hearing rumors of wise spiritual grandmothers, Sean had helped connect me with a new and real female power: the presence of Emily and her friend Constanza, with possible others still hidden in the shadows, waiting for timing.

"Emily," I began when I saw her now, social niceties never necessary in dreaming, "Sean and I would like you to help me *see* Colette and then try to heal whatever needs attention. Will you help me?"

Her form shimmered slightly, and then coalesced again as she apparently came to a decision. she nodded and without speaking, pointed off into the distance where a delicate strand of energy led to a dimly glowing form. We began to fly through the nighttime dreamscape, following the strand until we were almost upon the form. Then Emily signaled me to stop and observe, as we hovered over the strange glowing blob.

I knew we'd found Colette's dreaming body even though there were no identifiable human features. I was aware that Emily was fulfilling her commitment to help me *"see,"* to perceive in a non-ordinary state of awareness. I scanned the form before me, and was drawn to several areas that appeared to have brownish stains on them, areas where there was no glow at all. I looked over at Emily, who nodded and made little clicking sounds of disapproval. "She looks like a leaky sieve," she commented to me as she observed. "She's obviously been squandering her sexual energy like a spiritual lunatic, so it's to be expected. Not only that, but she's torn up different spiritual connections with Sean. That's a shame, since he'd been helping hold her energy in some kind of balance. Well, we'd better get to work, even though I must warn you not to expect the results to last very long. Unless this woman changes her life style and some of her attitudes, she'll probably be in the same shape the next time you pay her a visit. However, this will be good practice for you, both in healing and in detachment," and she laughed her unearthly laugh.

"Can she hear us?" I asked curiously.

"Her dreaming body is quite aware of us," answered Emily, "and is in total accord both with what I've said and with our intention to heal. However, I doubt if very much of this will filter from her *will* to her conscious thinking mind, if that's what you're wondering."

Emily then began to "breathe" intensely, her dreaming body expanding and contracting noticeably. As she did, the space behind her slowly thickened and coalesced into a mist. I watched the image of a large, silvery spider superimpose itself over Emily's "human" form, the spider's round belly aligned right over Emily's. Her powerful breathing then pulled some of the mist through her back and out her belly as a dense, luminous thread.

The spidery Emily drew more and more of this thready stuff through her, gently shaping it with her hands into a fine layer of glowing fabric. She then took this material and placed it over one of the stains that I could now see were holes in Colette's luminosity. Emily was literally patching her up! She then repeated the process a number of times, applying layer after layer of this etheric fabric over Colette's "holes."

Emily had me help her with the patchwork so I could practice handling the fabric and look for places to apply it. Finally the overall luminosity of Colette's form appeared to become a consistent whole. As we observed the results of our work, I was reminded of a musical instrument from Africa I'd once scrutinized in great detail. It was a type of marimba, and had a row of hollow resonating tubes along the back. And in the back of each tube, a silver dollar-sized hole had been carved and then covered by some kind of lightweight, semi-opaque material. As I ran my fingers over it, the marimba's owner told me the material was in fact hundreds of layers of spider web, glued together to form those translucent patches. They provided the instrument and its amplifying tubes with just the appropriate vibrational quality desired. So it was with Colette's dreaming body!

Our work completed for now, Emily and I parted and followed our own *will* strands back to our individual physical bodies. I stretched, sat up, and after walking around the house for a while to ground myself, I described my experience to Sean. He was not at all surprised by Colette's condition, nor by Emily's blunt comments.

I was somewhat surprised. Over the past month, I'd slowly gained a more solid picture of Sean's prior relationship to Colette. He had invested considerable time and energy on behalf of her *will* for several years, and recounted a number of powerful stories about her spiritual talents and how he'd tried to support them. It was difficult for me to grasp how she could be such a mess now.

"There are some things I haven't told you yet about Colette that will help answer the questions in your eyes," said Sean. "When I first met her years ago, I could see she had a powerful and unusual spirit, and we began working on ways to develop it further. But over time, it turned out she was a very complex woman with a lot of complex problems. She'd been around a physically and spiritually rough crowd for a long time, and finally became a cocaine addict on the verge of suicide. She'd periodically made money as a prostitute. And if all that wasn't enough, her back was so knotted up around her dreaming point that she was on tranquilizers and muscle relaxants half the time to try to get rid of the painful spasm. That's the shape she was in when I met her. But she had a ferocious *will* which, combined with her critical condition was a peculiar and invigorating challenge for me.

"Her *will* was more than ready for a change of venue, and as I worked with her she quickly began to get strong in certain ways. She finally got off cocaine, and I fixed a lot of what was causing the problem in her back. Then I guided her to other teachers and gatherings and supported her in learning to sort out the bullshit from real power, just like you'd been trying to do before you met me and more intensely after my first touch to your back. And as part of Colette's 'hunting,' I steered her toward meeting you."

"What do you mean?" I asked in astonishment.

"Colette was with me the first time I laid eyes on you and recognized you from my vision at Joshua Tree Park. I pointed you out to her. Since she already knew a lot of people at that gathering, it wasn't that hard for her to track you down and eventually meet you. I was hoping the two of you would bond and begin forming a nucleus of real female power.

"Anyway, for a while it looked like you women were going to be able to work together. While I stayed behind the scenes, I managed to introduce both of you to Brooke Medicine Eagle and some other women with unusual strengths. But over time, Colette became increasingly jealous of my spiritual attention to this growing circle of women and began to try to sabotage my efforts. That's why that first time she brought me to your home, I had to wait until she was out of the room before I could touch your back. She was getting dangerous! She had a fair amount of power by then and I didn't want her turning her energies against you out of jealousy.

"You first met Colette when she was at her strongest and most filled with light. But by the time you two took that trip to the Olympic rainforest, she was already starting to lose it. As Emily so bluntly pointed out, Colette's issues of her own value are still bound up with sex. The more jealous she became of my spiritual attention to others, the more she reverted to feeding her ego through her old sexual patterns with a variety of men. Her spirit began to collapse. For a while I kept pouring vast quantities of energy through that woman, but it became increasingly difficult to see so much of it being squandered through her lousy self-esteem. I've had to shift to a more sober detachment as I've watched her partly abandoning her spiritual life.

"I'm willing to continue trying to serve people's spirit up to the point where they withdraw their interest in my doing so. That's been true with Colette. You and some of your friends have already experienced my commitment, and I'm happy to serve you all as best I can. But I think Colette may be close to the point of finally shutting the door."

"I hope you're wrong," I said quietly. "I had some wonderful times with her in the past, and really looked forward to years of spiritual adventures together. But whatever the case, I still want to be there for her as a friend should she ever need me."

"The whole situation could break my heart if I let it," said Sean, "but then what good would I be to you, myself or anyone else? So I have to protect myself and pull back. Nevertheless, that dreaming was excellent practice for you," he commented, "and Emily is such a skillful a dreaming teacher. Perhaps some day you'll be able to turn around and teach the *art of dreaming* to someone else. Meanwhile, I'm going to bed to do some of my own style of dreaming. I'll leave you something to read before you go to sleep tonight, something I wrote on dreaming a few years ago. It's part of a letter to an anthropologist who had an interest in the role of dreams and dreaming."

After he went to bed, I thought about the dreaming I'd done with Emily. Her answer to my question about how aware Colette had been of our presence only addressed part of a larger body of questions. Sean felt that what I'd seen of Colette's condition was quite accurate, but I was still wondering if this dreaming business was really "real." Would anyone I touched in dreaming ever remember in his or her waking mind? And if not, how could I judge if I was in fact dreaming with them or only addressing phantoms of my own imagination?

No answers were forthcoming in the moment, so for now I let the issue rest. I turned to the letter Sean had left for me to read. It was somewhat complicated, but a few bits especially caught my interest.

...Dreaming is done with the "second attention will form" and the remembrance of the characters of second attention—dreaming—forms a praxis in every human being.

...(some dreamers) have modulated that special praxis of dream-memory in order to control time, to be able to pre-cognize and even pre-experience chosen portions of future reality. This is a selected fore-seeing of events, rather than the

somewhat common "accidental" effects of a deja vu—living through a dream
already dreamed by the second attention.

And some dreamers have even taken up their dreaming will like a lariat
and lassoed or captured segments of future reality like they were rounding up
young calves.

There is a definite end to things, but from the common viewpoint of
humanity the feats of these talented few dreamers are virtually past the infi-
nite realm of imagination. Vocabulary shreds and analogies fail their mark...

The next day I found myself alone once again. Sean had helped me
support Rose in her efforts toward recovery, bolstered my dreaming and
had loaded me up with new information and ideas for spiritual projects.
Then he'd once again taken his leave for parts unknown.

As I went about my domestic tasks that morning, I thought back on
Sean's descriptions of Colette. Although I'd known her for several years,
she'd apparently chosen to keep big chunks of her past to herself and had
seemed relatively carefree around me. Learning about the gravity of her
prior condition, what Sean had done for her and what was now taking
place in her life was very sobering. I wished I'd been more perceptive or
Colette more frank. Perhaps I could have been a better friend and support to this woman who'd been in a severe life and death struggle with
many destructive forces. But she hadn't allowed me to see through her
tough facade.

I then found myself reminiscing about the good experiences we'd shared,
particularly our journey to the Olympic rainforest of the Pacific Northwest.

I'd gone to the rainforest once many years earlier when I was living in
Seattle, and its lush, surreal energy had left a deep impression on my spirit.
For about half a year before Colette and I traveled there, the desire to
return had been tugging at me with a growing frequency and intensity. I
mentioned this in a phone call to Colette one day. We were immediately
swept up into a whirlwind of energy and arranged to meet two weeks later
in Seattle. Colette and I each had friends in Seattle, so our adventure

would include some socializing and a trek to the rainforest. Our friends informed us that the Pacific Northwest was being blessed with a glorious Indian summer.

The weeks sped me toward the green forests of my memories, and at last Colette and I were in a little rental car, cruising west along the northern coast of Washington State. We'd taken a ferry across Puget Sound, and then, passing from Port Townsend and on through Port Angeles, cities were finally behind us. I didn't know exactly where we were going, but a vague memory of a small Indian village somewhere near the rainforest pulled me further and further west.

The morning had been overcast and misty, washed in a watercolor palette of grays, but the mid-afternoon sun broke through and my hope for pleasant camping increased. During the drive Colette and I shared the comfortable silences and conversations of friendship, occasionally exclaiming over the glimpse of snow-capped mountains, the majestic evergreens, the Victorian quaintness of some of the houses in the port towns.

Late that afternoon we drove onto the Quillayute Reservation, finally veering off the main highway and arriving at the Pacific coast and the town of La Push.

"This is it, Colette! This is the place I visited fifteen years ago!"

"Great," she said. "Let's explore."

I gazed in curiosity at this vaguely recalled village: now older, more stores shut down, but calling to me with a wealth of mysteries despite its weatherworn appearance. Hoping there was a restaurant where we'd be able to have dinner, we began wandering through the town, breathing in the wonderful, tangy ocean air.

Some faded signs along the main road advertised a shop selling local Indian baskets. Colette and I looked at each other as we clicked into "hunting mode," grinned, and followed the signs. They led to what looked like a small combination gas station and general store.

"Do you think this is the place?" Colette asked dubiously.

"I don't know, but since we're here, we may as well check it out."

At first, all we could see in the somewhat dimly lit interior were half a dozen aisles of canned foods and basic household necessities. We turned to the white-bearded man behind the cash register and asked if he sold Indian baskets. He smiled, pointed toward the left, and there we found a small area of the L-shaped store we'd somehow missed before.

It was empty except for half a dozen unvarnished wooden shelves lining the walls. On the shelves, practically glowing with energy, was a breathtaking array of woven baskets. Colette and I approached them and began to pick up one after another, admiring the intricate handwork. There were several kinds of baskets. Some were made of broad strips of cedar bark, square and flat with an opening on one side. Others were round with woven lids, ranging from the size of a small plum to larger ones about eight inches in height and diameter. The latter were woven mostly from sturdy grasses, although some of the larger ones also had a few strips of cedar bark around the top and edge of the lid. All of the round baskets were colored with woven designs of black, green, red and purple-dyed grasses set off against the natural tan background. Whales, boats and eagles or thunderbirds were the dominant motifs.

The shopkeeper came over to see if we had any questions. He was soft-spoken, short and slender, with long and wiry graying hair held back with a rubber band, his skin slightly tan. He didn't look Indian, but I couldn't quite place his ethnicity. "Who made these wonderful baskets?" I asked curiously.

With quiet pride, he replied, "My wife did. Would you like to meet her?"

"Yes, we would," I responded with interest as Colette nodded in agreement.

He disappeared into the back of the store, and returned with his wife. In contrast to his diminutive stature, the woman beside him had the massive quality of a bear. She loomed several inches over him, moving slowly and deliberately, her dark eyes taking us in with a steady glance.

I introduced myself and Colette. "Your baskets are beautiful." I pointed at one and said, "I'm thinking of buying this one. Could you tell me anything about the meaning of its designs?"

The woman smiled, and the instant warmth this brought to her face offset the slightly overwhelming force of her size and presence. She gestured for me to bring the basket over to the counter, behind which she then settled into a nearby chair.

Colette and I ended up standing there for hours listening to her stories. From the theme of the specific basket that focused primarily on the power of the thunderbird, the woman proceeded to talk to us at length about her people and their spirituality. Alsinor herself was Quillayute, and her husband Joe was a native Hawaiian who she'd met years ago when she was living on the islands. I was entranced with her stories, but over time I noticed that Colette was becoming increasingly restless. I finally and reluctantly told the couple we were going to have to start looking for a place to eat and sleep for the night. Before we left, I not only bought the basket, but I pulled out a little cluster of crystals from my pocket as a gesture of appreciation for her generosity with her time.

"Well you must be psychic or something!" she exclaimed as I gave it to her. "About a month ago there were some Greenpeace people who came to do a ceremony on behalf of our situation here. As they finished, they offered a crystal into the fire. A few days later I went out on my porch, and there was that same crystal sitting there! I figured it must be tired from travelling around however it did, so I wrapped it in some cloth so it could rest for a while, and took it inside my house to place in a basket.

"Later in the week a friend of mine came over to visit, and I told her about that crystal. I went and pulled the bundle out of my basket, but when I unwrapped it, the crystal was gone. This one here that you've given me looks just like the other one. So thank you very much."

"Well thank you, Alsinor and Joe, for the wonderful afternoon. Maybe we'll stop by again tomorrow or the next day, after we go camping out in the Hoh River Valley area."

"Yes, do that," she said. "In fact, if you find a place to eat and stay tonight in La Push, come back after dinner and we can visit some more."

Colette and I did find a restaurant and motel in town. As we ate, I was bubbling with excitement over our new friends. Colette was more subdued. After dinner she said, "I'm kind of tired, Josie. I guess I don't really feel like going our again tonight. If you want to visit some more with Joe and Alsinor, you go ahead without me."

By now I was wondering if the mounting pull from the rainforest had been partly related to meeting Alsinor and Joe. "Okay," I said to Colette. "Have a good rest and I'll see you later."

I walked back through town, intrigued with the mysterious unfolding of this journey. When I arrived at the store, Joe was there alone.

"Hi, Joe," I said. "Colette was worn out, so I came by myself."

"Alsinor was tired too. She has heart trouble and went home early to rest. But she said to tell you she 'dreamed' with you after you left because she felt some kind of strong connection to you. She also wanted me to give you this little basket."

"Oh, it's lovely, Joe. Please thank her for me." I too felt an inexplicable bond to Alsinor, and was more than curious about the nature of her dreaming

Alsinor wanted Joe to tell us if we hadn't found a motel we were welcome to stay the night at their home. I told him we'd already found accommodations, though now part of me wished we hadn't, and thanked him for the offer. We began chatting about Hawaii.

"I wrote a short paper in high school on Pele, the Hawaiian fire/volcano goddess. I don't know why, but I've always been fascinated with her."

Joe smiled and said, "She's real powerful. A lot of times before a volcano erupts over there, people see Pele walking around as an old woman with a white dog. And over here, right after Mt. St. Helens went off, my wife heard of a lot of people from Washington all the way down to California seeing giant turtles swimming south in the ocean with a shadow of a serpent on their backs. She says its part of her people's prophecies, and that it fits with a lot of other prophecies about this time. That volcano power is something else!

"You know, unusual things have happened around me and Alsinor," he continued, a mischievous smile creeping across his face. "Once when we were over in Hawaii, the son of this Kahuna [Hawaiian sorcerer or shaman] told my daughter he was in love with her; but she wasn't in love with him. This guy went back to his Kahuna dad and asked him for some help. Well, a few days later Alsinor and I were at home relaxing, and somehow we made the mistake of leaving both doors open, which they say is bad luck. It sure almost was for us! All of a sudden, this great big ball of fire shot in through the front door, just missed Alsinor and me, and hit the wall behind us. Alsinor was really pissed off, and was pretty sure the energy had been sent by the boy's Kahuna father. She went and grabbed that fire ball, told it to go back to whoever sent it, and then threw it back in the direction it had come from. We didn't have any more trouble after that, and then I guess that boy kind of lost interest in my daughter."

It was becoming obvious to me that Joe and Alsinor were far from being an average couple! Joe was clearly delighted with his wife's unusual spiritual qualities and proud of her artistic abilities. Alsinor had briefly alluded to Joe's talent as a dreamer earlier, and the glances they'd exchanged periodically were deep and full of mutual respect. I couldn't remember ever having met a couple who demonstrated this kind of spiritual support of one another, and I *knew* I'd never met one with such an exotic spiritual history.

"I'll tell you one more story about something that happened to my wife in Hawaii," Joe continued, brown eyes glittering with enjoyment. "One day she got the urge to island hop, and took a plane to one of the smaller islands. When she got off the plane, this guy who was a total stranger came up to her in the airport. He told her he'd known she was going to be there, and asked if she'd come with him. So she did.

"First he took her to his house and fed her dinner, and when they were done, he said he had something unusual he wanted to show her. Right around dusk, he took her wandering for some way through the forest, until they got to this little cabin. They went inside, and there was a woman lying on the couch. They talked for a while, I don't know about what, but as night fell, something strange started happening to that woman. Alsinor told me later that at first the woman started looking more and more pale. Then, as the woman continued talking, she began to look kind of cat-like, and her words started sounding more like mewing sounds. This went on for a while, until finally the woman turned completely into a large yellowish-color wildcat, stretched, got up, and wandered off into the night."

He looked at me and shook his head slowly. "Yeah," he said, "me and Alsinor have seen a lot of strange things."

I felt that was quite an understatement, and told him so. He laughed and told me I'd just barely seen the tip of the iceberg. Joe was an excellent raconteur, and his stories saturated my mind like the Northwest rain. He seemed capable of going on all night, but finally the hour and the long day's drive caught up with me. I returned to the motel after thanking him again and telling him we'd stop back in a few days.

The next day Colette and I went camping in the rainforest, and had a wonderful time getting rained on. The forest was an enchanted place, soft and lush, with long moss hanging from the trees, ferns and fungi growing out of the ground and on rotting logs, layer after layer of life upon life. We saw deer and smaller creatures, and the mystic, hushed quality that delighted me long ago was pervasive. After several days of saturating ourselves in the energy, we returned to La Push and drove straight to the little store where we were greeted like old friends by Joe and Alsinor .

They immediately invited us to their home for lunch, and there we spent a thoroughly enjoyable afternoon. I sang and drummed for them, using Alsinor's large ceremonial drum that she graciously offered for me to play. Then she told us some of her people's creation myths, several of which were highly amusing and, as she called them, "X-rated." The latter included the efforts of a character—called "the Maker"—to sexually seduce young women. Eventually, despite my great reluctance, we finally had to leave, as Colette had promised to meet a friend the next morning back in Seattle. Joe and Alsinor warmly invited us to come back after we visited with our friends.

Colette had planned to return home after a few days in Seattle, and despite what I felt was an incredible opportunity being offered to us by Alsinor and Joe, she was unwilling to alter her itinerary. Rather than try to change her mind, I accepted her decision—figuring maybe the force that had originally pulled me to the rainforest was no longer pulling so hard on Colette—and worked out my own travel plans. Timing, or perhaps some turn of fate was on my side, and I had no difficulty changing my airline reservations. Soon I was making the long drive back to La Push, pondering the mystery of this journey and looking forward to the next phase of my rainforest adventure.

As I drove into the little coastal town, I almost felt like I was coming home. Crows and ravens greeted me as I pulled up the driveway of Joe and Alsinor's house, and I was filled with a pleasant sense of anticipation. Alsinor welcomed me with a strong bearhug, and immediately insisted that this time I stay at their home in the guest bedroom, so I accepted with heart-felt thanks. The next few days were full and rich on many levels.

One night she took me to a big Makah Indian ceremony being held for a couple who'd recently married. The hours reverberated with the coastal dances of her people, and with their haunting songs and drumming. I was completely absorbed, transported by the fierce masks of ravens and eagles, surrounded by a sea of glowing, copper-brown faces of all ages. While we were there, she introduced me to Laura and Tansy, two older relatives of Alsinor. We hit it off, joking and teasing long into the night. I was delighted to be embraced by this cocoon of older women, having never experienced anything like it. My own grandmother had lived a mostly difficult and dismal life, and never displayed the exuberant vitality of these coastal women. After the ceremony, Alsinor said she was amazed at Laura's behavior.

"Laura usually takes forever to warm up to strangers," she exclaimed, "and here she was treating you like a long-lost relative!"

I felt like one. I had a strange sense of family with these unusual older women who were bringing out my past ties to the Pacific Northwest and weaving them into a new basket of intriguing possibilities. They were also fulfilling something I'd sought high and low for years: female spiritual role models, each with a lifetime rich in experience.

On the day after the Makah wedding ceremony, Alsinor once again surprised me with her openness and confided in me how, long ago, she'd gotten her healing powers.

She had gone to a Shaker meeting with her grandfather. Shaker meetings were one of several nativistic Christian revivals that had sprung up some time after the Ghost Dance movement. A healer himself, her grandfather had been called to go to the meeting to doctor a man who'd just been badly injured and who was hemorrhaging. They sat in the room praying for a while, and then Alsinor saw a stranger appear in the front of the room with a large, glowing sphere that looked like the moon. He asked three times if anyone there wanted healing power. No one responded, and on the third time he said it was the last time he was going to ask.

"At that point," Alsinor told me, "I leaped up and went running to the front of the room. I made a grab for the globe, but the man lifted it just out of reach. After several attempts, I finally caught one edge of it and pulled it off. The piece became a little ball of light that filled my hands and arms with energy. Then the mysterious man led me over to the injured one and began to pass his hands over the patient's body, indicating that I should do likewise. After a while, the bleeding stopped, and the patient was healed.

"The man who'd held the globe of light then disappeared, and I wondered if anyone had even seen him besides me. But you know, since that day I've had the power to heal. Every time someone calls on me for healing, the power flows into my arms like I'm wearing a long, glowing pair of gloves."

"That's an amazing story. But I bet it's only one of many more, right?" The big woman laughed and agreed.

After that initial contact, I returned to visit Joe and Alsinor several times over the next two years. Each time was rich and varied, and I came to care immensely about both of them. Alsinor would regale me with exotic tales of her people's legends, her own encounters with *tziatko*—little people—and with a Sasquatch who she swore once touched her arm. On one visit she took me to another ceremony, a potlatch put on by a Hoh River man which lasted an entire day and was filled with even more wonderful dancing and singing than the Makah wedding ceremony. Alsinor was greatly respected not only as a healer but as a powerful singer by the coastal Indian people. She was asked to sing several times during the potlatch and her deep voice filled me with delight.

After one round of songs, she shocked me by waving me up to stand with her. She introduced me to the large crowd of hundreds, and then handed me her sacred drum and asked me to sing a song for them. I was so nervous my first few notes came out like croaks, but eventually I relaxed enough to execute a passable rendition of a Pueblo song I knew. Alsinor's gesture was a great honor and made me feel even more included among her people.

As we got to know one another better, she began telling me I should come and move out to La Push, that she loved me like her own daughter and had things to teach me. At the time of her first such offer, I was very entrenched in work and friends, and had trouble thinking about living in such a remote place, much as I was drawn to this older woman. But around the time Sean arrived at my mountain retreat, I'd been considering the possibility more frequently as the frustration with my circumstances intensified. Then Alsinor died suddenly of a heart attack, and I never got that chance. I grieved intensely. I missed her a great deal, and deeply regretted never taking her up on her offer.

Looking back now, I saw a rare spiritual opportunity had been presented to me and had passed by, pulled forever out of reach by the hands of the final reaper. Alsinor had leaped for the globe of power when the spirit-man said it was his last offer. But Alsinor had not been able to tell me when her offer to me would run out. And I had not leaped. She died shortly before I left on my first trip out to Arizona to meet Sean. Within two months I had taken up a different offer from power, leaping myself into the unknown, and was now living in a place even more remote than La Push.

***

For several days after Sean left for the week, I strengthened myself by returning to some of the areas that he'd taken me to. His confidence in driving me to unusual and out-of-the-way parts of the desert had originally mystified me. At first I thought he was simply following various whims that led us to these locations. After experiencing them, I revised my opinion and sensed he was being drawn to various power spots. I was partly right and partly wrong. As it turned out, Sean had criss-crossed the Southwest numerous times throughout his life, going in all directions as he followed power to these very places years ago. His present confidence was well grounded in familiarity, and he resembled a spider retracing strands woven long ago to see how they had weathered over time.

One day he'd driven me to the edge of a mesa overlooking the little Painted Desert—a relatively unknown place compared to the more popular Painted Desert National Park. As we stood looking down on the multi-colored dunes, we heard some scuffing, muted steps behind us, and turned in curiosity. To my surprise, I saw a small herd of very rough-looking, slightly gaunt and dusty cattle heading our way. The leader was a stately white hump-backed Brahma bull. The rest were a line of scruffy mixed-breeds. Astounded by this unlikely apparition, I momentarily felt I'd been transported to India. Sean later told me the Brahma cattle had originally been brought from India to Mexico long ago, and that it was a half-breed man from Sonora who'd first brought them up to the Southwest.

As the cattle plodded toward us, I briefly wondered if we were in any danger; but Sean seemed calm, so I relaxed a bit. The creatures proceeded at a leisurely but purposeful pace along the edge of the mesa, temporarily obstructing our view of the painted hills. Once they were lined up, they stopped and turned so they were all facing us, back-lit against the blue horizon, and utterly still. They looked like they were waiting to be photographed. Suddenly, dozens of large brown unblinking eyes fixed their gaze upon us: calm, undemanding, but wholly attentive. We all remained motionless for about fifteen minutes until, once again in unison, they bowed slightly, turned around, and left in the direction they had come from. This was most mystifying behavior!

Once they were gone, I looked west across the desert to the San Francisco peaks near Flagstaff, some sixty miles away, and then back to the ground beneath out feet. The mesa we were standing on dropped straight down about 300 meters, colored with layers of mineral deposits. As the mesa wound its way north, rising slowly like a painted serpent, it eventually encircled the many small villages of Hopi land, holding them up like an offering to the elements.

The total effect of the landscape and the cattle had been utterly surrealistic, and I had no desire to talk for some time afterwards. Later, Sean commented on the event.

"Once again, Josie, what took place was an exact replica of what happened to me in the same place fifteen years earlier. This time, the event made me feel strangely at home. The main difference is that in the earlier version, I was slightly nervous around the cattle. I had had a fair share of prior experiences with aggressive bulls charging at me and chasing me in my rural childhood, and had to save my skin more than once by throwing rocks at them, using a slingshot or running away," he laughed. "But this time there was clearly no threat, so I was pretty relaxed."

He went on to remark that the Brahmas had come to pay their respect to both my years of East Indian meditations and my connection to Mexican dreamers and sorcerers. I thought this a hilarious interpretation, but sobered up when Sean remarked dryly, "You could at least accord the Brahmas the same respect they gave you. They were beautiful and utterly focused, and I seriously doubt if you'll ever experience anything like it again. Not only that," he said in a lighter tone, "but, just like you, they made a bid for power fifteen years ago, and they were there to defend it. You might have thought that parking area made the mesa a human domain, but I think the real situation is that those cattle have made it their own personal power spot."

I considered this novel perspective. Being with Sean was like living in an ancient myth in which animals paid their respects to spiritual power and the wind could be one's dance partner.

A few days after first moving to Arizona, we'd driven to a different area of the Painted Desert. Although I prided myself on regular exercise and being in good physical condition, Sean exhausted me that day. Not for him the flat, winding dry riverbeds. No, this wild character was drawn to the roller coaster mode of running up and down the painted hills. Not wanting to get lost or be left behind, I tried my best to follow in his foot-steps. But due to old knee injuries, racing downhill on slippery and unsta-ble surfaces such as these made me quite anxious, and I had to proceed much more cautiously than Sean. More than once I would watch in amazement as he ran in a state of exuberant abandon along the sides of these hills. At times I would gasp to see him racing at almost a ninety-degree angle, practically parallel to the flat ground below. I dared not keep the same breakneck pace, and struggled along more slowly, fearful of aggravating my old injuries.

Despite being almost in tears more than once from the stressful hours of trying to keep up with Sean, for reasons of pride or stubbornness I could not bring myself to ask him to slow down. Finally, panting and ragged, I caught up to the place where he stood waiting for me. He placed one finger over his lips to indicate silence, and then pointed ahead of us, indicating our destination.

There in the distance, in the middle of a wide valley flanked by high red canyon walls, was a solitary tree, the only one in miles and miles of visible terrain. We set off toward it across the level ground at a slower, more deliberate pace. When we were within about thirty feet of the tree, Sean gestured for me to follow him, and we walked four times in a large circle around the solitary sentinel before approaching it directly from the south side.

The tree was a magnificent, ancient juniper, one of the largest I'd ever seen. Gnarled and twisted from age and the driving desert winds that often raced through these valleys, the juniper was a tribute to strength and resourcefulness. Nearly half the branches on one side were naked and dead. The rough bark had fallen to the ground in ragged peels here and there. The earth beneath the tree was also littered with an amazing abundance and variety of animal droppings from creatures who had been drawn to the shade and nourishment of this ancient, generous matriarch. A few dry purplish juniper berries from the previous year still lay on the ground, hard and wrinkled, no longer tempting food for the desert creatures.

A large, long-dead branch rested on the earth some yards away from the tree's furthest-reaching limbs. As I wandered over to it, I saw its bark was gone, and I touched the exposed wood that was bleached silver-gray from years under the desert sun. Lying there on the sandy soil, it looked like a smooth piece of driftwood on a beach, but it had been polished by blowing winds and sand rather than by the salt and pounding waves of the sea. I looked at the tree again, and went over to stroke the place where the branch had broken off. The break must have happened at least a hundred years earlier, judging from the way the wound was covered in barky scar tissue. I wondered briefly how the heavy branch could have arrived at its place away from the tree, and then forgot the issue as Sean gestured for me to sit near him on the earth.

He gathered up a large clump of dried juniper needles from the ground and touched a match to them. Popping and snapping into flames, the juniper burnt bright until Sean blew the little fire out. Then smoke burst forth. The intoxicating fragrance of juniper incense enveloped us in its sweet embrace. I sighed contentedly, pulling more smoke toward myself with cupped hands, happy with everything: the scenery, the company, my life.

After a blissful period of rest and meditative absorption in this delightful setting, Sean coughed abruptly and then began to speak.

"That tree is about seven hundred years old. It was born in a very different age, before there were white people in this land.

"I believe that long ago, Apache long-distance runners passed through here regularly. I felt their lines of power twenty years ago, when I first came to this tree." My eyebrows lifted as I once again tried to determine if Sean was exaggerating about having been in this spot before. He continued on uninterrupted by my silent skepticism.

"Peyote once confided in me that some of the Apache runners used to eat him to keep up their stamina, and to be able to go all night long without water. Although they were famous for their remarkable endurance, I'm sure that on long, hot days, those runners looked forward to rest stops in the shade of this tree. It was their power and dreaming here, as well as peyote, that first guided me here. This place, those men, they have a deep hold on me. The tree and I are both rooted, grounded here by a certain link to *intent* that is connected to this earth, to the Southwest."

Here, his voice trailed off, only to whisper a few moments later, "They knew I was coming. They dreamed through time that I would one day be here."

"What?!" I exclaimed, not believing my ears. But Sean was staring off into the distance, a strange and remote expression on his face, and I didn't want to disturb him by questioning him again. A fragment of his letter about skilled dreamers dreaming through time into the future flashed through my mind and then floated away. My mind was just not ready to consider the implications of his comment nor the content of that letter.

After another period of silence, I went to explore the tree more thoroughly. I found numerous swirls and whorls in its intriguing surface, and the animal droppings brought out the amateur tracker in me. I thought I could identify rabbit, coyote and owl scat as well as that of several other birds, and possibly deer or antelope.

I was just about to go sit by Sean again when the tree pulled me back to show me her secret. Nestling in the large crotch of one of the lowest branches and the trunk was the unmistakable design of a serpent, complete with eyes and coiled body. It was not a man-made design, but one created by the artistry of the tree herself. I traced it with my fingers, enjoying the tactile nuances of its textures. Then I noticed that off to the side of the snake's head, nature had clearly carved a vulva. When I finally looked up, Sean was smiling at me through the branches from his spot on the on the ground.

"I see you discovered the hidden message," he said. "You might want to think about the original story of Eve and the serpent, and the way it's molded the human mind for several millennia. And then look at the tree's snake again. That design could become the starting point for a much better story, a link to a new creation story for yourself and other women. Touch and rub it again with that intention in your heart, mind and *will*. Other people have touched it before you, and gone deep into dreaming."

It hit me that Sean really had been here years ago. At first I'd wondered about some of his statements, since it seemed like, if his stories were all true, he'd been almost everywhere in the Southwest. Over time he'd displayed a trucker's intimate knowledge of Route 66, naming restaurants from Needles to Tucumcari. But his familiarity went much deeper than this. Not only had he already visited the ghost town and power spots like this juniper site, but the Brahma cows, the fingerprint in the sky and other phenomena he'd witnessed years ago were now repeating themselves for both of us. And he remembered the serpent in this tree. I was a believer, even though my belief did nothing to eliminate the mystery of the situation. I had no idea how and why Sean had been involved with the power of those events years ago, how he'd held onto those strands of power all this time, and why so much of it was now dropping into my lap as well as coming back to him in these weird "winter repeats." I couldn't fathom it. I could tell myself Sean had been following *intent*, power and his own *will*, but these words barely satisfied mental reason, and the magic around Sean was *un*reasonable.

I gave up and went back to concentrating on the serpent, trying to let my mind stretch out toward new myths and potentials for women's spirits. Finally I emerged from under the tree and joined Sean again on the ground.

"Last time I was here, about twenty years ago," he continued, "I carried that big branch from under the shade of the tree and set it out there in the sun pointing south. It had two indentations in it that looked perfect for sitting on, but I didn't sit on the branch then. It wasn't the right time, just like it wasn't the right time to start the ghost town ashram, even though I was aware of the power of both the branch and the town. I waited very patiently for almost two decades. I waited for *intent*, and *intent* waited for you."

Sean then stood and walked over to the weathered limb. He reached down and dragged it into the shadow of the tree, turning it about a quarter turn before setting it down again. He then patted the branch invitingly as he sat in one of the indentations, gesturing me to occupy the other.

"Time for a new direction in life," he smiled, his eyes sparkling.

Fourteen

...Muerte, el muerte, eres mi amante.
Como un novio, me llevas el diamante
De tu presencia, frio y brillante.
Eres el espejo de mi alma flameante...

(...Death, o death, you are my lover.
Like a suitor, you bring me the diamond
Of your presence, cold and brilliant.
You are the mirror of my shimmering soul...)

from "Verses of Twilight Meditations"

Taoism was making its debut in the little Arizona ghost town. Sean had returned, and was taking me through several hours of various Taoist breathing exercises to add to my power-gathering and _will_-strengthening repertoire.

Over the past several months, there were two related themes Sean had consistently brought up to my mind and _will_. Both were involved with strengthening what he called my "western" face.

The first theme was the awareness of energy, or _chi_, moving through the body, and how to direct it and make it more powerful. I already had decades of prior experience with these processes through martial arts, meditations, energy-based healing work and the training with my shamanistic dance teacher. Sean added the awareness of _will_ moving in and through the body by teaching me exercises, postures and gestures he had developed as well as practices from Taoism and other spiritual disciplines.

Since his first touch to my back, Sean had encouraged me to believe in my *will*, to strengthen and act with it. *He* believed in it from the beginning, and it responded over and over to his energy and to other forces such as the wind, peyote or Emily's dreaming presence.

Sean's dealings with his *own* body were completely unique and initially incomprehensible to me. His gestures, his eyes and the manner in which he displayed his spiritual intensity all appeared very strange at first. He might grab his own belly, touch the top of his head, or raise his arms to meet a gust of wind. Over time, this approach had washed over me and begun silently integrating into my own awareness and actions, sneaking up on me at first, and finally transforming me. I was learning pieces of a vast spiritual system by observing Sean, imitating him, from his direct touch, and finally from my own *will* moving in and through my body.

My earlier training in dance and psychology had taught me that to imitate someone else's gestures, posture or style of movement creates a powerful rapport between the two people. It also brings the "imitator" direct knowledge of the other's reality. Some psychologists will imitate their patients' breathing or subtly reflect their posture for this purpose. Mirroring Sean's spiritual "body language" brought me knowledge and an energetic rapport with him and the spiritual forces he was touching.

Many spiritual and religious teachings would have us deny the body, calling it a source of sin, or at the least, a distraction of lower vibrations to be transcended. But Sean and I believed in the body as a vessel of—and potential door to—Spirit.

The second major theme Sean consistently encouraged from the beginning was my relationship to "Mother," his term for both the Earth herself and the forces of nature related to the Earth.

Sean himself was Mother's devoted son. He had an overwhelming affection for her. His attention to Mother was vast, and she in turn rewarded him with an abundance of spiritual experiences that filled each day of his life with power and beauty, surprises and solace. Over the years, they had interwoven their energies through countless interactions, to the extent that there was a fierce and sustaining umbilical connection between them.

Sean was not in the least bit self-conscious about where he and Mother might dance out their connection to one another. From the city parks of Los Angeles to the barren "badlands" of Arizona, any time was a good time to display and strengthen their ongoing dance of power.

Sometimes Sean would express exasperation over the current human fascination with the non-terrestrial. One of his pet peeves was the space programs, which he felt were largely a waste of time and money. He'd said, "Not only do we have plenty of the unknown left to explore right here on Earth and inside our very bodies, but real planetary challenges need our full attention," he'd said. And he sighed over what seemed like a growing collective fantasy/longing for UFOs to come whisk us away from our earthly problems.

In addition, he disagreed with popular theories that an alliance between God and the Earth was about to create apocalyptic natural disasters sent to wipe out large populations of people as some kind of divinely ordained revenge for human disrespect of nature.

"I know these kinds of doomsday prophecies abound from Native Americans to some Bible-brandishers alike, and have been around through-out history," he said, "but I've never believed in a murdering, destructive God. Nor in a vengeful Mother Earth. Human beings are more than capable of creating both problems and solutions here on Earth, and there is plenty of available energy to do either. And while we're here, why not enjoy and take advantage of our spiritual connections with Mother?"

Sean had said that developing my spiritual connection to "Mother" was a means of "turning my mind around," and of strengthening two of my "directions": my western and northern "faces."

Many systems use the number four to categorize the outside world and describing human personality types. Humans have long oriented them-selves to the four cardinal directions, have related to the four elements, the four phases of the moon, the four seasons. Scholars of human psychology have frequently divided humans into clusters of four basic personality types, and sometimes even body types. The mind's waking and sleeping activities have also been broken up into classes of four.

"In each of these cases, four is actually pointing to a totality," Sean commented. "The four directions encompass the totality of space or geography, the four seasons create the entire year. The human personality types are all found in each individual, as are the various types of consciousness. It is a matter of personality or circumstance that all aren't equally developed."

He'd then described the way he looked at the four directions and their spiritual counterparts in humans.

"The east is the place of dawn, and for a human, it is the face of openness, beginnings, and a certain childlike quality of naivete or innocence. It is like the Buddhist 'beginners mind.'"

"The southern face reflects an embracing warmth, nurturing, fertility, growth and maturation."

Sean felt I had developed both of those faces along my spiritual path. I'd played out the innocent beginner's face, full of hopes, confusions and fantasies. I'd also come to a certain southern maturity before meeting him, wishing to nurture the spiritual growth of both myself and of others. Now he was encouraging me to strengthen my western face and prepare to act from the north.

Sean saw the west as deep, dark and mysterious. Place of the setting sun, it is the reflection of several powerful elements. "It is the Earth, because of her increasing dominance once the sun has set. It is also death, the end of a cycle, but it points to the future as well. Once people truly confront their own mortality, knowing their days on Earth are finite, their priorities and the quality of how they spend their remaining time often go through intense reorganization.

"The west can also contain expressions of irrationality, even insanity, as well as completely non-thinking states like the Buddhist 'empty mind.' These three elements relate to how one deals with death. The mirror of death can loosen our attachments to our own past by reflecting our patterns, fantasies, our loyalty to—or betrayal of—our true nature. As everything shakes loose, one can feel and even be 'insane' for periods of time. Since death is a profound spiritual force unhampered by reason, its impact may also cause one to feel irrational or lead one to non-thinking states."

I wondered how much stamina I'd need to strengthen my western "face."

Sean felt his own strongest face was that of the north. This direction—with its qualities of clarity, coldness and soberness—motivated and colored many of his actions. For me the north could be a balance from emotionally based actions and reactions into a place of seeing myself and others more clearly, and then acting with power.

These four faces, or directions, reflected the totality of the Self. Sean's experience was that each directional wind carried the spiritual qualities of its direction and could help strengthen the corresponding "face" in a human being. He was helping me learn to become a balanced "woman of the four winds" by having me repeatedly absorb power from each wind into my *will* and womb. The winds were also aspects of Mother and non-human sources of power. Sean believed that relating to these non-human energies could help people rebalance from their entire history of social interactions and help them face future relationships with more power and freedom. I was trying to see if it would work for me.

***

Now, while we sat resting, calm and energized from the Taoist practices, I could tell that Sean was getting ready to say something. As was sometimes his habit before launching into a particular subject area, he sat silently for some time, holding one of his bare feet with his thumb pressed against the instep. Sean once told me the center of the thumb corresponded to the pituitary gland and the brain, while the point on the instep corresponded to the *will*'s center in the belly. Bringing the two together was a type of "mudra," in Eastern terminology, which helped him be *will*ful and focused in a non-thinking state. Often he would continue to hold this mudra while he talked. Following his suggestion, sometimes I used the same mudra to help me concentrate.

While Sean sat in contemplation, I surveyed the interior of my new home with satisfaction. Several beautiful hand-woven wall hangings from Mexico and South America glowed in the candlelight. Softly colored but sturdy cushions were scattered in inviting clusters around the edges of the living room. The sofa had bright-colored woven blankets draped over it, a few piled at one end and available for warding off the evening chill.

I'd experimented with limiting myself to sparsely adorning the various shelves with only a few favorite rocks and ethnic decorations. In addition to their being more easily seen, I liked the overall effect. The general feeling of the living room was warm and hospitable, with a culturally eclectic aura. And now Sean would be less apt to accuse me of laying traps for people's attention!

"Tonight I thought we could talk about spiritual power, shamanism and sorcery," Sean began. "Let's start with sorcery, a mostly unfamiliar practice in the West. At its core, sorcery is simply the recognition and application of spiritual power." Seeing my brow already furrowing, Sean waited for my question.

"But isn't that the same as shamanism?" I asked.

"Yes, and the definition fits both. But where shamans and sorcerers sometimes differ is in their interface with society. The line between them is not completely clear cut, and it varies from culture to culture. I'll get to that shortly. Now, for people who've read Castaneda's books, the term sorcerer has taken on a unique meaning, especially because the way he uses it is pretty much outside any anthropological data. But since you're familiar with it and sometimes think of me in similar terms, I'll use that definition some of the time in this discussion. I do have to say, though, that many people who have read Carlos's books then toss around terms like "power," "will" and "sorcerer" like some intellectual Frisbee. Most of them aren't really grounded in experience with any of those realities, so it's mostly mental entertainment.

"For most Westerners, a sorcerer is something fantastical that doesn't really exist. And often when they do hear the term sorcery, they usually equate all sorcery with dark sorcery. That is one reason why I don't usually use the term to define what I do or sometimes teach.

"Anyway, in reality, you can divide the practitioners of sorcery into dark and light, with both sometimes drifting toward a neutral or gray zone. From now on I'll use the term 'witch'—as do many Native Americans— to indicate dark sorcerers. We'll say it's their goals that separate witches from sorcerers.

"Witches don't have altruistic goals. When they focus toward others with their *will* and power, it's to bend people to their purposes. They've traditionally exerted control over others through drugging them, sometimes entrapping them sexually, and almost always by heavily manipulating their emotions. Or all of the above. Their goals are invariably to feed their own egos, increase their material wealth, and sometimes to trap new apprentices.

"Witches are immoral, and have been known to even kill in order to steal or otherwise increase their own power. They tend to draw their power from death, violence, fear and sex, and won't hesitate to provoke or directly cause any of these energies if they feel they can manipulate them to their purposes. Power *is* most definitely released from any of those elements, and witches may know how to gather it up."

"They sound like the ultimate ugly control freak," I said, grimacing. "I guess this kind of blows the theory that only good guys can wield real spiritual power. I mean, witches don't use death, violence, anger and fear the way psychopaths or terrorists would, right? Their 'spiritual' power is for real? This isn't just superstition that people have always had about witchcraft?"

"No, it's not superstition, although I'm sure there have been plenty of unfounded accusations of witchcraft. People often look for a scapegoat for their troubles, and if their culture believes in witchcraft, innocent people may often be labeled and attacked as such. And innocents have been branded as witches when someone wanted to get rid of them, as in the infamous era of witch burnings in the West. Many innocent women were tortured and killed by men greedy to gain those women's material wealth and possessions after their death. Those men masked their greed and ego as piousness."

"It seems to me that the supposed witch hunters were the real witches," I interjected. "They were using all four of those elements you mentioned, and getting off on the power, control and material goods that resulted from their actions."

"In a sense, that's true. The main difference is that they weren't spiritually trained, so their efforts and the results had a more worldly aspect. But yes, the tactics were similar.

"The freedom-seeking sorcerers have a very different set of goals than witches. Rather than serving ego, a great portion of their spiritual practices are aimed at shrinking their own self-importance and that of their apprentices. Rather than seeking to control others, they try to exert impeccable control over *themselves* and encourage others to do likewise. And, although this is usually more typical of shamans, occasionally some sorcerers even turn part of their efforts to benefit a larger community. But when they do, they tend to operate from behind the scenes rather than call attention to themselves.

"I want to talk a little more about the differences between sorcerers, shamans and other kinds of spiritual practitioners," I said. "Since I've been studying this subject for years, I'd like to hear more about your point of view and see how it matches up to what I've learned."

"All right," he grinned amiably, "but can we take a short break first?"

"Fine with me."

We put on our jackets and stepped out into the crisp desert night. The moon was a glowing crescent, the starry sky at its crystalline best. We strolled down the quiet road. I was relieved to be moving after the intense concentration of our talk. We didn't speak, and I listened to the sounds of our footsteps, occasional muffled birds calling briefly in the night, a dog barking somewhere in town, and rustlings of the wind or small nocturnal hunters.

While we walked, I reviewed some of the Taoist breathing practices Sean had taught me earlier in the evening, trying to synchronize them with the rhythm of my footsteps. By the time we approached the adobe house, my efforts were more coordinated.

"To address your burning question," Sean picked up where we'd left the discussion, sipping on some of the spiced apple cider I'd heated up, "I see one major difference between shamans and a sorcerers. As I said before, it has to do with their interface with society.

"Shamans function very much within their society. They use their knowledge and power to assist people who come to them for healing, dream interpretation, family and crisis counseling, and to mediate with the spirit world for an individual or the entire community. They live within the community to which they are available as would be a doctor, therapist, minister, or even a lawyer in Western society.

"Shamans tend to be fairly innovative and spontaneous in their art. When called upon for help, they respond as they see most appropriate to meet the needs of the immediate situation. These days in the Anglo new age, however, the term is wearing pretty thin. Everyone with a crystal, a drum or the occasional unusual experience wants to call him or herself a shaman. Most of them are spiritual neophytes, and rarely are any of them being called on by their community to handle heavy issues of power. There are probably a handful who've got the talent and power for the title and who actually serve some community, but they are in the minority."

I recalled the numerous New Age publications I'd seen that listed shaman services in their classified ads. I also thought over the thousands of hours I'd invested in spiritual practices, and was more than aware that owning a few accouterments of the trade was no substitute for hard work and real access to power.

"But back to the subject," Sean went on, "there are a variety of other spiritual practitioners who also have knowledge and experience of spiritual power. These are the priests, ministers and medicine men and women of various cultures. Where they most differ from shamans and sorcerers is in their attachment to form. They tend to follow either dogma or prescribed rituals and rules of behavior established some time in the past, and are discouraged from deviating from their particular religious framework. Such people are the spiritual glue holding their community in place. They maintain a certain balance and order which can encompass not only spiritual behavior, but sets of rules and ethics for other social behaviors as well. From the Pope and the Vatican with their far-reaching influence, to the Dineh *hataalii* (medicine men) and their on-going efforts toward restoring the community to *hohzho*, (order, harmony and beauty), all follow time-honored practices and rarely deviate from those methods. In a sense, these people stand in the center of their aggregates, holding the society firmly in place while the eyes of their followers focus expectantly upon them.

"Sorcerers often tend to live outside society. This full or semi-isolation is frequently the cause of suspicion and fear in the rest of the community, even if the individual sorcerer has no inclination whatsoever toward the darker practices. I believe the distrust is a result of the sorcerers being an unknown element, and you know that many people react to the unknown with a certain amount of fear."

I nodded in agreement, quite familiar myself with fears of the unknown. Sean continued.

"One of the things to remember is this: the primary currency of exchange in most human interactions is self-importance and how to maintain or increase it. This is the opposite of the sorcerers' goals. In order to complete their training and become balanced, eventually sorcerers must venture back into society to test themselves and further hone their practices toward defeating their biggest enemy: their own self-importance. It's one thing to be detached, calm and serene on a mountaintop or in a lonely cave, but what about with a mean, demanding boss, unreasonable customers, loud snobs or obnoxious drunks?! And society is also a great stage on which sorcerers can practice becoming more fluid. They will sometimes even use various disguises and personalities to enhance their *art of stalking*."

Sean paused reflectively for a few minutes, then laughed softly to himself and continued.

"I'll tell you a funny story," he said, "one that illustrates how I once functioned in the role of a sorcerer.

"One day some years ago, I was driving east through Utah. Near the Wyoming border, I picked up three Indian hitchhikers. One was Navajo, one Arapaho, and I think the third was Sioux. After they'd settled in and we'd been driving for a little while, I pointed to the dashboard, where some time in the past I'd placed the bottom of a broken green glass bottle. In it were five black cedar balls: the dried cedar berries.

"'You know what that is?' I asked them innocently. They, of course, said no. 'Well,' I said, 'that just happens to be my antelope-hunting altar.' These guys stared at me, then at each other, and tried their best not to choke at this revelation.

"'Yep,' I said, 'and I'm in the middle of an antelope hunt right now.' Then, for the next quarter of an hour, I proceeded, with great solemnity and deliberation, to move those five cedar balls around. I'd place one in my hand, then sometimes I'd stick one in my nostril, or in my mouth, or back in the jagged glass 'altar.' The three men were mesmerized by my performance. But under the surface, I was exerting my *will*, sending it out on the antelope hunt.

"As I juggled my cedar balls, I asked if any of the men had ever hunted antelope. Although one of them remembered a grandfather who'd done so, none of them had themselves. They'd rarely even seen one their entire lives.

"Right about then, I pointed up ahead, and said, 'Well, guys, there they are.' There, lined up on both sides of the highway and stretching ahead as far as the eye could see, were hundreds of antelope. Those antelope were standing right up against the highway fence. Some were sticking their heads as far through as they could, and all were almost militarily shoulder-to-shoulder. They were standing absolutely stock still, looking dazed and frozen, their eyes fixed and unblinking, watching as we passed.

"I'll tell you, the three Indians were absolutely floored. After having probably thought my broken bottle and cedar balls were the poorest excuse for a holy altar they'd ever seen, lo and behold, here were the ante-lope in mind-bending array. Not only that, but this situation continued across the *entire* state of Wyoming! In some ways, I was as amazed as the other men. For at least four hours, we were never out of sight of hundreds of antelope, sometimes scattered along one side of the road, sometimes crowded along the fence on both sides. My passengers were stunned into silence and ended up looking as dazed as the antelope!

"Finally, when we got near Cheyenne, a thunderstorm appeared up ahead. Just as suddenly as the first rain hit us, the antelope disappeared completely and mysteriously. Looming above us about five miles away was an enormous thundercloud, intersected by a brilliant rainbow whose cen-ter was obscured by the cloud. As we approached, we went in and out of rain and sun. I rolled down the window and started yelling, 'there's got to be more, there's got to be more!' while taking the rain that fell on my hand and rubbing it on my head, my chest, my belly, shaking my hand toward the thundercloud, and yelling periodically.

"The men were riveted, and looked almost afraid, like they'd gotten trapped with some total maniac. In truth, it was power we all were trapped with. 'Where's some tobacco?!' I yelled, 'I need some tobacco!' One of the guys rolled me a cigarette, and I started blowing smoke toward the broken rainbow and waving the cigarette out the window.

"Then, a second rainbow appeared alongside the first one, again bro-ken in half by the massive cloud. Now there were four half arches. I kept up my show, getting more and more intense, breathing hard. Just as we drove directly under the thundercloud that had lightning crackling through it, both rainbows finally connected and became complete.

"There was utter silence until we got to Cheyenne. I dropped those men off at the bus station at their request, waved, and drove away.

"So in that situation, Josie, you could say I acted like a shaman. But because I wasn't part of the tribal community of any of those three men, and because I simply volunteered my energies rather than responding to a formal request and some kind of payment on their part, my role toward them was as more of a sorcerer. And that's it for tonight."

My mind was probably almost as dazed as the three men had been. Sean was quite the dramatic storyteller, and the stories of his own life were of mythic proportions.

It was late by this time, so I suggested a good night's rest. Soon I was drifting into sleep with a slight smile on my lips as Sean's antelope hunt danced across the dream-screen of my inner vision.

Fifteen

...Hold me tight, hold me tight,
Danger water's comin' baby, hold me tight...

from the old folk song "Danger Waters"

Some nights are stranger than others, and some go so far beyond the definition of strange they enter into another category entirely. Or even into another dimension.

Another surprise visitor had arrived at my doorstep. After answering a knock at the door, Colette walked into the house, pulling some man I'd never met before behind her. I was astonished by their unexpected presence. With a bold look at Sean and myself, right before our eyes Colette immediately began making flagrant sexual advances toward the man she'd brought, running her hands over his body with lewd suggestions spewing out of her brightly painted lips. *Good heavens,* I thought to myself, as she rubbed her pelvis against him, *she's practically having sex with this guy right in the middle of my living room.*

As she continued, she began taunting Sean, making increasingly negative remarks about him, his masculinity, his spiritual worth, on and on with the most wicked, vindictive look in her eyes. She finally ended her ugly display by dropping a nasty poem she'd written about Sean onto the carpet. By then, I'd had it with her disgusting performance. I grabbed her by the shoulders, and started shaking her violently. I wanted to shake the evil energy from Colette and bring her out of her terrible state. Sean, who'd remained rather calm and detached during the whole episode, finally came over and gently disengaged me, eventually managing to quiet my fiery outburst.

Then, something strange came over me, and the next instant, as I looked around, I realized I was no longer in my home in Arizona, but was actually in Mexico in the house of a powerful male witch. The lighting was very dim, and I could see nothing in the room except for the man himself, who was sitting directly across the room from me. As I sat studying his cold, almost reptilian eyes, feeling both fascinated and repulsed, he began to remind me of someone else I knew. His skin had an unhealthy pale cast, and his hair, which was longish and pulled behind his head in a short ponytail, was graying and oily. I realized that he vaguely resembled a more obese, distorted version of Cecil, a man from whom I'd once taken some spirituality classes.

As soon as I had that thought, the witch trapped me with a gaze of power, locking my eyes with his. As the seconds ticked by, I began to have the most horrifying realization that this man was slowly but powerfully pulling my spirit and *will* right out of me, and I was growing weaker by the moment. I knew if this went on for long I'd be completely helpless, perhaps die or become a zombie pawn of this witch. In desperation, I gathered what of my *will* remained and acted. Quickly and suddenly, hoping to startle the witch enough to break his hold, I locked my arms over my belly to protect my *will*, and crouched low to the earth. While I stamped one foot vigorously on the ground, I yelled "Sean! Sean!" hoping somehow to alert him to my predicament, wherever he was.

Immediately, I felt a weird fluttering at the back of my neck, as if a giant moth was behind me, and suddenly I was back in Arizona with Sean. I started telling him frantically what had just happened to me. Even as I spoke, I could tell I was in bad shape from my encounter, and was even losing my perspective on Sean. Before I could finish my story, I felt a violent yank and found myself back in the evil witch's house in Mexico.

This time things became rapidly much worse. The witch trapped me once again in his cold, inhuman gaze, pulling my *will* out of my belly like spiritual entrails from a fatal gut wound. I kept trying to break his hold, but my struggles were becoming weaker and weaker. With my last bit of strength, I cried out again for Sean, felt the strange flutter at the back of my neck intensify and then, with a popping sound, I was once more out of the witch's house and back in my own room in Arizona.

"Sean!" I screamed, but he'd already arrived. "Mexican witchcraft, oh, you've got to help me, don't let him get me again or I'll die!" I was almost out of my mind with combined fear and relief, trembling uncontrollably on the edge of convulsions.

"Shh, shh, you're all right," Sean whispered, sitting me up and holding my body tightly against his from behind me, with his hands laced over my midsection. "I know what was going on, and you're all right now," he continued soothingly.

It took quite a while, but I finally stopped shaking and calmed down enough to realize it was dark out, and that whatever had taken place from the moment Colette had walked in the door until I woke myself screaming had happened to me asleep and dreaming. However, even after I woke up, the dream energy continued with strange lights and noises hissing through the room. A sense of being in the middle of a battle gripped me with ongoing, jolting intensity.

As I was still covered with sweat and on the edge of spiritual and physical shock, Sean suggested I take a shower. I stood under the hot water until my body was warmed and relaxed. Then I cooled the water from tepid to ice cold for a short while to try to help make myself more solid. After drying off briskly with a thick towel, I slipped into a sweater and sweatpants and joined Sean in the living room.

While sipping on some hot ginger and mint tea that he had prepared for me, I said, "I'm doing better, Sean, but I've got to tell you what happened to me. I don't think I've ever felt as spiritually threatened as I did tonight. I need some kind of catharsis before I can even think about sleep again."

"Okay," he said. "As I told you before, I already know what happened. I was in dreaming with you, both awake and asleep. But if you need to talk about it, go ahead."

I *did* feel I needed to. Even if Sean thought he already knew every detail, I needed the release of speech to help me deal with the soul-crushing terror I had just been through. And so I recounted my ordeal as thoroughly as I could recall. By the time I finished, the first pale tendrils of dawn were stretching their way through the sky, as if seeking to consume the pale remaining stars with their growing power.

"You must get some sleep now," said Sean, after listening quietly to my experience. "This has been a wonderful challenge for you, and you rallied your resources, including me, and came through it fairly well."

"You've got to be kidding!" I exclaimed. "It didn't feel even remotely wonderful, and I don't think I came through it well at all. I feel like I just barely survived, and if you hadn't been here when I woke up, I'm not sure what would have become of me."

"It's useless to speculate," he said, "and for now, maybe you can take my word that you did well. Try to get some rest. You still need to replenish your energy, and I assure you, nothing else will disturb your sleep and dreaming tonight. I'll be close by, so don't succumb to unnecessary anxieties."

He must have been reading my mind, as the thought of sleeping and dreaming had begun to make me nervous again. I finally agreed to try to rest. Sean sat beside me for a while, with one hand resting securely over the top of my head, and one over my belly. Slowly, I unwound and began to feel my limbs grow heavy with relaxation and fatigue. As I entered the twilight realm that midwifed deeper states of slumber and dreaming, I heard Sean slip out of the room to go begin his morning meditations. And then I slept undisturbed, as he had promised I would.

***

"There are strange things going on in your life," said Sean that evening. "I have felt the edges of some of them since I met you, and was considering whether or not to include them in our earlier discussion yesterday."

I promptly began to feel anxiety flood through me. My hands turned cold and sweaty, and I wrapped my shawl more tightly around my body as if it could protect me from some as yet unseen threat.

Sean had held off talking about my dream all day, choosing instead to accompany me on a lengthy hike in the desert, where he regaled me with humorous and exotic stories from his past, and encouraged me to gather power. Until this moment, the tactics had successfully held the previous night's terrors at bay.

"Your dreaming last night was the deciding factor for me," he stated, "since you're now more consciously engaged with some of the forces I was debating bringing up.

"I believe what happened to you last night was real. It wasn't 'just a bad dream'. You were involved in an actual battle, and it wasn't between one part of yourself and another, as many modern dream analysts would claim. No, I believe there was a force outside you that was trying to weaken and perhaps even destroy your spiritual *will* and take it prisoner."

"What do you think this force is?" I asked as my anxiety level rose. "Is there really some Mexican witch out to get me, and if so why?!" I'd traveled extensively in Mexico earlier in my life, sometimes staying for several months at a time, and had come in contact with a number of unusual people. I'd walked through sorcerers' markets and met various healers. I wondered if perhaps I'd unwittingly made an enemy down there who was now taking his revenge on me. Even though the man in my dreaming didn't resemble anyone I remembered ever meeting in Mexico, still, it was possible it was someone I'd forgotten. Or someone skilled enough to alter his image in dreaming.

"I'm not sure how to answer that specific question," Sean replied. "There are some things I know and some things that are still wrapped in mystery. Let me try to explain what I perceive as best I can."

He then spoke to me at some length. What I heard during that time described issues of spiritual and worldly power that criss-crossed much of human history.

"As you already know, there are and always have been people in this world driven by a great need to control and wield power over others. Such people can be found in all walks of life from the secular to the spiritual. Historically, sometimes such tyrants have operated alone and influenced few, while others have made liaisons with like-minded people from a variety of professions.

"Take for example, the kingdoms of old where soothsayers and magicians, political advisors and priests formed strange alliances in order to influence the actions of the king. Their goals were power and material rewards. Or consider the younger brother of the village chief in some remote jungle tribe. He offers the local witch wealth and women in exchange for helping arrange his older brother's death. *His* goal is to assure his own succession to power.

"On the surface, these examples may seem irrelevant to the lives of most people in the Western world. But this is not so. In modern times, deals are made and favors curried for power and control between many strange bedfellows, with goals of success in big business, politics and even positions in our Western churches.

"I'll give you one fairly ugly example from this century, not widely known, but with some written documentation available to the public.

"When Hitler was reaching for power, he amassed not only a group of political and military supporters to aid him in his diabolical plan, but also cultivated a relationship with various members of the occult. He acquired a group of occult Tibetan practitioners to join him in Germany and to combine forces to further influence and inflame people's minds.

"A great European mystic by the name of Rudolph Steiner lived at that time, whose work in philosophy, education, and even a spiritual dance form called Eurythmy, is still fairly well known even today. He was a gifted seer and dreamer, and would frequently send his astral body, or *double*, to eavesdrop and run interference with the plans Hitler and his Tibetan goon-squad were making. They eventually became aware of Steiner's efforts, and made several attempts to assassinate him, all of which failed."

Sean handed me a book that had been resting at his side since the beginning of our conversation. It was titled *The Spear of Destiny*, written by Ravenscroft, and described in detail much of what Sean had just told me about the relationship between Hitler and the occult.

"Now, what does any of what I've been saying this evening, or in our discussion of sorcery yesterday, have to do more personally with you and me? What I'm going to tell you is based partly on deduction, and partly on the perceptions of my *will*.

"Ever since I was a young man, I have dealt with a variety of strange spiritual energies, some positive and some negative, while awake and dreaming. This has caused me to develop an extremely strong *will* and *dreamer*. As I began reading about the world's history and exploring the information with my mind and *will*, I started examining uses of power in the world. I became aware of the role of Tibetan sorcery in World War II, and learned of other occult groups of European origin such as the Illuminati that were connected to intellectual and political elites.

"I believe that in the present there are still individuals who practice witchcraft. Some of them practice it alone, and others work together either with others of their kind or with those who wield secular power. My *will* tells me some of them are able to travel in the astral to gain spiritual knowledge of people and to influence them. Witches are extremely possessive and jealous of power, and think nothing of trying to either dominate or destroy anyone who might pose a threat to them. There's no reason to think they're behaving any differently now than they always have. And I feel that some of them are either directly involved in—or working from behind the scenes to support some individuals and groups in places of political and financial power.

"Like Steiner and others over the course of human history, I don't appreciate that kind behavior. My *will* sometimes picks up those negative

energies in mid-air, in dreaming, or occasionally around other people
who've become targets of some sort. Then I roll up my spiritual shirt-
sleeves and do what I can to bring a more positive balance. Every time I
get involved with people spiritually, I try to foster their awareness of both
positive and negative forces in the world. During and since the peyote
ceremony, I've been encouraging you to get better at identifying various energies, and your dreaming experience last night gave you a great
opportunity to deal consciously with some negative forces.

"I'm not telling you all this to frighten you unnecessarily, but rather to
arm you with knowledge and to catalyze your fighting spirit. There has
been both good and evil in the world for a long time, and ignorance of
darkness is not bliss. You don't want to play ostrich, do you?"

"No, of course not. I've done my share of looking at the ugliness that can
grow in people or societies. But that's been from more of a psychological or
sociological perspective. I'm not sure if I'm ready yet to do battle with spiritual darkness."

"I think it's too late," Sean laughed. "You've already started.

"To combat evil in any form, including witchcraft," he continued, "you
need a thorough understanding of your emotional weaknesses. Scrutinizing
your personal history as you've been doing, helps you identify those weaknesses and brings you power. The emotional knowledge is key, because
witchcraft often works on exacerbating people's vulnerabilities so they can be
more easily manipulated."

"But Sean," I asked, "why would this awful attack happen to me at this
particular time of my life? I just don't get it."

"Because you are becoming more powerful, Josie. Power attracts power,
and you'll continue to draw powerful people with both good and evil
motives the stronger you get. And this isn't a completely isolated incident
for you, although it's one of the more dramatic so far."

He went on to point out and analyze various incidents in my own life
and human history where forces of darkness may have been operating
from behind the scenes, attracted to various kinds of power. After several

hours of this, my emotions were in great turmoil. On one level, the perspective Sean was presenting had a certain kind of cohesion and inner
logic. On another, parts of it seemed like something out of a very grim
fairy tale. I kept trying to figure out how to get any concrete proof that
what he'd described about witchcraft was a present day issue in *my* life.
Yes, I knew greed and power-lust motivated some people, and I could see
how such a situation *might* exist. I was also aware, however, that once one
develops a belief system about one's world, the mind is quite adept at then
being able to tie anything and everything that happens into that system,
leaving everything accounted for.

If I hadn't already experienced Sean's powerful *will* and his many
insights into human motivations and psychology, I could more easily have
dismissed some of his theories about dark occult forces as paranoia. As it
was, I couldn't. However, it was quite difficult to embrace these concepts,
as this would mean changing my perspective on my own life as well as on
the nature of the world in which I lived. Could I keep my balance and sanity while acknowledging I inhabited a world that contained hidden spiritual enemies bent on human destruction or distress, including mine?

One of the main things Sean suggested these dark forces and witches
might attempt would be to weaken me or distract me from my spiritual
goals. That wasn't a major surprise, once I thought about it, since I
assumed that evil had long opposed light and spiritual illumination. Sean
also implied that efforts might be made to create conflict, disharmony, or
possibly spiritual separation between us. I'd felt the edge of those elements
in the dream and was alarmed at the thought of more such tactics.

Then I began to wonder if this was all a big set-up created by Sean. I
remembered an incident in one of Carlos Castaneda's early books. The gist
of it was that his teacher don Juan had said that his own life was being
threatened by a powerful female witch, and that, unless Carlos helped him
defeat her, don Juan's days were numbered. Don Juan then led Carlos
through a series of preparations and strategies leading to several confrontations between Carlos and the witch. Carlos had been frightened

when don Juan had first described the danger from this woman, and had
had to intensely rally his resources, wits, and courage to deal with her. His
loyalty and concern for don Juan finally overrode his own fears, and he
had acted with power.

The strange irony of the situation was that the "witch" turned out to be
none other than la Catalina, one of don Juan's sorcery associates. The
whole story had been a well-planned set-up to help Carlos learn to act
with his *will*, driven by a combination of fear and loyalty. Later, la
Catalina even became a unique spiritual benefactor to Carlos.

What if what Sean was using fear and loyalty in the same way and for
the purpose of strengthening my *will*? If so, he wouldn't reveal his strategy
if I asked him. I was caught between taking him at his word, or not believing but going along with him anyway to try to get what good I could out
of the situation.

What *was* obvious, whether Sean's theories about present-day witchcraft and darkness were correct or not, was that my dreaming experience
of last night had been truly terrifying. Certainly I'd had nightmares before,
but nothing—even from my childhood—began to approach the quality
of that experience. It was just too real, too visceral to be dismissed. If there
was a real threat, I was going to have to arm myself spiritually and develop
a tougher *will*.

In the midst of my efforts to sort all of this out, the phone rang. It was
Tess, sounding slightly agitated.

"I hope I'm not calling too late, Josie," she began a bit apologetically,
"but I really need to talk to you."

"Oh, I was wide awake, I assure you," I said dryly. "What's going on,
Tess?"

"I just got home from attending one of Cecil's classes where I had a very
strange experience." *Oh no*, I thought. Cecil was the person the witch in
my nightmare had resembled.

Tess continued. "Cecil was going on and on about something, I don't
even remember what, when all of a sudden his face began to change. It

wasn't a dramatic change, but a subtle shift into someone who looked like him, but slightly older, heavier, kind of foreign-looking, somehow, and rather evil. I was both fascinated and unnerved, and I felt a bit weird for a while. Then the other image faded and Cecil was back again. It was really quite disturbing. Nothing like that has ever happened to me before. I'd be grateful if you would tell Sean about it too, and maybe the two of you can help me figure out what this was about."

My heart raced as I listened to Tess's story. I told her, without going into detail, that I'd seen something similar in a dream last night, and that I would most certainly relay her story to Sean as one more piece in a strange mystery we were trying to unravel.

"Thanks," she said, "I sure appreciate it."

"What else did you want to tell me?" I asked hesitantly, hoping it wasn't more disturbing news.

"I just found out from a friend in Los Angeles that in a few days Carlos Castaneda plans to speak at a bookstore there. I'd very much like to go there and meet him, and thought you and Sean would probably be interested as well."

"Oh, yes, most definitely," I exclaimed. "Let me tell Sean, and I'll call you back and see if we can figure out a rendezvous spot so we can go there together. I'll tell my friends Rose and Selena too. Maybe we could all meet up somewhere before seeing Carlos, and gather our focus and energies."

"All right, great! Call me soon. We don't have much time to make plans. And Josie, I'm really looking forward to seeing you and Sean again! Well, I know it's late, so I guess that's it for now."

"It was more than enough!" I laughed.

After a few more words, we hung up. I was quite intrigued by the prospect of seeing Castaneda again, and it was just the news I needed to counterbalance the heaviness of the last twenty-four hours.

I repeated the telephone conversation to Sean. He was enthused at the prospect of seeing Carlos again after his first encounter with him eighteen years earlier. He became a bit more grave when I described what Tess had just experienced in Cecil's class.

"Do you think that witch in my dream really was Cecil?" I asked him anxiously. Since Sean had met Cecil once, I figured he must have taken some kind of energetic reading of the man.

"No," Sean shook his head, Cecil doesn't have anywhere near the power nor training to be a witch. No, I think what Tess saw was more like a dark mask descending over his face, a mask set there by forces he has aligned himself with over the years through his own bad habits. Cecil is one of those petty tyrants who has a consuming need to control the people in his small kingdom of authority. Perhaps between that and the lies he's told about his connections to powerful secret societies, he's unwittingly aligned himself with darker hidden groups such as I described earlier. Tess's experience and your dreaming certainly indicate a connection between Cecil and some strange business."

I stared at him and nervously twisted a loose strand of hair.

"I know some of what I described tonight was unsettling," he continued after a brief pause. "However, you need to be knowledgeable and you need to get a lot tougher. You should be utterly delighted that you have such challenges for your *will*. And the fact that I was in your dream with you, pulling on you as you reached out to me, shows a powerful bond between our *wills*. Perhaps that will be of some comfort."

"I don't think I'm quite to the delight stage," I said. "And I'm having difficulty accepting some of what you've told me. I will consider it all anyway, Sean, especially in light of my dream and now Tess's experience. Something weird *is* going on, but I need to learn more about its nature. In the meantime, let's plan our trip to see Carlos."

***

The long drive to Los Angeles provided me with the perfect opportunity to reflect on all that had taken place over the last few months of my life. Much had changed, including my social aggregate. I began to mull over the interactions that had taken place when I'd introduced Sean to some of the people I knew.

When Sean interacted with my friends, he would often zero in on where they were leaking their power away, and would help lead them in directions that were less wasteful. Much of the advice he gave them was to stop wasting so much power in talking, and to stop chasing leaders or trips that were primarily talking-oriented. The key to real power and experience, he told them, was to connect more with themselves and with the Earth in states of internal and external silence. He showed them power moving right out of their bodies or the earth or a snake, and assured them they didn't have to sit around and wait for messages from UFOs or crystals from Atlantis. There was plenty of mystery right inside them and close at hand.

In one of our conversations about this Sean had said, "I've tried to stay in touch with the various aspects of the New Age, including where power is moving in some of the groups and their teachers or leaders. There's definitely some there, but often it's the combined power of the group attention that's making the leaders look as good as they do rather than just what the leaders themselves have to offer."

"Are you trying to discourage me from ever attending anyone's lectures or workshops again?"

"Definitely not," he'd replied. "There are things to learn about the world, and the information can come from a variety of sources. Simply go as a hunter of knowledge and power, and be discerning with your mind and *will*.

"The thing is, a lot of people don't want the responsibility of strengthening and developing their own spirit and *will*, which takes time, energy and devotion. They'd rather talk or listen to someone else talk about what's possible than to have a daily practice and experience of spirit. Maybe being brought up on Walt Disney's 'Peter Pan' has a whole generation waiting for Tinker Bell to sprinkle us with magic pixie dust," he laughed.

"But seriously, I feel too many people in the New Age spiritual movement are just waiting to be hypnotized by anything that glitters. And we all know that not everything that glitters is gold."

Once, I'd asked him about the popular reincarnation and past life fascination that abounded in the New Age. Sean gave his impressions. "I feel that in most 'past life readings,' the reader is mainly playing off the emotions and self-importance of the person seeking the information. In other words, people are getting what they want to hear."

"That sure makes sense," I said. "I've heard at least a dozen women who claimed they were Cleopatra in a past life, or people who were Merlin or some great shaman or mystic or other important beings. None of my friends has ever come bragging to me about their past life as an ordinary farmer or garbage collector, accountant or housewife."

Sean smiled. "That's part of what supports my disbelief in reincarnation. But some people do have powerful dreams or visions from which they emerge convinced they have just had a past-life experience."

"Where do you think those experiences are coming from then, if not from past lives?"

"Well, the stones and soil of Mother Earth's body hold memory of everything that's ever taken place on the planet. I believe that a lot of what people think is a past-life memory experience is actually their contact with a memory held by the Earth herself. If people are in an area where an event took place—or even have an object from there—their connection to the past can be so strong they really feel like they were there in another life. And those can be very powerful experiences."

En route to Los Angeles, we stopped for lunch at the popular Cafe Espress in Flagstaff, and then began the slow descent toward the first ruthless touch of the Mojave Desert. Except for the one night dancing in New Orleans, most of the time I'd spent with Sean had been in nature, at home or in interactions with my friends. I realized our attendance at the peyote ceremonies was our largest communal activity since I'd met Sean.

"Where did you first get to know or know about peyote?" I asked him as we sped west. I was curious, since he was obviously familiar with the plant before our first ceremony, and was also knowledgeable about the ceremony's history and form.

"I first learned about peyote and other power plants in Mexico," he replied. "As in most parts of the world, there is a long tradition of local power plant use there, and some of the form of the Native American Church ceremony is a gift from the south. I studied peyote use in the Native American Church and then attended their ceremonies for many years off and on before our Arizona experience."

Sean had been spiritually active in a variety of settings throughout his life. As we drove, he entertained me with numerous and colorful stories of unfolding his *will* at Johnny Winter rock concerts, on dance floors, at restaurants and at New Age gatherings. He seemed comfortable in most environments, whether it be in the city or the desert, with people or other forces. With me, however, he was most dedicated to the development of my *will* and its contact with nature, and to strengthening my dreaming.

My efforts in both directions were meeting with success, I decided as I leaned back in the car seat. Emily and her silent partner Constanza continued to guide me through the intricacies of my daily efforts at conscious dreaming. And after my frightening dreaming encounter with the witch, Sean suggested asking Emily to show me some methods for spiritual self-defense. I was looking forward to that project, and hoped I'd learn techniques I could some day share with others as well. And I was glad Sean had encouraged my relationship with "Mother." With each passing encounter with her power, I was grounded deeper in delight with the Earth herself.

In one season, I'd shifted the focus of my interactions from thinking and emotions to *will* and dreaming, and from the social aggregates to the non-human forces of plants, the winds, of "Mother." As we raced west, I gave thanks for the fullness of life.

Sixteen

...Walkin' down the highway as the ravens fly west,
Dusk is the hour that my spirit loves best.
Twilight paints the mesas from daytime red to blue
And nighthawks trace the ways that my spirit touches you...

from "Canyon Country"

Standing before us in his well-tailored brown suit, Carlos Castaneda cut a handsome and debonair figure. The only other male in the room wearing a suit was Sean, which shocked me as I hadn't even known he owned a suit before that night. It was as difficult to imagine this urbane Sean racing up and down the hills of the Painted Desert as it was to imagine the suave Castaneda running about the Sonoran desert.

Shortly before entering the bookstore, our attention had been captivated by the omonic appearance of a multi-colored Mexican parrot squawking loudly from a nearby tree. It was flamboyant and out of its normal context. Sean told me late rthat he felt the parrot's presence was a comment from Spirit about the content of Castaneda's books.

Carlos's only two props as a speaker were his body and a chair, both of which he utilized dynamically and inventively over the course of several hours. Never once did he sit on the chair, though he kept us in suspense several times as he hovered over it like a hummingbird, almost sitting, and then leaping up again. Sometimes he paced around it like a cat sneaking up on a mouse. Other times posing with one foot on it, he took on the demeanor of the consummate professor. On this level alone, he gave a wonderful performance.

Throughout the evening Castaneda displayed an adeptness for moving his audience through a variety of mental and emotional hoops. He was intimate and personal, filling in certain details of his life which, after he'd been such a reclusive figure for so many years, was a great delight to the small but thirsty crowd perched on the edge of their metal folding chairs. I sat near the front with Rose, Tess and Sean. Selena arrived after Carlos had begun speaking and remained separate from the rest of us in the back of the room. Our little group had traveled from three different states, drawn from afar by the famous storyteller.

Carlos's books had partly shaped the spiritual expectations, hopes and goals of the baby-boomer generation. Were they true or were they powerful allegory? I still wasn't sure, but the story he now told, like his books, had its own reality. He said he had witnessed Florinda, one of the members of don Juan's party, leave this world. She had remained behind, Carlos said, when most of the rest of don Juan's associates achieved the formidable goal of leaving *en masse* years ago through an act of unimaginable power. Years later, Carlos and his own party of sorcerers watched Florinda choose her mode of departure which, as the others had done, was to consume herself with the internal heat of spiritual fire. She was aware enough in advance to invite Castaneda's party to witness the event.

His personal experience, Carlos confessed, was a sorry illustration of loss of emotional control. As he watched Florinda glow and then begin to disappear into the fire, he lost the composure of the detached witness, and went from awe at such a feat to a sudden response of emotional horror. He lunged to pull her from the fire and immediately experienced an excruciating pain in his abdomen, a pain which didn't diminish and left him gasping and unable to reach her. This action was ironic, as Sean commented later. Since Florinda supposedly *was* the fire at that point, Carlos in effect was trying to save Florinda from her "enlightened" self!

Whether allegory or truth, I felt the story was a lesson about the need for careful and impeccable relationships to power. This feeling increased when Carlos concluded the anecdote by telling us he was later diagnosed as having developed a hernia as a result of his sudden lunge! As in his books, Carlos in person displayed an utter lack of self-consciousness or embarrassment in relating his moments of weakness.

Having lost his detachment during Florinda's final gesture, Carlos continued, his role as leader once again was in question by the members of his party. When don Juan was here, the latter had endeavored to teach Carlos to live with power. Then he departed from this world, leaving Carlos to do just that. Carlos expressed this with an air of deep meaning and intimated that, on his own, it had been difficult to hold to and live with the teachings of don Juan.

Over the years since don Juan left, the teachings had taken Carlos to making many changes in his outer identity, as part of the *art of stalking*. He said this had included working as a short-order cook in a major city in Arizona, as well as menial jobs in other urban areas. Spiritual discipline wasn't only to be practiced in exotic places like the Sonora, he was telling us, but was something to be applied anywhere and everywhere.

Then he went off on a particularly jarring tangent. After don Juan left, Carlos said he had explored a variety of spiritual teachings from many cultures. He'd even gone to see a Taoist master who allegedly took one look at Carlos, fell down the stairs and died as a result. I became uncomfortable with Castaneda's cavalier rendition of this story, and my feelings intensified as he continued. He maintained no teacher or spiritual path came close to offering what don Juan had taught him, and so he had abandoned his search and set himself beyond future outside help. I noticed that Sean had a wry expression from hearing this total invalidation of all the world's spiritual knowledge.

Sean glanced around and took an energy reading of Tess, Rose and Selena at that point. He told me later each one of them appeared to be in a rigid state of hypnotic trance. He became concerned about their passive fixation on Carlos. Selena was too far away for him to deal with directly, but he immediately touched Tess and Rose on the back and used his *will* to shake them out of their trance. To my relief, they responded by sitting up straighter and appearing more dynamic in their involvement.

Sean then nudged me and whispered, "Someone else arrived late besides Selena." I quickly scanned the back of the room, and there were three women sitting together who had not been there earlier. They looked unlike anyone else in the audience, elegantly dressed and wrapped in shawls, each with silvery-gray hair. It was hard to guess their ages as they were all heavily made-up, and they could have been anywhere from their mid-fifties to mid-seventies. I turned back around, wondering who they were.

Castaneda was moving into the last phase of his talk. Sean later dubbed this as Carlos's "end of time" speech. Carlos began telling us he might be the last of his line's naguals—their spiritual leaders. His emotional dance with the audience now entered its most poignant and powerful stage.

Rumor had it, in recent years, that Carlos had been showing up quietly here and there around the "New Age" spiritual scene, particularly on the West coast, looking for a possible nagual successor. Evidently he hadn't found one, for he was now before us quietly explaining that their line was doomed, there was no new junior nagual, no new sorcerer's party, nothing but himself and the remnants of the party don Juan had put together for him before leaving. Despite my various unanswered questions about Castaneda and his stories, at this point I found myself being drawn into his pathos and had to restrain an impulse to leap up and volunteer Sean, myself and my friends to carry on the tradition.

Then Carlos switched tones, and moved from this heart-wrenching lament to a mode of "not-caring." He assumed a rather existential stance, telling us that don Juan himself had sensed perhaps this would happen, and that there was nothing left to do but to use the teachings as best he could for his remaining time on earth. There were a number of people dabbing at their eyes by now.

Last came the third tone, what Sean later called the final pitch. Carlos began to tell us that in fact, he was looking for a group of people who would take don Juan's teachings seriously. As he warmed to his subject, he said he would be willing to return again and again, free of charge, to teach such a group. He vowed he had nothing to gain from this, if only he could teach. Among the audience, tears were now being replaced by naked expressions of eagerness and hope.

Over the next half hour, he went through each of these three modes several times over, whining about the end of the line, then turning cold and disinterested, and again begging for people who would take the teachings seriously, even though he had nothing to gain from this himself. The audience moved from practically choking over the end of don Juan's line, to being stunned that Carlos might be offering to teach, to gripping the edge of their seats as it appeared he might retract the offer, over and over until almost everyone was limp from the process.

The fact that Carlos was even bringing up an apparent willingness to teach was surprising. After all, since the early seventies people by the thousands had been swearing they'd follow him anywhere, do anything if he'd teach them, and he'd been staunchly refusing and retiring to anonymity ever since. What was suddenly pulling on Carlos so strongly to cause this radical turn-around?

Suddenly Carlos turned in our direction and, beaming toward Sean and myself, asked us to become his apprentices.

Carlos's closing words were lost to me in the stunned aftermath of his offer. I realized he was finished when he walked past us, heading toward another area for the last minute questions and greetings of his audience. Never once over the course of the evening had he sat in the chair that had been placed there for him.

When he was almost out of the room, someone called "Carlos!" The author stopped in his tracks and turned slowly around. There at the front of the room in the formerly empty chair sat Sean like the young successor to the throne, glowing with suppressed mirth and energy. Their eyes met, Carlos laughed and made a gesture that was almost a salute, and then turned again to continue out of the room.

As I watched Carlos disappear with Tess, Rose and Selena trailing after him in the crowd, I shook my head and tried to figure out just what had transpired over the last few hours. But it was a futile gesture. I would have to wait, meditate, integrate and dream.

In the meantime, I wandered off to browse through the book store. A few minutes later Sean came up behind me from between a row of books and whispered, "Well, Josie, I think something happened between you and the last paperback hero."

"What do you mean?" I laughed.

"Of all the major spiritual authors of the new age, Carlos was the one you had most wanted to meet. And your *will* has gained a great deal of power and knowledge from this encounter—and from the first one as well."

"Well, if that's so, I hope my *will* confides in me some day, because my mind hasn't a clue what was really going on tonight!" I replied.

Then a flurry of motion caught my eye. After spending time with his enthused post-speech audience, Carlos was finally leaving the building. The three older women who'd come in late swept out after him, lining up quickly on either side of him once they were outside, and clasping elbows with each other and Carlos. Sean nudged me and teasingly asked me if I thought they might be the "little sisters," the supposed remaining women dreamers of Carlos's party known as Rosa, Lydia and Josefina.

As we watched them, slowly following behind them at some distance, it appeared as if the women were almost lifting Carlos off the ground as they strode energetically forward.

When they reached the end of the block, they suddenly stopped, and the whole line turned as a unit to face us. We gazed at each other across time into an unknown future and a mockingbird suddenly exploded into song. Then a warm Sonoran wind came up from behind Sean and me, and as it reached the others, ruffling their hair and clothing, Carlos and his line turned again and disappeared around the corner. They left an empty space that shimmered briefly before being engulfed by the dark, mysterious night.

***

That empty space was soon filled by more mysterious power. Several days after returning from Los Angeles, we were invited to another all-night ceremony with our Dinch friends. Although Emily wasn't physically present, through our dreaming bond she began teaching me how to strengthen my *double* or astral body. I also sent my *will* out to connect with Carlos, hoping to take him up on his offer to teach us before such time as we were to meet again in person. But in this effort I was disappointed, for he seemed vague and unable to add anything to Emily's knowledge of the *double*. I was baffled, for this was the person who had supposedly learned so much about the subject from his teacher Don Juan. I finally set this riddle aside for the time being and went on to enjoy the rest of the ceremony.

Afterwards Sean and I spent a number of hours visiting and eating with the other participants from the ceremony before finally leaving for home. It was now early afternoon, and as we drove south through the desert heat, I was finally getting groggy and looking forward to a shower and bed. I'd been sitting on hard, dusty earth for fifteen hours, felt as grimy as a fillet dipped in corn meal, and every bone ached.

My mind was wearily but doggedly trying to sort out the many experiences I'd had throughout the night when suddenly Sean gestured to something ahead of us. I searched the horizon, wondering as I often did at moments like this, what kind of thing to start looking for. I did not have Sean's acuity of vision, nor was it clear if he was pointing out something near or miles ahead, up in the air or on the ground, plant, mineral, animal or Other.

Then my eyes locked onto it and certainty gripped my mind. Roughly five or six miles away was a giant whirlwind, a true *diablando* churning up sand as it roared along. It was one of the largest I'd seen, looming hundreds of feet in the air like some mythical, imperious Mongol warrior about to conquer the desert. It was an awesome presence.

"Grab it with your *will*!" Sean said. "See if you can hold on till we catch up to it."

The prospect seemed to me like trying to grab a tiger by the tail. Not only was I uncertain if it was even possible, but I wasn't convinced it was advisable. Then Sean pressed on my back, all thoughts ceased, and my *will* made its own decision. It gathered its energy, coiling in my belly like a snake about to strike, and then launched itself through space and hooked onto the whirlwind. As we barreled down the road, fatigue was left in the dust and I was filled with a fierce exultation.

That day riding along in the desert, I had an appointment with power, an appointment Sean had predicted long ago when he had led me to face the four winds at my mountain retreat. As the *diablando* swirled up ahead of me, I held onto it with all the *will* I could summon. When we came within about a mile of it, I was amazed the swirling monster was still going strong, for most whirlwinds usually dispersed fairly quickly. Finally we had to leave the highway and make some zigzags on a few back roads until we got as close to it as we were going to get by car.

The giant was poised a few hundred feet away, throwing sand and debris into the air. From this close, it looked totally intimidating.

As soon as he braked the car, Sean yelled "Go!" and once more my mind stopped and I leaped out of the car. I took a few running steps toward the *diablando* and suddenly it exploded toward me. Within a breath it was twenty feet away and coming *fast*.

Then it split in two, and the first half raced at me and crossed the front of my body, grazing my belly, almost knocking the wind out of *me* and sending me reeling. In a moment it was gone, and I was totally absorbed in catching my breath and watching the other half, which had been barely restraining itself.

Moments later, the second half was upon me *and around me until I was at the calm center…Energy shimmered everywhere. I was in a dream, another world. Breathing deep into my belly, I felt my* will *being pulled taut into the wind. My hair was electrified, serpentine in the air.*

Power flowed through me like lightning down a lightning rod, and I gathered it and grounded it deep in my womb.

Ecstasy filled me in that timeless space, and I had to dance, to dance with the diablando, *with this swirling gift of power that had embraced me like I belonged there at its center. I had to dance my thanks to the wind, to the earth beneath my feet, for all the mysteries large and small, for the breath within me, for the magnificence of being alive, and for the light pouring through me.*

And so I began to spin myself, there at the center of creation. My arms came up, my head tipped back, and I turned and turned. And it almost seemed the diablando *was still and I was all that was moving. I was Whirlwind Woman, spinning through time, spinning through the desert, landscape of dreams...*

And as I danced with the four directions, embracing them all, singing to them, laughing, urging them on in a spiraling gyre, past the exuberance, wild ecstasy and motion, I found the calm center at the core of my whirling body, the shimmering absolute dancer's center of stillness.

***

A few days later, Sean and I talked briefly about the experience. As he'd done with Rose when he first met her, he often advised me to wait at least several days after encounters with power before speaking of them. I learned to appreciate this over time, though at first it felt like trying to suppress a nervous twitch. Like most people, I was used to seeking a listening ear as soon as possible for important happenings in my life. Over a period of following Sean's recommendation, I found that if I didn't speak of an event for a while, it not only continued to reverberate longer inside me, but more details of it would surface in my memory. He said this was from "holding the self sealed."

When we discussed my encounter with the *diablando*, I told Sean I'd felt massive power flow into my entire being as I spun in its center. Sean *saw* this energetically, and told me my body appeared to turn white, as if it were illuminated from within. He felt that what happened to me involved a deep spiritual bond between myself and *diablandos*, and over time I found this to be true. After that day I had some kind of eerie connection with the whirlwinds. They would come and chase around my house, sometimes pounding on the roof and making the house shake, sometimes dancing outside in the garden as if waiting for me to come out and play. And in the future, I was to have many other opportunities to dance in the center of their power.

***

As the weeks passed in the little ghost town, spring sashayed in dressed in all her green finery, the earth warmed and I planted a large spiral of the pink women's corn, looking forward to the time when I could give ears of it to some of my friends and students. I was integrating more and more of my recent experiences and knowledge and beginning to plan a new format of seminars for the future. I also spent time dreaming new dances for awakening people's spirits and ecstatic nature, as Emily had suggested, and anticipated teaching them somewhere down the road.

Meanwhile, on my own or with Sean when he was around, I continued to explore my strange surroundings. Sometimes power would meet me just outside my doorstep as I would sit and soak in the sun's increasing heat. When I first began doing this, the little lizards that also loved to bask in the sun would scurry away. But eventually they came to know me, and would stretch out near my feet. We would enter into a silent communion during which they occasionally nodded and winked at me, or with a turn of the head would alert me to a passing hawk or raven. Sometimes they came to my feet hungry, and would devote hours to scarfing up all the ants they could catch, in the same way that I was gathering power from my surroundings.

Sometimes I would read as I sat outdoors, and this led to another interaction with power over a period of four days. Power came disguised as a large black spider, whose body was so shiny it glistened with iridescent rainbow colors in the sun. Each day this spider would come and hop up on my arm, my hand, and especially on whatever book I was holding.

It seemed intent on distracting me from reading, and I wasn't sure whether to be irritated or amused. On the fourth day of its insistent activities, I finally asked the spider if there was something it wanted to tell me. I reached out and touched it with my *will* and waited attentively for its answer.

Finally I heard the spider's response. "You spend a lot of time reading other people's stories. But one of these days you need to write your own. The world needs a true story of a woman of power. Write your story. Weave together the strands of power from your experiences and create beauty that will touch others. That's what I came to tell you." And with that, the spider jumped off the book I was holding and scampered away, never to interrupt my reading again. I took its words seriously, and shortly afterwards began to write.

Sometimes power would call in the night, and Sean and I would go racing out to witness the spectacular lightning storms leaping back and forth across the big desert sky. Our *will*s loved the raw intensity and would surge out of our bellies to gather some of the crackling energy back into our bodies. Other times we would slip outside in the middle of the night and Sean would move behind me, hold my belly and shake out my *will*. Almost every time he did this, a star would shoot across the sky, exploding with light and leaving a brief afterimage of its streaking flight.

Sean himself was a reflection of power. I made various efforts to learn more about Sean the person. He accommodated me to a certain extent, but getting to know him like I'd gotten to know other people in my past just didn't happen. Over and over, he turned me back to knowing myself, my *will* and my own link to spirit. Over time I grew more accustomed to living with a mystery named Sean, who became part of Mother's backdrop as he harmonized and blended in with the winds, the insects, the birds and the earth.

Day after day, night after night, we made numerous efforts to pay attention to and interact with Spirit. I had traded my past social circle for a life with Mother and other non-human forces. Although there were a few people still living in the ghost town on the edge of the Dineh reservation, I wasn't trying to meet them and create a new social aggregate. Instead, during this season while I lived in the "eagle's house," I was saving myself for my most constant friends: Spirit and power. Every night I slept and dreamt wrapped in their cocoon, every day I gathered them to me and walked with them.

There were many ways to experience power in all directions from my home. Some of its mysteries stretched across great distances to other places I'd been: to Joshua Tree Park and Los Angeles, to New Orleans and eagles crossing over Texas, to Mexico's sorcerers and bat caves, and to the mystical rainforests of the Pacific Northwest. But power was also close at hand, and frequently I'd walk alone or with Sean to feel its varied textures in each of the four directions. Often before starting a walk, Sean or I would pick up a magical stick he'd once found at a power place in Wyoming. The stick was a rich golden brown, and came from a tree whose branches had been twisted by the wind again and again until the grain of the wood had spiraled. Holding the stick, we would march to the end of the driveway, lift it up into the wind and let it choose the direction of our walk.

The east walk took us into the "twilight zone": down Main Street past the ghost town's only restaurant whose small, almost anonymous interior with its Formica tables and counter nevertheless gave forth the bounty of wonderful homemade pies. Occasionally we'd stop in at the old, abandoned church a little farther down the street, passing through the doorway framed by two ancient, still living cedar trees, and Sean would tell me about his original dreams of starting an ashram here in this church years ago. Finally there was the post office, its American flag proudly announcing it was still open for business, and where I would occasionally get letters from the outside world.

The west walk took us outside the town proper, as did the other two directions. The west walk was actually like stepping into a Western movie set, and we often took this route to catch the sunset. A few ramshackle old farms and stores were scattered here and there, any paint stripped long ago by the sun and wind to a pewter gray, boards missing, windows gone. A faded sign in front of one old structure advertised real desert petrified wood and Indian curios, and we'd stopped there more than once to poke around the dusty interior which now contained many shadows and minimal relics of former merchandise. A few farmers still grazed some of their cattle in the meager, scrubby fields, and startlingly large jackrabbits occasionally burst across the dusty road: the only traffic besides us. As the golden sphere of the sun would sink into its own sea of colors at the horizon and splash the snow-capped San Francisco Peaks in a final, fiery benediction, the meadowlarks would thrill us with their liquid evening concert.

Our southern walk took us down the wide, mineral-stained arroyo of a now-dry tributary of the Little Colorado River. Lined with massive cottonwoods and salt cedar, it eventually wound its way like a red snake toward the White Mountains, pinyon trees and the occasional majestic elk. The south held its secrets. Sean had often intimated he'd had contact with unusual men of power from southern Arizona and Mexico. Now and then on our south walks, a sudden wind would roar down the arroyo, sending huge tumbleweeds racing toward the Mexican border and threatening to carry Sean's hat to the finish line.

The northern route took us to my vast desert playground with its always-enticing striped hills, crystals and petrified wood. The ravens or darting flocks of tiny white birds that would suddenly erupt out of the desert scrub always matched and danced with our energy as we walked. It was in this desert that I felt the most free. There were no fences, buildings, human sounds or technology; nothing but Mother in her dreamiest of moods, calling me home and home again. Her soft-colored robes wrapped around my heart and claimed me as she had long claimed the ancient Bedouins wandering their beloved desert on the other side of the world.

Mother was sometimes gentle, sometimes threatening, but whatever her mood, my *will* and I always had to be prepared for action. There was always some underlay of order in her manifestations, unfathomable or more readily discerned, and my *will* sought to harmonize itself with it. I then used the energy I gathered on these four-direction excursions into Mother's domain to strengthen my *will* and its waking and dreaming activities.

After returning from Los Angeles, I'd given some more thought to the "witch dream" and the subject of enemies that had disturbed me so much. I realized that I did have enemies, although I still wasn't certain if they included the type Sean had described. From a certain perspective, they were all internal, the kind that everyone on the spiritual path has to deal with sooner or later. Self-importance, laziness, fear, losing sight of goals and energy-draining indulgences all ended up on my personal inventory. I could endlessly seek excuses for my habits and remain a prisoner of my past, my conditioning, or I could pursue freedom through awareness and the exercise of choice.

The inertia of social interactions was another potential enemy. I'd seen how with familiar people in a familiar environment, we humans can easily allow ourselves to drift toward spiritual unconsciousness. Moving to the eagle's house had been a wise choice for me at this stage of my life. Getting out of the city and breaking free of the known was giving me a chance to solidify new ways of relating to myself and to spiritual power.

There was one more element I could see that was antagonistic to my spirit, and to the spirit of many women. This was the continuing oppression of women's minds, hearts, bodies and spirits, and the battlefronts were everywhere, from the New Age community to the mutilation rituals still practiced in other cultures. And yet, even this oppression which seemed so much to be coming from the outside—from patriarchal or sexist attitudes—was an internal issue to the extent that women had internalized the attitudes and were still oppressing themselves.

I hoped some day to be free of the clutches of all of my enemies, whether inner or "outer," and knew I'd need a good deal of energy and awareness to do so. One aspect of the battle was still raging in my dreams.

One night as I slept, an old woman had suddenly popped into the dreamscape. She had a long gray braid and terrifying, hard black eyes. The woman caught me in her powerful gaze in a manner similar to that of the male witch of my other dream. She stood immobile except for a rhythmic contraction of her throat. The weird movements continued and she slowly began to open her mouth. Something was between her lips. As I stared in horror, a lizard's head emerged, its eyes a miniature reflection of the old woman's, and equally intimidating. Bit by bit, the rest of the creature crawled out of her mouth, eyes fixed on mine, slowly gathering itself to pounce on me.

Somehow I knew if the lizard managed to land on me, I would be in deep trouble. With that realization I was able to break my paralysis. I brought the palms of my hands together and aimed my fingers like a weapon at the lizard. Then I summoned *will* and began to direct it up from my belly and out through my fingertips. I kept pushing and pushing with my *will*, trying to drive the lizard back into the old woman's body. Finally the creature began to retreat, until at last its head disappeared and the woman's mouth closed, her throat rippling once again as the lizard made its way downward. She glared at me for a moment, then bowed her head slightly and disappeared.

I awoke feeling energized and victorious after this dream, in contrast to the state I was in after my nightmare with the male witch. However, this was not the end of my dreaming battles. I began to have a long series of confrontations with a hostile group of men who would appear individually or in twos and threes, varying from night to night. Some of the men looked vaguely familiar, some did not, some were white and some were amerindian. And the figure of the male witch was one of them. Every time one or more of these men would appear in my dreams, they would first appear to be flirting, then would begin taunting me, and finally would become menacing and try to physically attack me.

In each of these demanding dreams, I used every tactic I'd learned in women's self-defense courses to try to overcome those tyrants. First I would try to walk away from them, then I would try to verbally defuse the situation, and finally, when none of these attempts succeeded, I would begin to physically fight for my life, using the kicks, punches and other maneuvers I knew. I'd even kick them really hard in the balls, and they'd just stand there smiling. The men were completely immune, invulnerable to my every effort. For a long while nothing worked, and I would waken from the dreams exhausted and frustrated.

Finally, as my months of power-gathering practices began to pay off and my *will* grew stronger, I began to turn this dreaming strand around. Emily also helped in the sense that she began to teach me methods of spiritual self-defense, methods I applied consciously in both normal and dreaming states. The cumulative power of all these practices resulted in success. One by one my dreaming enemies were vanquished, never again to darken my dreams with their evil intentions. Who they all were, I may never know, or from what reality, inner or outer. What I am certain of is that I summoned power and *will* to defeat them.

Seventeen

The clouds are hovering close to the hills of New Mexico,
The ancient magic lays in the earth, gold of New Mexico.
Children are dreaming as hawks soar high keening since long ago,
Apache songs echo from holy mountaintops quiet as snow.

And the road is a river that carries us on
To the spirit that never has ever gone
From New Mexico...

from "Dreams of New Mexico"

One afternoon as I stood in the spiral of women's corn whose young green leaves were brushing at my ankles, I heard a car pull up in the driveway. I peered through the high, dry stalks of last year's weeds and saw a slender woman with a long dark braid step out of the car and make her way toward the front porch.

"Hey!" I yelled, racing the length of the garden and rushing to greet her. It was Brooke Medicine Eagle, come to visit for a few days.

I'd first met Brooke over a decade earlier at the shamanism seminar at Esalen. Since then our paths had crossed from time to time. We had several interests in common: singing, a love of nature, and human spirituality. What I hadn't known until more recently was that Sean had worked with her some years ago.

Sean had played some similar roles in Brooke's life and mine. He'd told me power originally directed him to rescue her from a spiritually and socially stagnant situation in Oklahoma, where she was living at that time.

Once he'd helped her liberate herself, he'd taken her through the Southwest and on to the West Coast, connecting her more deeply both to places on the land and to other people he'd been teaching. She'd been struggling to integrate his impact on her ever since.

At this time of her life, Brooke was somewhat overwhelmed with lecture tours and writing a book that included much of what she'd learned from Sean. Given the circumstances, her coming to visit us for several days in Arizona was an unusual break in her schedule, one Sean hoped to pack with spiritual practices and events.

"Howdy," said Brooke as we embraced. "So this is the ghost town."

We laughed and I helped bring her luggage into the house. Sean had been sitting at the kitchen table writing, but he put down his pen and looked up as we entered. Without speaking, he fixed Brooke with an intense gaze, then strode across the room and silently touched her belly, her back and the top of her head.

"Well," Brooke said finally, breaking the silence, "find anything interesting?"

"Sure," Sean replied with a smile, and the atmosphere lightened slightly. The next few days were spent in desert walks, relaxation and conversation. It became obvious early on that Brooke was fatigued from her travels and was not up to the rigorous spiritual demands Sean might have otherwise made on her time and energy. However, they did spend time discussing some of her recent dreams, visions, and the progress of her book. Having read a great deal of the New Age literature, Sean's *will* had told him that some of the alleged "true journeys" of spiritual discoveries and teachers were at least partly fictional. He'd encouraged Brooke to write her story as a counterbalance to the situation.

Brooke was a strong woman who'd had her share of life's challenges. During her visit, I learned a little more about the difficulties she'd experienced being part Nez Pierce and Sioux but growing up on the Crow reservation with old intertribal animosities. Crow kids used to literally spit on her and insult her about her background. She'd had to defend herself physically in more than one fistfight, and had become partly toughened as a result. Later in life, she'd moved through the predominantly Anglo community at college, and then through the Anglo and Native interface of shared spiritual interests. In these milieus, she'd often struggled with issues of identity and questions about where she belonged.

Brooke had faced a variety of obstacles and challenges in her search for spiritual teachings from her own Native people. The one powerful Indian woman who had spent time with Brooke—Stands Near the Fire—was an exception in Brooke's experience, and one for which she was deeply grateful. However, despite her earlier dreams of becoming more of a traditionalist, Brooke had a different destiny. The inexplicable reluctance of Indian elders to teach her forced Brooke to rely on her own experiences and knowledge from many paths, not only for her personal development but to create the seminars she now offered. Sean had supported her in her efforts as much as he could.

We'd all just finished a late breakfast the last day of her visit, when suddenly Sean and I heard a strange rustling in the nearby field of last year's cornstalks. We grabbed Brooke's hands and dashed outside. Across the road a *diablando* was tearing through the field, pulling hundreds of dry corn leaves from their stalks as it flew toward us, rattling and hissing loudly like an airborne sidewinder.

The whirlwind came to within about thirty feet of where we stood, and then it gathered itself and jumped! The massive leap carried it just in front and above us, where it began to lose some of its intimidating momentum.

As it moved higher, gentle slow-motion swirls of corn leaves floated there dreamily for a few moments like a golden halo against the turquoise sky. The initial swirling motion had all but disappeared, and yet the leaves stayed clustered by an invisible magnetic force. Then, hovering directly above, the formless *diablando* began to drop its bounty, which descended lightly upon the three of us. When this surreal shower ended and the *diablando* held only a few remaining leaves, it jumped again, landed on the garden behind us, and went racing and spinning off until we lost sight of it. We were left standing in a small and becalmed sea of the *diablando's* golden gifts.

Sean and I were stunned by this unique demonstration of power's artistry, but Brooke went nonchalantly back into the house as if nothing had happened. Perhaps such events were commonplace for her. Nevertheless, the omen had come to bless her, this part-Indian woman, with the energy of corn, the food of her people, and with the power of the wind. Just as with all of us when Spirit touches our lives, it was up to her what she would do with it.

***

Not too long after Brooke's visit I acquired a new neighbor. Sandra was one of my friends who had been touched by Sean and the spirit wind that blew through my circle of acquaintances shortly before I'd moved to Arizona. Apparently she had taken her experiences to heart. She and Selena were close friends, and the two of them had decided that Sean was a "nagual" like Castaneda's don Juan. Sandra's life had been rearranged by her encounters with Sean, and she began asking me to keep an eye out for possible nearby rentals so she too could move to the ghost town and have more access to Sean's teachings.

I was delighted she was even considering such a move, and when occupants of the house nearest mine left the ghost town as so many others apparently had, Sandra made her decision and moved in shortly thereafter.

Sandra already had a partly developed *will*. It was in strange shape because much of its strength was due to having survived repeated struggles with a dark sorcerer to whom she'd once been married. Among other things, this Indian man had a predilection for strange rituals, and had repeatedly tried to convince Sandra to let him ritually "initiate" her teenage daughter into sex as one of his practices. Sandra had refused to allow this and left him soon after, as she wasn't sure she could trust him to honor her demand. Although this man who she'd originally seen as spiritually knowledgeable and intriguing turned out to be a monster who'd dominated her for years, a core of her spirit had remained intact. However, at the time she met Sean, her *will* was still partly angry and jumpy from the ordeal and from the fact Sandra had never mastered dealing with her ex-husband's domination. Her *will*, sensing its opportunity for freedom, was extremely demanding that Sean help her.

In many ways she didn't look like most people's fantasy of a prime candidate for being a woman of power. She was plump and middle-aged, had several grown children, and her subservient and retiring qualities, especially around men, completely masked the power of her *will*. Because of the kind of social conditioning most of us receive, Sandra, like many other women, was somewhat insecure, emotional and often moved to jealousy. She also had a very warm, nurturing side, and loved to mother people of all ages. But if one wasn't nurturing or being nurtured by her in the ways she was used to, insecurity would set in.

Sean was delighted at the challenge she presented. "Sandra's *will* has a life of its own," Sean exclaimed several weeks after she'd become our neighbor, bemused at the juxtaposition of her *will*'s powerful displays and her emotional outburst of anxieties just moments earlier.

Often, if Sean was in some interaction with power, Sandra's *will* would respond and make her belly jerk, or cause other strange motions in her body. This would happen regularly if Sean was touching her back or *will* center, but sometimes took place just being in his general proximity. Because of the intensity of response, Sean was convinced that Sandra was consciously aware of what he was doing with power. Yet most of the time she wasn't, and would endlessly beg him to explain what he was doing and what was going on. It was as if her *will* was a team of horses, and the burden they were dragging behind them was her mind. I was more than sympathetic, having experienced the same dilemma numerous times myself.

I faced my own challenges with Sandra. On the one hand, it was nice to have the companionship of a woman friend, and to know there was someone with whom I could spend time when Sean was on one of his numerous travels. However, ostensibly our reason for living out here in the middle of nowhere was to have a concentrated environment for focused spiritual development. Conditions for this were optimal. Sandra had a part-time business she operated out of her house, and I could choose my seminar teaching schedule, so our time was much freer than that of most people. And there was nothing nearby in the way of entertainment as a distraction from our goals. The biggest potential distraction soon became our relationship.

Occasionally I would tear my hair and tell Sean, "I don't know if Sandra is a blessing or a curse in my life at this point!"

"Maybe she's a blessing in disguise—a very powerful disguise," he once commented.

Every time Sandra and I were together, I had to struggle against the tendency to drift into the ever-present jaws of social habit. Sandra loved to gossip about mutual acquaintances, go over the astrological forecasts for the next month, and a variety of other engaging but non-essential topics. These subjects were more than enticing for my mind, which relished the opportunity to be set loose from the focused grip I'd tried to maintain on it for the past few months. I attempted to find a balance between allowing some time for this kind of social interaction and more *will*ful activities. But frequently I'd try to remind Sandra about our spiritual goals and our need to support one another in sticking to them.

"You know, Sandra, Sean and I try to follow some basic practices here, and some of them have to do with talking," I commented again one day.

"I know, I know," she said, her round face tightening in irritation. "But I have this real adversity to spiritual rules since living with that man who ended up being such a creep. He was always bossing me around and telling me what I could and couldn't do with my spiritual life. Once, when I wanted to go to a Native American Church ceremony, he told me if I ever ate peyote, it would kill me. And now, here I am in Arizona, with a new set of rules and you two offering to take me to a N.A.C. ceremony some day."

"But Sandra," I said, slightly taken aback by her response, "you're the one who wanted to come here. You'd already met Sean, and you and I had talked on the phone a number of times about our efforts to be focused. So it wasn't like you were lured out here under false pretenses. You said this was what you wanted: an environment with certain spiritual structures—like an ashram—that would help you get out of your old habits! And that you were excited about going to the Church with us some day."

Sandra stared at me intently. Finally she said, "I know I'm being irrational, Josie. When I do succeed at keeping my big mouth shut and focus more on *will*, I can really feel myself becoming more centered and powerful. I know that's the purpose of the rules, guidelines, whatever, that you two have suggested. It's just hard sometimes to separate out my past experiences and to remind myself that the goal of your practices is very different than those of my ex. My ex wanted to imprison me with his rules, and you and Sean want to help set me find my freedom with yours."

"And old habits die hard, too," I smiled. "I've got plenty of my own I struggle with."

Despite the difficulties in avoiding the shark's teeth of habit which were always waiting to consume all our energies, we managed to practice various exercises of *will* together and enjoy Mother's ever-present mysteries. Sometimes we would go over Sean's "lecture series," as we affectionately termed them, to try to better understand them.

These sessions took place frequently whenever all three of us got together. One afternoon Sean had spent some time talking about ways in which spiritual power had been used both appropriately and inappropriately over the course of human history so that we could all better understand issues of power in the present. Sandra and I were silently trying to absorb the information as we sat in her living room. Suddenly I felt something grab my *will*. I looked up. Sean was already on his feet striding rapidly toward the front door. I immediately raced after him, knowing instinctively a *diablando* was on the way and that Sean intended to meet its power as he often did.

This day however, by the time Sean got to the door, something about the power made him alter his plan. He stopped, and like the perfect butler, opened the door for me as if my carriage had just arrived. He'd had enough time to see the *diablando* through the window, and decided in an instant that this one was not for him.

I stepped out the door and had a few moments to watch a distinctly feminine *diablando* that seemed to be shyly tiptoeing down the road, hesitating and hiding here and there. It was small in stature, perhaps twelve feet high, and was slower spinning than the giant I'd danced with after the ceremony months earlier. As it touched the front of the yard, it picked up bunches of freshly mown green grass. Meandering toward us, it then threw small portions out to one direction or another, like a young girl tossing flower petals for a processional.

Finally and gently, the *diablando* and I intersected, and I spun once again in the welcoming center, amidst the slow and delicate spiraling of grass cuttings. The mood was delicious, light and playful, like a champagne bath. Sean later told me I'd changed colors again, that a rosy flush of youth and vitality had come over me as I whirled.

After our brief and lovely duet, the *diablando* moved on, trailing its green garment behind until it disappeared from sight.

Sandra caught only a glimpse of our dance before the *diablando* left. According to Sean, after I'd rushed out the door, rather than swinging into action herself she'd become sluggish and started trying to talk to him and ask him what he was doing and what I was doing and what was happening. By the time she finally got outside and around the corner of her house, she'd missed most of my dance with the spiraling visitor, but saw enough to immediately feel jealous and left out.

"How ironic," Sean commented to me afterwards. "Power came right to her house, practically to her doorstep. And in fact, she was standing closer to the door than you. When I opened it, I was thinking the *diablando* was waiting for her, if not both of you. I opened the door to power for her, but because she hesitated in going through, she missed its gift. I think she's still a little confused about her relationship to power and to her own *will*."

Power presented countless other opportunities to Sandra, but like most of us, her struggles with her past and personal insecurities sometimes got in the way of her taking advantage of them. She was often a mirror of both my own frailties and strengths like other friends—and family—have been. And even her ongoing love of gossip provided us both another chance to learn about power in one unusual situation.

"Guess what, Josie," she told me with a gleam in her eye one evening as she burst into my home.

"What's up?" I asked. I could see Sandra was on the verge of exploding with news.

"I've just been on the phone with a friend of mine, and there's a whole lot of turmoil going on about L. and her books."

The woman Sandra spoke of—and who I will refer to as Laila—was the author of a series of "woman power" books. Curious about Laila and the female teachers of her stories, I'd gone to see her shortly after her first book was released. At the time I'd had my fill of male teachers and their antics, had not yet met Alsinor, and was hoping to find some women of knowledge who could enhance my spiritual development. I wanted to meet Laila primarily so she would introduce me to her teachers. The results of our several encounters were—for me—both disappointing and hilarious.

Laila made it fairly clear at the beginning that it was unlikely I'd have a chance to meet her teachers, which was a letdown. However, she said they had approved her to carry out some of their teachings to those who were interested. So despite my disappointment, I decided to see what Laila might teach me and we agreed to meet a few times.

At first I'd hoped that I'd learn something substantial, and I tried some of her suggestions of exercises and guided journeys. She told me the journeys would enable me to find my spiritual guides. And I actually did encounter one female character as I journeyed into the world of spirits. Upon asking her what I could learn from her, she promptly told me Laila

was a fake! I was a bit taken aback by this information, but when I
returned from my journey and Laila asked for the details, I faithfully
reported the results.

Laila became quite flustered and then tried to cover her emotions by
insisting this character I'd met on the spirit journey must be a *heyoka*—a
contrary—who always said the opposite of what he or she meant. I was
somewhat dubious about this interpretation, especially after, at Laila's
insistence, I went back to the spirit realm and confronted the character
again. This time the latter became extremely irate and said she was no
heyoka, that she was calling the shots as she saw them, and that I could do
whatever I damned well pleased with the information.

Shortly thereafter, I terminated my brief relationship with Laila and
continued my search. But over the years I would occasionally hear rumblings about the veracity of her stories. By the time Sandra brought the
issue back to my attention, I'd found a number of discrepancies in Laila's
books that pointed to the likelihood that they were allegorical fiction. My
attitude about this alternated between two primary points of view. One
was irritation that her readers—largely women—were being misled.
Second—and partly from my own experience—was that we are capable of
learning from—and despite—a variety of situations, including fiction and
even charlatans. When Sandra brought the issue of Laila's books to my
attention, I found myself once again in the middle of a sorting-out process
on the subject that was apparently still ongoing.

"What kind of turmoil?" I asked in response to her statement.

"Well," she said, her brow furrowed with concern, "it's beginning to
sound like Laila didn't even write her own books. A close friend of 'Jack'
says that Jack is the real author, and his friend would have no reason to lie."

Sandra then proceeded to track down Jack's phone number, a man who
had been included in a minor but powerful role in Laila's early books. I
decided to pursue the mystery further, called Jack on the phone and
responded to his invitation to meet him in person. Sean accompanied me.

***

Since the drive to see Jack would take us the better part of a day, Sean and I headed east early in the morning. At Albuquerque we turned north and began the gradual ascent toward the Sangre de Cristo Mountains and Santa Fe, where we stopped briefly for lunch. The picturesque center of town was replete with Southwest architecture, a growing proliferation of art galleries, and with tourists. In the outdoor plaza, Pueblo artisans hawked their wares of jewelry, pottery and woven rugs, creating a colorful palette against the dusty rose backdrop of the surrounding adobe buildings.

After eating, we managed to escape town without succumbing to Santa Fe's siren calls to buy, buy, buy, and continued north. The highway cut through the famed Rio Grande Valley which was flanked on both sides by the green, higher ground of the Santa Fe National Park. We slipped by little towns with Spanish and Pueblo names—Nambe, Pojoaque, Chimayo—as we climbed steadily toward Taos.

We left the highway some miles outside of Taos. Over the next few miles, the road sloughed off its pavement like a desert snake shedding its skin, leaving us on the kind of deep-rutted and washboard dirt road now familiar to us from our many back road adventures in Arizona. Finally we pulled into a long, dusty driveway and parked in front of what, according to our directions, was Jack's house.

Sean and I sat in the car for a few minutes as we'd grown accustomed to do when we visited our Dineh friends. As we gave Jack time to get ready to greet us, I pulled out a cloth bag of gifts I'd brought for him. Among its contents was some of the pungent, silvery Chumash sage Sean and I had gathered in California, some fragrant cedar, and tobacco—a traditional Native gift of exchange for teachings or ceremony.

"Are you ready for your hunting expedition?" asked Sean quizzically, as I sat gathering my power together. "Do you know what you're after?"

"I think I'm about ready," I replied. "What I'm after, Sean, is knowledge. Ever since I was a child I've considered books to be my friends and companions. I realize there's such a thing as 'poetic license' on behalf of a good story, but total fabrication is something else. I want to know the truth about the books. And for my own peace of mind and trust in my spirit guides, I want to know if that long-ago, supposed *heyoka*'s statement about Laila's authenticity was on the mark or not. So that's what I'm after."

We got out of the car and walked to the porch of the sprawling, one-story adobe house with its small, covered veranda off to the side. The door opened several moments after my knock, and I had my first look at Jack. *Irish?* I wondered, taking in his fair skin and the faint streaks of auburn among his mostly graying hair. His facial complexion was that of a man who'd lived hard, and he later confirmed he'd recently put the bottle and other substances behind him in an effort toward cleaner living.

"Hello," I said, extending my hand. "I'm Josie, this is my friend Sean, and I'm hoping you're Jack."

He smiled as we all shook hands. "Pleased to meet you both, and yeah, I'm Jack. Come on in and make yourself at home."

As we sat in his living room, Jack offered us iced tea. "I'm not going to offer you any coffee or booze," he said. "I used to drink, smoke, and indulge in a few other things, but no more. My health started slipping, and when you feel death breathing down your neck at my age, you either pay attention and change your ways or you're asking for trouble. I decided I'd like to live out my remaining years in good health, so iced tea is what you get. Hope you don't mind."

"Not at all," I said. "I think it's great you're taking care of yourself that way."

We chatted a while longer until I felt the time was right to move on to more serious pursuits. I pulled the cloth pouch from my jacket and offered it to him, saying, "As you're already aware from our phone conversation, I've come seeking knowledge. I'd like to offer you these small gifts in exchange. I hope you'll accept them in the spirit given and be willing to help me out."

Jack accepted the pouch, opened it and peered at the contents, smiled broadly and nodded. Over the next few hours he told us his version of "the Laila books," thus responding first to my question.

"Are the rumors true? Did you actually write all those books?" I asked. "I wrote the first four," he responded.

He then recounted the circumstances surrounding the initial ideas for the books and some details that I cannot write at this time.

"But since the original four," he continued, "Laila's been reneging on some of our legal arrangements, so she's going to have to use another ghost writer now." His eyes flashed with anger. "I'm just about pissed off enough at her that I can't decide what to do first: sue her or sic one of the local witches on her. And believe me, there are some witches around here with real power. People are always seeing their green fireballs flying around the valley."

I looked at Jack in alarm. It was obvious he was furious over losing control of what he had created and of Laila. His own image was at stake. As he spoke, his eyes darted wildly about like a man possessed. It felt like these witches he was referring to already had *him* under *their* control. I became increasingly uneasy about him and his threats toward Laila. Much as I could understand angry feelings resulting from unfair treatment, I didn't think Jack's idea of resorting to witchcraft would be very good for his own spiritual health, let alone for Laila's. If Jack was speaking the truth about the books, he and Laila had *both* contributed to fooling numerous readers and would have to learn from the circumstances they'd created. But bringing even *thoughts* of witchcraft to deal with the situation was, I felt, a doomed approach. In an effort to diffuse some of his fury and intensity, I suggested taking a short break.

"Sure," he said, looking slightly baffled at the change of venue. "What do you have in mind?"

"Let's go outside," I gently suggested. "I'll get my rattle from the car and we can enjoy the late afternoon sun while I sing."

Jack trailed behind me as I collected my rattle and some more sage and cedar. I used the blessing of my rattle as an excuse to thoroughly smudge Jack as well with the soothing, fragrant smoke of my two plant friends. He slowly began to mellow out of his stormy mood. Then I sang some healing songs and peyote songs, silently calling on peyote to help this man resolve his problems without resorting to assistance from witchcraft. The sagebrush flatlands of the valley extended west from Jack's house until they finally disappeared in the greener embrace of the distant mountains. I sang softly at first, but as the power gathered around us, my singing grew stronger until I felt it could easily reach those snow-capped mountaintops. I became filled with a calm and confident strength, and knew Spirit was effectively touching both me and this strange man. Finally I stopped, breathed the fresh high desert air, and glanced over at him.

Jack's face had smoothed into more peaceful lines, a slight smile playing on his lips as he sat with closed eyes, and I felt like I might have succeeded in averting a spiritual disaster for both him and Laila. We sat quietly in the sun's warmth until finally he sighed, opened his eyes and nodded. "That was good," he said. A few moments later he added, "Maybe I don't need to sic any witches on Laila after all. She's already caught in a trap she gave her consent to and it's getting stronger all the time."

"What do you mean?"

"She's trapped in a mask."

I stared at him, starting to understand what he was getting at. He added a few more words.

"She has to keep up the image now, because if she admits I wrote the books and that the stories are made-up, her whole world will crumble around her. But you know, there might even be some good in her situation. In clinging to the mask, she's being forced to hunt around for a little power to back up her image. So maybe she'll actually learn a few things along the way."

We went back indoors, where Sean had remained sipping tea. I silently sifted through everything I'd learned so far on this "hunting expedition." Meanwhile, Sean joked around with Jack who in turn told a few tales of his own search for spiritual knowledge and experience.

"The odd thing is," Jack said pensively after recounting some of his stories, "I had some real powerful visions a while before I started working on those 'Laila' books, and they kinda provided some of the fuel for the more far-out content. And the women teachers in the books were modeled in part after some of my own female relatives. So in a way, I guess you could say there's a little reality in those books."

As the house filled with shadows and the setting sun began to paint the desert mauve and rose, I sat contemplating the world of power. It certainly wasn't what it had seemed many years ago when I first set out on my path. Apparently there were people willing to mix large portions of fiction with bits of the real thing, people who had rather diverse goals. I still felt fiction should be called fiction, but Spirit and power were moving in their mysterious ways no matter what I thought, and who defined reality anyway?

In the face of so much conflict over the nature of reality, a sudden need for something spiritually tangible washed through me with great intensity. And so I turned within, meditated and drank deeply of the only truth I would ever know for sure: my inner connection to Spirit.

Eighteen

Eshe Meo Woona, Blue Star Woman, Dawn Star Woman,
Morning water woman, come to us.

We have sat, we have sung, we have prayed from dusk to dawn,
In our hearts grows a thirst that has deepened all night long.

In the center fire burns a fire, we are purified anew,
Now the sky reflects its light and the earth is bathed with dew.

    Eshe Meo Woona, Blue Star Woman, Dawn Star Woman,
    Morning water woman, come to us.

We've been touched with vision bright and clean and medicine of pure green
dreaming
Spheres of sacred breath, each of us is clearly blessed.

Now she enters through the door, soft winds dancing with her shawl
By her hand the water's poured, she's the goddess in us all.

    Eshe Meo Woona, Blue Star Woman, Dawn Star Woman,
    Morning water woman, come to us.

                               from "Eshe Meo Woona"

When Sean and I returned to Arizona, I decided to sponsor a Native American Church ceremony. One of the peyote roadmen we'd met was

willing to take on the big job of leading the meeting, finding the necessary crew, and helping spread the invitations to any and all who wished to
attend. My role was to supply and prepare most of the food, bring tobacco
and corn husks for the prayer cigarettes, and to appoint a woman to bring
in morning water. Sean was to bring as much firewood as he could find.

I had several primary goals for sponsoring this ceremony. One was to
return the hospitality the Dineh had shown us through including us in
their homes and peyote ceremonies by being responsible for one myself.
The second was to celebrate my move to Arizona and further ground
myself here through this ceremony. I also felt like I needed the supportive
energy and prayers to sort out the turmoil following my visit with Jack.
The combined strength of the ceremonial attendees, peyote and my other
spiritual allies would undoubtedly help me come to more clarity. And
finally, I wanted to invite some of my friends to come experience the
beauty and power of this kind of ceremony.

I decided to invite Tess, Rose and Selena in addition to Sandra. These
four women were those who had been touched most strongly by the spirit
wind, and all accepted the invitation with interest and enthusiasm. To
my delight, Emily had also agreed to come and, at my request, to take on
the major role of bringing in morning water: water of life, as the Dineh
called it.

In the Native American Church ways, from dawn and morning water
on into the preparation and distribution of food, the ceremonial roles
were taken over by the women. The Dineh often spoke about how the
Church originated from a vision peyote had given to a woman, and that
the ceremony really belonged to the women. Even the moon altar was a
symbol of the feminine. Despite the fact that during the night it was the
men who served as the ceremonial leaders, at dawn it was a woman who
brought in water and grounded everyone's experiences of peyote and spirit
back into the community of humans. I felt Emily would do an impeccable job as morning water woman.

The two days before the ceremony were going to be slightly hectic. Not only would I suddenly have a house full of guests, but I also had a great deal of shopping and cooking as part of my responsibilities as sponsor. But when Tess, the first to arrive, pulled up in my driveway, I felt a surge of excitement that overrode my worries. This was really happening! After Tess and I embraced, I was glad to see that she seemed strong and happy.

Selena came next. Before I could do much more than wave at her, Sandra came dashing across the yard from her house, where she'd apparently been keeping vigil, and immediately whisked Selena away with offers of tea and a shoulder rub.

Finally Rose pulled up in her rental car. She bounded out the door with great exuberance, almost skipping up to the door where I waited, and gave me a surprisingly crushing hug for such a tiny woman.

"I feel like I'm home, y'all," she exclaimed with enthusiasm. "And you can just wipe that little bit of worry off your face, Josie, 'cause I'm in great shape this time."

"I'm more than delighted to hear that," I smiled.

"And you and Sean will be very proud of me. I've been keeping my energies more contained, feeling more powerful, and I did not tell one soul that I was coming here this weekend. I learned my lesson and I'm a reformed woman."

"Wonderful! Come on inside and make yourself comfortable."

Early that evening, I rounded everyone up in the living room and said, "It's really great you all could be here. This is a special occasion for me, and I think it will be for all of you. I want you to enjoy each other and have a chance to see some of the desert I've come to love. I'm going to be pretty busy cooking, and if anyone wants to help that would be fine with me. But I also want to make sure we have some quiet time so I can help prepare you for the ceremony itself. And I'd like to start everything off with a small blessing ceremony if that's okay with everyone."

All heads nodded in assent, so I got out my bowl of cedar and sage and my smudging fan and said a short prayer of thanks for the safe arrival of

my friends and requested that Spirit and beauty bless each of us in the following days. Then I went around with my fan and blessed each woman
with the redolent smoke of burning cedar and sage. We sat quietly in the
twilight, relishing the magic hour and tranquility. Then the spell broke,
Sandra stood up and said, "Anybody hungry?"

Sandra was in her element as Mother Hen Superior. Over the next few
days, she spent a good deal of time clucking and hovering over the rest of
us, making sure we were fed and that the three travelers had their basic
creature comforts. I was also pleased to see her struggle not to ask the others for the latest gossip, and slightly amused to overhear her shushing
them from time to time and inviting them outdoors to stand silently in
the wind. I was happy to have Sandra shepherding my guests about, as I
wouldn't have much opportunity to relax with them until after the ceremony, and Sean was out looking for firewood much of the time.

Launching into food preparations, I made an enormous stew and salad
to be served at both the pre-ceremony supper and lunch the next day. One
of the Dineh women I'd met at a previous ceremony said she'd make the
fry bread, for which I was grateful, not yet having mastered that art. I also
baked a number of deserts, some for the main meal and some to serve with
coffee or juice during the mellow extended breakfast that went on for
hours after the ceremony. Next on the list came the three traditional
dishes—meat, fruit and corn—that would be brought in with morning
water. First I cooked and diced about five pounds of beef and mixed it
with raisins and walnuts. For the fruit dish, my friends helped me make a
salad of grapes, melon, apples, oranges, coconut and peaches. And finally,
I prepared a large bowl of blue corn meal mush.

While we chopped fruit together, Tess said, "Have you done much travelling around the Southwest since you got here, Josie?"

"Some. Sean and I went to New Mexico recently."

"Yeah," said Sandra. "They were trying to find out if the rumor was
true that Jack—was the real author of the Laila books."

"Josie, didn't you tell me you'd once met Laila?" asked Rose.

"Mmm-hmm."

"Well," inquired Selena, "what did you find out on your trip?"

Sandra stopped with her cutting knife poised in mid-air. After Sean and I returned from New Mexico, she'd asked for details of our visit with Jack. Sean had told her we couldn't talk about it yet, that the power of the event was still sealing itself up. Now she was in a state of anticipation over the possibility of getting some juicy details out of me, hoping that since Sean wasn't in the house, I might be a more willing informant. But she misjudged power. I was silent for a moment, weighing whether or not to speak about the situation at this time. Suddenly a crack of thunder erupted from east of the house.

Sandra jumped slightly, and then looked around at the others. "We can't talk about it yet," she said in a small voice. "The timing's not right."

The other women stared at her, then at me. I shrugged and said, "Sandra knows what she's talking about. We better do as she says."

Meanwhile, Sean was busy scouring a nearby arroyo for dead cottonwood branches he could saw and load into the back of his car. He found enough to make several deliveries over to the ceremonial site. On one such trip, some of the roadman's helpers arrived with a large load of wood and bragged that the wood had come from all four of the Four Corner states plus one cottonwood branch from Oklahoma. They also teased Sean mercilessly for having included some salt cedar in one of his loads. Apparently salt cedar didn't burn well, its smoke stung the eyes and was generally considered "hard-up" wood to be used only if nothing better was available. Sean took the jokes in good humor, squared his shoulders and went hunting again for more cottonwood.

Finally, the evening before the meeting, we all gathered in the living room so Sean and I could talk to my friends about the structure of the ceremony. A few minutes earlier, Sean had gestured for me to go outside with him for a minute. As we stood on the porch in crisp air, he asked me if I wanted him to share some things about *will* and peyote.

"I think it would be fine, as long as you don't totally overload their circuits with a five-hour discourse," I said, remembering the mini-seminar
he'd given me before our first peyote ceremony together.

"Sure," he smiled, "but don't underestimate how alert and hungry their
wills are for more knowledge and experience. On some level, I believe
they're here to follow up on the residual power from the spirit wind that
swept through their lives a few months ago.

"Not only that, Josie, but being here with you and going to meet peyote at the Church is the culmination of some of their deepest fantasies.
They've been languishing in the cities with their crystals, consulting their
horoscopes or rubbing shoulders with a few of the "road show" Indians.
Now they're here in Dinetah, meeting real power and getting to go to a
ceremony with the Navajo, including Emily. Selena's dreaming may never
be the same after this! Your little Rose might just find her true snake
power. Sandra is overcoming her ex's threats about peyote, and who knows
what could happen to Tess. So I think they're ready to hear whatever we
have to tell them tonight."

"Okay," I laughed. "We'd better get to it, because I don't want to be up
two nights in a row."

We went back indoors where my friends were assembled expectantly in
the living room.

"Sean is going to talk to you in a while about peyote," I began, smiling
with affection at the four women, "but first I'd like to say a few things
about my experiences with 'Mr. Green'—Sean's nickname for peyote—
before describing the ceremony. Peyote is a real being, who Sean sometimes refers to as an archangel of sorts. Even without having him in my
body, peyote sometimes meets me in the wind and in my dreams, or he
comes and gives me new songs. He's a serious power, so don't approach
him like some recreational drug. In fact, peyote and the Native American
Church have helped many Indians stop drinking alcohol and taking
drugs, like the smokehouse ceremonies have done for the Northwest

coastal tribes. So a lot of Indians have a great deal of respect for peyote and the N.A.C.

"The Native American Church isn't some pagan free-for-all where people go to get high, and its also pretty different than any of our past fantasies about eating peyote with Castaneda's don Juan. The N.A.C. has a structure within which people pray and get help, healing and power. You all know I've done years of meditations and vision quests, and I've experienced incredible sweat lodges and other ceremonies. I have to say that the Native American Church is right up there at the top of the list as a serious spiritual event."

I looked around at the women. It was clear from their fascinated expressions that I wasn't boring them, so I continued.

"Like I was saying, the ceremony isn't at all pagan, despite what some ignorant or misleading authors have written. The N.A.C. really is a church. People pray and sing to Creator, to Jesus, and sometimes to the Holy Spirit. Some roadmen even place a Bible near the altar with an eagle feather on top of it. So the ceremony is a unique blend of Indian spirituality and Christianity. In the case of the N.A.C., the sacrament is peyote instead of the wine and wafers, and it's treated in the same manner: as a bridge to the Creator. The attention of the entire group is focused solidly on Creator at four specific times during the night: at the opening prayers, midnight water, the main smoke and at morning water. But peyote and the songs bring people's connection back to the mysteries of Creator and creation countless times during the night.

"As a church, the N.A.C. is different than what most Westerners have experienced. Instead of the service lasting just an hour or two, the formal service lasts about twelve hours. But most people arrive hours before it begins and stay a good four to six hours after it ends, so the communal involvement ends up being almost an entire day.

"Some Dineh go to a Native American Church meeting every weekend. And they're very proud of any family history with the church. Sometimes people will bring old fans and staffs that have been passed down to them by their parents or grandparents, and ask to have them blessed during the night."

I then went on to describe the basic structure of the ceremony from beginning to end. After I was done, Sean gave his talk.

"Before I talk about peyote and *will*," he said, "I want to tell you in advance that I won't be sitting with you during the ceremony."

I looked at him in surprise, having assumed he'd be sitting next to me as usual.

"I don't want it to look like I'm there with a harem," he scowled, and my friends nodded their heads. "I'm just going as a nobody wood-gatherer who they'll probably make more jokes about. I know Josie will do all she can to serve you throughout the ceremony, and I hope you'll be focused and supportive of her. Being the sponsor is a fairly big responsibility. Not only that, but she just might be the first *bilagaana* woman in Dinetah to sponsor a meeting, and the fact that she'll be there with four other mostly Anglo women will also be unusual.

"Now, even though Josie has described the roadman's role, in my perspective peyote is the chief, the *real* master of ceremonies. He's a strange green being who's going to take up residence in each of you for a night," he added with an intense look that belied the slight smile on his face.

My friends began to look somewhat unnerved, reminiscent of my own experience when Sean told me peyote was a Martian who was going to temporarily inhabit my body. Then he changed moods.

"Even though Mr. Green will wake up your spirit, he'll also put you in a dream state—one that can affect your nighttime dreaming forever. In fact, he can carry you off into a virtual riptide of dreaming when he's in your body, so you need to stay alert and *will*ful during the ceremony."

Selena perked up at the references to dreaming, as I was sure she would. Sean then went on to describe the importance of maintaining awareness with peyote and being active with *will*, including much of what he'd told me before we went to our first Native American Church meeting together.

After a brief period of questions, we were able to wind up the evening and get to bed at a reasonable hour, with everyone satisfied they were as prepared as they could be and looking forward to the ceremony.

The next day arrived sunny and fresh. By mid-afternoon we were packed up and on our way to the roadman's home where the meeting would take place. All the advance preparations had increased my appreciation for just how much effort went into these events. Even though my friends helped me with some of the cooking, by the time we arrived at the location for the ceremony and unloaded all the food and utensils, I was already a little tired. I started worrying about staying awake all night, about having enough energy to fulfill my goals for the ceremony, and about the two "speeches" I would need to make.

The person who "puts up" a Native American Church meeting—the sponsor—is responsible for explaining its purpose at the beginning. Later in the night at the "main smoke," he or she reminds everyone about it once again and makes some serious prayers. During those times it's common for the sponsor to thank everyone who has helped in any way, including the roadman, the firetender and the drummer. If anyone has come from a great distance, like my friends, usually they are given verbal recognition as well. These speeches would be my responsibility.

However, I wasn't the only one with responsibilities. Other people had been working hard to get ready for this ceremony as well. After storing the food, I stepped outside and gazed in admiration at the beautiful tipi that had been put up for the night ahead. It was quite large, big enough for fifty people to sit in a single circle in its interior. Hours of hard work had gone into setting up the lodge poles and draping the heavy canvas over it until everything was properly balanced. I looked up and saw a dark and magnificent white-tipped feather hanging from the air flap at the top and felt a small flutter of excitement. Eagle power would once again be with us.

As I stood in the late afternoon breeze, I could overhear my friends chatting away. Tess and Sean were off to one side of the tipi sharing witty repartees. Sandra and Selena sat on the porch together like long-lost sisters, and I could hear Selena interpreting the meaning of a dream Sandra had described to her. Rose had braided her hair and donned moccasins for the occasion, and I could hear her telling one of the young Dineh women about her Indian heritage. She'd come up to me earlier in the day full of excitement.

"Sean told me he's going to introduce me to Brooke Medicine Eagle when he gets the chance! He said she and I have some things in common 'cause of us both being mixed-bloods, and that we'd probably be good for each other. This is all just so fantastic. I'm so darn grateful you and Sean are in my life and that you included me in this gathering, Josie. Thank you, thank you, thank you!" And off she whirled like a spinning top.

I was enjoying having my friends here, despite the fact that having so much human company over the last few days—after months of mostly Nature for company—had partly worn me out. They seemed to be getting along well with one another. We'd even spent a little time meditating together the day before, to focus and remind ourselves of the spiritual purpose for all of us being together at this time.

Over the next few hours other people arrived, were fed, and began to drift into the tipi to visit in the warm glow of the fire, and the now-familiar tones of the Dineh language mixed with the conversations of my friends. Emily arrived safely in the company of her husband, and I was quietly thrilled to greet her once again in person. The sweet scent of burning cottonwood now filled the air. Having finished my kitchen obligations, I could briefly rest in the tipi and gather myself for the ceremony I had set in motion when I'd decided to sponsor it some weeks earlier.

As sponsor, I sat to the left of the roadman and cedar man, who were in the west opposite the door. My four friends sat to my left, on the north side of the tipi, and Sean sat across from us in the south, facing both us and the north—his direction of power. I was still a little nervous about being more on my own this time without Sean next to me to touch my back or to talk with if I needed him.

Despite my anxieties, after a slightly awkward beginning my initial speech went relatively smoothly. The Dineh outnumbered we six Anglos about that many times over. A few seemed to regard us with some curiosity, but all were cordial and listened attentively to my opening words. After I was done, the roadman translated for those who didn't speak much English.

Prayer cigarettes were then made, and I helped my friends struggle to master the art of corn-husk rolling. As the glowing cottonwood "lighter" stick was passed around and we began to smoke, I offered my prayers and requests for help to the Creator, peyote, and to other spiritual powers that had assisted me in the past. I blessed myself with the sage bundle as the drummer, roadman and cedar man each sang their first four songs to the accompaniment of the water drum. Then it was my turn to sing, and once again felt my love of singing these songs and the small ripple of surprise from those Dineh who had never heard me—a woman and *bilagaana*—lead a set of peyote songs.

Next came the peyote tea and powder, which went down only slightly easier than I'd experienced it other times. I saw my friends do as I'd suggested—waiting until the tea was close at hand before trying to eat their green medicine.

As the first round of singing progressed around the circle, I spent most of the time praying for the wellbeing of everyone there and for help with my personal goals for the night. Occasionally I would look over and check on my friends to make sure everyone was doing all right. Rose's eyes were as big as saucers as she took in every detail of the ceremony. In contrast, Selena's were closed and I imagined her already pursuing the trail of some dream. Tess looked bright and alert, and Sandra looked demure, eyes downcast and skirt gathered carefully around her folded legs. And across the tipi, Emily sat serenely while Sean gazed at the fire with his usual intensity.

I used the "adjustment period" before midnight water to exercise my *will* with peyote and to remind him that I needed his help and power to accomplish my goals. I also tried to take a *will*ful reading of those guests with whom I was not acquainted.

As I did, I picked up some undercurrents of ambivalence here and there around the tipi. Although everyone present had known in advance that the ceremony was being sponsored by a non-Dineh *bilagaana* and had decided to attend, apparently not every heart was completely at ease with the situation, especially because there were six of us. I sighed as peyote and my *will* helped me sort out the mixed ripples of curiosity and concern. It felt like the concern was over the possibility that a host of Anglo thrill-seekers might start inundating their ceremonies in the future.

I prayed to Creator and then asked peyote if there was anything I could do to help alleviate any such worries; to let them know our intentions were sincere and that it was most unlikely Sean and I would be showing up with hosts of Anglos in the future. Since part of my purpose tonight was to do what I could to ground myself not only in the land and my new home, but to seek good relations with those people I would be in contact with, I wanted to do what I could to further that goal.

"Send out your *will* with soothing, healing intentions," said peyote. "Pray for harmony among all of you and do what you do naturally anyway: create more beauty every time you sing."

I followed peyote's advice and I could feel my efforts having an effect. Midnight water was a turning point, with its blessings and soothing qualities and the energizing four-direction eagle-whistle prayers performed outside by the roadman. We'd all come through the adjustment period together. Peyote was helping unite us all with his "green" power, and issues of race became irrelevant. We were all bonded to one another and to the great mystery of Spirit.

Now we were moving rapidly toward the main smoke, when the prayers for the ceremonial purpose would become even deeper. I intended to make the most of the opportunity to share my hopes of living at the edge of Dinetah in peace and harmony with the land and my Dineh neighbors.

When the singing and drumming stopped for the main smoke, the road-man passed me a cornhusk, a pouch of tobacco and one of aromatic herbs to add to the smoke. While rolling my prayer cigarette, I spoke of my gratitude for this ceremonial way and thanked those who had welcomed Sean and me at other such meetings in the past. I also thanked those who had helped with the preparations and leadership of this ceremony, and introduced my friends who had traveled long distances to be here this special night. I spoke of my love for the land, and said that during the smoke I would offer prayers for the wellbeing of the Dineh who lived here now and in future generations.

After continuing on for several minutes more, I nodded to the fire-tender, who came around the tipi with the cottonwood lighter. I touched the end of my cigarette to the glowing tip and puffed a few times until the fragrant smoke began to rise. After blowing a puff to the four directions, the earth and sky, I then used one hand to bless my head and heart with the smoke. The drumming and singing began again, a powerful backdrop to the prayers I now offered up to Creator. When my prayers and four songs had been completed, I offered the smoke to my four friends. Each woman puffed four times in turn. Then I signaled the firetender to come over once again, and asked that he carry the smoke around to Sean. Once Sean finished smoking, the firetender carried the cigarette back to me.

As I had seen done at other ceremonies, I then stood and walked clock-wise around the fire until I was in front of the roadman. I extended the cigarette out toward the fire, bringing it slowly back across the peyote chief on the altar, and then handed it to the roadman to smoke. I returned to my seat by walking counter-clockwise to avoid crossing in front of the roadman and his smoking prayers. When he was finished, he then passed the ciga-rette to the cedar man, the drummer, and finally the firetender, who, as the last to smoke, then carefully placed the cigarette onto the altar coals.

Before the music began again, the roadman stood, picked up his eagle feather and a pouch of cedar and came over to me. He threw a generous handful of cedar onto the coals. Then he used the feather to waft the sweet, smoky incense in my direction, and blessed me thoroughly while murmuring prayers for my wellbeing. I felt the bit of residual tension that I'd picked up from some of the guests melt away as the cedar smoke enveloped me. Then the roadman enacted a briefer version of the same blessing for each of my women friends and finally for Sean. When he was finished, I asked for the cedar, was offered both cedar and eagle fan, walked again around the tipi and blessed Emily, her husband, and the roadman. Finally I returned to my seat, my ceremonial responsibilities complete for the moment.

I could see that my friends were doing fine, so as the singing and drumming commenced once again, I held my lovely fan of blue-green macah feathers in front of my face as others were now doing, closed my eyes, and sent out my *will*. The time was finally right to enter into dreaming with Emily. After eating the last round of peyote, I'd told him I wanted to use his energy for this purpose, and he agreed to help.

I had no problem making a strong dreaming connection with Emily. Not only had I practiced doing so many times over the past months, but now she was also in physical proximity and we were both bonded in a mutual link to peyote.

"Emily," I said as soon as I saw her moth form, "thank you for coming to the ceremony."

"My pleasure," she said. "I always enjoy the opportunity to be with my old friend peyote, and I appreciate your invitation. Is there something I can help you with tonight?"

"I hope so," I replied. "You know I've been sorting through spirituality teachers, both in person and through their books, for years now. And since I met you, I've been trying to make dreaming contact with some of them, including Carlos and his group and Laila and her teachers. There just aren't that many people who are aware dreamers, so I've tried to focus on those I thought might have the best chance of consciously remembering our contacts and developing them further. I recently discovered what I believe is probably the truth about the 'Laila books,' so I can stop banging my head against a brick wall trying to do anything with her and her 'teachers' in dreaming. And now I'm wondering about Carlos and his crew. I was hoping you could answer my questions about that group, since you've helped me with some of my dreaming efforts toward them.

"Are those people for real? They seem unable to follow through with anything they tell me they're going to do when we're in dreaming. And dreaming is supposedly one of the arts they've mastered. What's going on? Maybe it's me, and I'm just not a strong enough dreamer yet. I'm so frustrated! I don't know what to believe any more."

Emily was silent during my outburst, and then waited patiently for me to calm down a bit before she responded. When she did, it seemed at first that she was avoiding answering my questions.

"You know, dealing with issues of power is a very tricky and sometimes hazardous path," she began. "Look at you, Josie. Power came and touched you when you were just a baby, and your life has had many difficult challenges since that time." She paused and the memory of the gold light flickered through my mind once again.

As Emily had said, my path had not always been as ecstatic as that golden moment decades earlier, and she now addressed some of my difficulties.

"You have played a part in creating one of your main dilemmas. Can you guess what I'm talking about?"

I thought for a few minutes and then replied, "Has it been wanting too much, having too high expectations for my life?"

"Not exactly," Emily responded with a slight motion of her beautiful wings. "It's good to dream big. Where you and other spiritual seekers sometimes get into trouble is with your human teachers. You have a tremendous amount of spiritual energy, Josie, and throughout your history of searching for a teacher comparable to your image of don Juan, you've often draped your own power over your teachers and then mistaken it as theirs.

"Look at that old charlatan Cecil, the one you told me you took some classes with years ago. Sean was right when he said Cecil had nowhere near enough power to have been the witch in your dream. Nevertheless, when you tried out some of his suggestions for spiritual practices, you some-times had profound experiences. Isn't that right?"

I agreed, not entirely sure where Emily was going with this topic.

"And what happened after each of those experiences? In one way or another, Cecil took most of the credit, credit that you allowed him to take out of your desire to believe in him as one of your spiritual teachers. Your experiences were the result of your *own* efforts and connection to Spirit, and had nothing to do with Cecil. You were the one empowering *him*, Josie. You fed him with power over and over again, the power of your belief in him, just as you've done with other teachers in the past. But with each one, somewhere down the road you would see that teacher more clearly, move on, and go through your sorting-out process with the next one.

"The first time you met Carlos Castaneda, once again you draped some of your own power over him. The power your *will* pulled out of him the second time you saw him in person was largely your own, and your *will* was taking it back."

"That first time you saw Carlos," Emily continued, "your own *will* and *double* invested a great deal of energy into him. By the second time, what his books once represented to you had already become a reality in your own life. You didn't really need him anymore. Your *will* drew back the power it originally had surrounded Carlos with and left Carlos standing on his own. At this point in time, your own spiritual experiences easily take the place of any fantasies you once had about him or Laila and her supposed teachers.

"Now let's look at you and Sean. To a certain extent, you've also given some of your power to him. Fortunately for you, he does his best to send power back your way and encourages you toward a greater degree of *will-ful*, spiritual independence and action than others have. And Sean also encourages you to learn directly from power: from Spirit in nature, from other realms and from within yourself so that your spiritual focus isn't too centered on him.

"Your relationship to Sean isn't a one-way street, either. Your own spirit has had positive effects on him. So has your move to Arizona. When Sean was a young man, I used to feel his energy buzzing back and forth across the countryside. He did incredible acts of power out here for such a young person, but his pace was so frenetic he couldn't really ground himself. Now, partly because of you, he has a chance to let the power from the past catch up with him. He's taking time to sort things out, integrate them, and share some of the results with you. Maybe it's time for you to stop thinking you need human teachers so much, and to see that you can be involved in mutually beneficial spiritual relationships. After all, you're a teacher with a lot to share yourself, Josie."

Emily's words impacted me on many levels. What she was telling me was very empowering, even though some of it was uncomfortable. I agreed that at this point I'd amassed a great deal of spiritual knowledge, some of which I was already teaching others. My tendency to put human teachers on a pedestal was also obvious. Undoubtedly most of them had encouraged me to do so, but I'd certainly contributed to the pattern. I now felt somewhat embarrassed about this, even though I knew the pressure to give power away to authority figures was thoroughly imbedded within our culture, and perhaps in most societies. It starts with our parents, and later our teachers, bosses, politicians and even clergy continue where our parents left off.

"I feel like we humans have created a big trap for ourselves, Emily. I've been trying to learn and teach self-reliance and self-esteem for years, but it looks like I'm still in the web with everyone else. This is depressing. Maybe it's true that we teach what we need to learn."

Emily's ethereal laughter echoed through the dreaming space. "This is no time to be morose, Josie. Power is close by waiting to pounce, and if it catches you in this pitiful state, your depression will become so empowered you'll be sucked into a black pit like you've never experienced! Focus into your *will* before it's too late."

Heart racing, I glanced around the dreaming space. I could see the dark abyss she'd warned me of yawning open near my feet, and behind me a wall of pure, crackling energy loomed massive, overwhelming. Emily was right. There was only one escape. I took a slow breath into my belly and summoned *will*. Then I took another, and another, and gradually a sense of calm neutrality displaced my panic and former gloom. Although the wall of power remained nearby, the abyss receded to a safer distance.

"Good," said Emily. "We don't have time for indulgences right now. And I'm getting older by the second, so you'd better learn what you can from me as fast as you can.

"You're absolutely right when you say you're in a trap with every other human being. It's inevitable. As babies we're dependent on our parents and trust them without reservation. The pattern to elevate people who seem in charge comes with birth. But freedom is just as inevitable. Every trap contains the potential for gaining knowledge, and with it, freedom. The problem is that most people grow comfortable with the security of their imprisonment and keep postponing the inevitability of freedom."

As Emily paused, I seemed to hear Janis Joplin's faint refrain about freedom being another word for nothing left to lose. What was it we humans were so afraid of losing?

"Self-importance," came Emily's answer to my silent question. "Self-importance and our known reality. We cling to our self-importance like babies to the breast, thinking it nourishes our identity when in fact it masks our true identity. And we cling to the known because the vast realms of the unknown frighten us. Your self-importance has latched onto being a student. A good student, but one in need of a teacher, preferably a very great and powerful teacher like your long-held fantasy version of don Juan or Carlos who, by association, could elevate your own importance."

If it were possible for my dreaming body to blush at that moment, it would have done so. Emily laughed again.

"Don't be too embarrassed, Josie," she said. "Like I told you before, it's fine to aim high, to seek quality teachers in any sphere of learning. Just don't keep giving away your power in exchange for self-importance. It's a bad trade. You need that power for your spiritual growth and journey. And you need to believe more in yourself.

"Now let's look some more at power and its relationship to Carlos and his stories," Emily continued. "Because Carlos's don Juan was described as being a Yaqui Indian, people wanting to believe in his spiritual power and knowledge started looking around for Indian teachers. Until that time, very few Westerners had much interest in native spirituality, with the exception of some anthropologists. Even a lot of us Native Americans had either been losing interest or contact with our own spiritual traditions.

"Carlos's books came out, and suddenly people were looking for don Juan or some Indian with his kind of his power. Any Native American became a potential don Juan. I've been keeping track of all this for years, Josie, even though I am just a frail old woman living out here in the middle of the desert."

I snorted at the idea of this formidable woman being anything close to frail.

"Those books—and others as well—have helped create an interesting situation. Many Anglos are putting any Indian who waves a feather around on a pedestal, and some of the Indians are getting a little arrogant and acting like we're the only ones with any spiritual know-how. It's a very ironic turn-around after having our spiritual ways put down by Anglos for centuries. But the other irony is that these books and the Anglo interest have contributed to Indians feeling like our spiritual ways have value in the world, and so we're valuing them more again for ourselves.

"So whether or not Carlos's stories are fiction, they've made quite an impact, both positive and negative. There are many fictional stories that contain truth and depth. We humans are storytellers and love a story that enriches our lives. Look at the many creation myths or the great dramas of the Greeks and Shakespeare. All have had staying power because their truths still speak to people's hearts, minds and souls.

"And think about how much power a creation story has. It can mold people's beliefs for thousands of years, and what people believe partly shapes their reality. Look at the effect of the Bible, or as in the case of my people, the Dineh Bahane. Both have affected the way millions of people have lived their lives.

"A good story is powerful, and Carlos created a powerful story. His books even suggest that gathering power is more practical for spiritual seekers than giving it away to their teachers or anyone else. So if his readers, including you, practice that, they will reap the benefits. Keep your own connection to Spirit strong, Josie. All the rest will fall into its proper place if you just take care of your own path of beauty."

Suddenly the dreaming space shuddered as if touched by an earthquake. I gasped and glanced nervously about. The wall of electric power seemed to have shifted closer to me and was emitting an eerie sound.

"What's going on, Emily?" I cried, as she began to fly in circles above me.

"Enough talking," she called, her voice becoming more faint as she spiraled higher. "All of this knowledge is turning into more power, and power is dancing tonight. Will you dance with it, Josie? Do you really want freedom? You had a chance to move through the wall long ago in Joshua Tree Park, but you became paralyzed and couldn't step through it. You didn't have enough of your own power yet. But now, now you might be able to withstand a moment or two on the other side. It's your choice Josie, but whatever you decide, don't forget *will*."

And then Emily flew through the crackling wall and disappeared, as her words, "believe in yourself, believe in yourself," echoed faintly behind her.

I froze as the wall of power loomed ever closer until I could almost feel it touching me. Then it stopped and waited for my decision. Fears of total annihilation mixed with curiosity and something more: an unfathomable longing for the unknown. I heard Emily's last words again in my mind and breathed, breathed into my *will*, leaned into my *will* like a ship into the wind. A few words from a Dylan Thomas poem echoed through my mind: "...and I sang in my chains like the sea..." Then I gathered more *will*, trusted it, turned, and flung myself through the wall...

...and heard a sound I'd only dimly heard before. The marrow of my bones congealed into gravel and then melted into lava as the strange reverberations poured through me. Its increased volume knotted my jaws and threatened to shatter my teeth in one moment, while in the next my womb vibrated with liquid waves of ambrosia at its touch.

The sound. Ah, the sound. It wrapped around me like a mother, like a lover, like death's cape at the end of the road. It brought to mind fresh raspberries in a chilled crystal goblet and dew-studded ferns in the rainforest, the flight of a hummingbird and the descent of a vulture, the brush of a moth's wing and the dust of gold.

The sound rose and crashed over me, a wave so great it must still be breaking somewhere along the shores of eternity. Drowning in sound, I felt the flutter of angels and the fury of demons, all wanting to possess that impossible sound. And for a timeless moment, I became one with the power's song.

It was the sound of freedom.

Some infinite time later, the sound of the approaching water drum brought my awareness back to the tipi, and as I opened my eyes I once again saw Emily rising from her unusual dreaming position. I immediately remembered to press on the top of my head to seal my energy back into my body. I'd shattered into billions of little pieces and then reassembled in my journey back and forth through the wall of power. I wasn't quite sure who the new me was, but I felt an eerie sense of serenity nonetheless.

I glanced again at my friends, suddenly concerned that I'd abandoned them for too long, but they all seemed well. The pre-ceremonial preparations and these women's own spirits were effectively harmonizing them with peyote and the greater Spirit present here tonight. I relaxed, and as the staff and rattle were handed to me, I launched into four of my favorite peyote songs. As I sang, my body filled with light. I sent some of it around the tipi and watched everything became incandescent. The fire, the chief peyote, the people, Sean's eyes all seemed to glow more brightly from within. Joy coursed through my veins, my heart, my *will*, as I sang out my love for this ecstatic moment of life and purity of purpose.

The singing then continued around the tipi and I immersed myself in the sheer pleasure, beauty and power of my surroundings. And there was more to anticipate. Dawn was approaching, and after singing one more round of songs, my last for the night, I began looking forward to the moment when Emily would bring in morning water.

I saw the roadman walk around to Emily, undoubtedly to check on any last-minute details for her part of the ceremony. As he crouched beside her, his head nodded several times, and then he stood up and came over to me.

He knelt beside me and said, "I just spoke to Mrs. B. about morning water."

"Yes," I smiled. "Does she have everything she needs?"

"Well, she says she's a little tired and is wondering if you would like to bring that water in yourself. You can think about it for a few minutes. If you don't want to do it, you could ask another woman to do it for you. I'll come back pretty soon and find out what you want."

I sat and tried to calm my racing heart as the roadman circled back to his place. Why was this happening? I glanced over at Emily, concerned that she might not be feeling well. Her head was slightly bowed and her eyes were closed, but suddenly they opened and she looked my way. Her dark eyes glittered with intensity as she gazed at me unblinking. Then they softened, she smiled slightly and nodded, and then turned away and closed her eyes again. Once more I heard her words, "believe in yourself" chiming in my head, and I finally realized what was really going on. Emily was giving me another opportunity to express my own power and link to Spirit. The moment this became clear, my question was answered and I made my decision. I would not reject the offer. I would not tell Spirit to go find another vessel.

"I will bring in morning water," I said when the roadman returned for my decision.

"Okay," he replied, and proceeded to outline my responsibilities and the order of events. When we were both satisfied that I was clear on the details, he handed me his eagle feather. I was to use it later for water blessings. Once the roadman had returned to his seat, the fire keeper began his ritual cleaning of the earthen floor and altar, sweeping up stray ashes and then using a long stick to arrange the coals in their half-moon pattern. Finally he built up the fire so it would not need much attention after I'd brought in the water. As morning water woman, I'd be kneeling in the east—right in front of the fire—possibly for several hours, and the fire keeper was not supposed to do much fussing with the fire during that time.

When all was in readiness, I draped my ceremonial shawl around my shoulders, grasped the eagle feather, and began to walk toward the tipi door. As I did, I passed my friends who sat like the four seasons. Rose was the babbling, effusive spring river, I decided. Sandra was the nurturing warmth of summer. Tess, with her bright wit, was like the crisp autumn air and leaves, and Selena was the imperious dreaming queen of winter. Just before I reached the door, I turned for a quick look at Sean. His piercing eyes were blazing silver-blue, twin versions of the Evening Star I'd seen sparkling so brilliantly when I'd briefly gone outdoors earlier in the night. He glowed like a fifth season: a season of eagles and magic.

The fire-tender opened the door flap. I ducked my head, stepped out into the soft breeze and colors of dawn, and gasped with delight. The Earth glistened with the silvery dew-drops shimmering like tiny stars across against her rich, red desert skin. Pulsing green with pure energy, the new spring sage, wild grasses and other plants I had no name for rose from the Earth's body. A delicate scent of damp soil and the glorious trill of the meadowlark caressed me with the touch of Mother herself.

Several feet to the east of the tipi door, a silver bucket full of water sat on the earth. Peyote's waterbird emblem in turquoise and coral proudly adorned one side. The mirror-like water's surface reflected the subtle peach, lavender and pink tints of the dawn sky above. I heard the water drum throb with its liquid tones from inside as the roadman began the first of the two morning songs he would sing before I was to enter the tipi with the water. A solitary bat skimmed rapidly past me in its search for shelter from the sun's first rays.

I faced the east as the morning breeze stirred the fringe of my shawl. Images of Changing Woman—one of the most beloved Dineh Holy People—riffled through my awareness. Like the Earth herself, Changing Woman was transformed with every season. By the end of four seasons she would complete her journey from infancy to old age. Then, as an old woman, she would turn toward the dawn light of the east. There she would renew herself through the touch of her husband—the sun—become young once again, and her eternal process of change would enter yet another cycle.

I lifted the eagle feather as the glowing rim of the sun surfaced above the horizon, catching its first light on the feather's tip. I blessed myself and the water. The golden vision of my infancy swirled around me, renewed me, filled me again with calm, hope and love.

The water drum rolled to a stop as the second song ended. In the silence, I wrapped my shawl and the power of light more tightly around myself. Holding the eagle feather in one hand, I carefully knelt down, grasped the cool handle of the bucket with the other, and lifted it up. The tipi door-flap opened suddenly like the wing of a great bird. As the voices within burst into the third of the four dawn songs, I stepped toward the dancing fire....

...and brought morning water, water of life, to the people.

About the Author

Josie Raven Wing, BA in dance movement therapy and MA in clinical and humanistic psychology, had her first visionary experience when she was about 10 months old, and this set her on a lifelong journey of spiritual explorations and discovery.

In the early 1970s, she began her work in the field of human development as an innovative pioneer of dance therapy and holistic healing. She also started exploring shamanistic traditions, which she has incorporated in her work since that time. At Antioch University in Seattle, she developed and taught courses in the first Holistic Health graduate program in the U.S. During that same period, her growing concern about women's issues and self-esteem inspired her to organize one of Seattle's first women's support groups, and later led her to create a variety of workshops and retreats to meet women's needs for spiritual exploration and growth.

Josie continued to expand her work, including with men and women. Throughout several decades as a psychotherapist, she has integrated Western theory with spiritual, shamanistic and hands-on healing practices of many cultures. She applies her grounded, ongoing synthesis in counseling work with individuals and as an accomplished seminar leader. She has lectured at college campuses and offered her seminars in the United States and abroad since 1983.

In addition to her workshops and individual healing work, the "Desert Visions" retreats she offers in Dinetah (Arizona's Navajo land) and her healing journeys to Brazil (which include sessions with Brazil's most famous healer Joao de Deus, subject of the book *The Miracle Man)* are some of the most exciting programs Josie makes available to the public.

RavenWing's creativity also expresses itself through her songwriting, poetry, ceremonial leadership and spiritual dance choreography. She is the author of *The Return of Spirit: A Woman's Call to Spiritual Action* (published in 1996 by Health Communications, Inc.) and her poem "Song for the Journey" is featured in Michael Harner's well-known classic on shamanism, *The Way of the Shaman.* RavenWing continues to explore ways to inspire people toward a life of awareness, beauty and spiritual fulfillment.

To receive information on her music tapes and other products, as well as to learn more about her workshops, the "Desert Visions" retreats and healing journeys to Brazil; or, if you would like to invite Josie to conduct workshops in your community, please send your request with a SASE to Josie RavenWing, PO Box 13162, Des Moines, IA 50310 or email her at *jravenwing@aol.com.*

You are invited to visit Josie RavenWing's web site at: **http://www.healingjourneys.net**

Printed in the United States
112493LV00003B/190-207/A